Disclaimer: This book is a recollection of the author's memories, which are based on true events. Some of the names and identifying details of characters in the book have been changed to protect the privacy of those individuals. Names, dates, places, events and other details may have been altered, invented or embellished for literary effect. The reader should not consider this book anything other than a work of fiction.

Cover photo: Flash Parker (www.flashparker.com)

BACKPACKER BUSINESS

One girl's journey
from wide-eyed traveller
to worldwide entrepreneur.

NIKKI SCOTT

DEDICATION

This book is dedicated to my dad -
my inspiration to always 'grasp the day'.

CONTENTS

ACKNOWLEDGMENTS

I would like to thank everybody who is mentioned in this book for being a colourful part of my adventure and every place I travelled to for teaching me something important along the way.

I would like to thank the following Southeast Asia Backpacker Ambassadors and friends for helping to proofread this book: Laura Davies, Charlotte McCarthy, David Noakes, George Reed, Will Hatton, AKA *The Broke Backpacker*, Jarryd Salem and Alesha Bradford of *NOMADasaurus*, Tom Rogers and Anna Faustino of *Adventure in You*, Nick Wharton and Dariece Swift of *Goats on the Road*, Caitlin Galer-Unti of *The Vegan Word* and my wonderful Uncle Dean (UD).

Finally, I would like to thank my chief proofreader who is still waiting for payment for her time and effort - the best mum in the world.

1

Getting the Kathmandu Cough

Kathmandu was mind-blowing. All the more so, because it was my first ever experience of Asia. I felt like I had just stepped off the aeroplane into a completely different world. It was a world that I had seen on TV documentaries, but one I guess I hadn't actually believed was real until now. As a 23-year old female traveller on my first solo backpacking trip, I left Kathmandu Airport feeling terrified and alone. I was immediately swamped on all sides by offers of rides from enthusiastic Nepalese drivers, describing a variety of vehicles that would escort me safely into the city. I wasn't so sure.

Intimidated by their eagerness and feeling very conspicuous with my brand-spanking new backpack, comfortable and practical travel clothes, money belt bulging under the trousers and that 'just arrived ever so pale face,' I was, what is known, as a complete 'travel rookie'. I was overly suspicious of everyone that spoke to me, and concerned about my obvious inexperience in such situations. I clutched the piece of paper with details of my hotel on, that I'd printed out back in England in tight sweaty hands, as if my life depended on it.

I managed to find a car with a sign saying TAXI on the top, which somehow made my English brain feel more comfortable, and I told its driver the name of my hotel. We sped off towards the city and my eyes widened. Once we veered off the main road out of the airport it became a free for all. Cows, buffaloes, trucks, cars, lorries, bicycle rickshaws, motorbikes and crowds of people shared the same roads as my ramshackle taxi, which manoeuvred through the chaos. The surface of the road worsened, and each pot hole or stone threatened to whack my head against the roof of the car. I winced at each motorbike that came within inches of the rickety car door. Like a frightened child, I wedged myself down on the floor between the seat and my backpack, and wrapped my arms around my knees. I looked around at the craziest traffic I had ever seen in my life and finally it was real.

What had I done? I had quit a promising career in an advertising agency, left my house and friends, sold my car and flown half way across the world, on a one-way ticket, to a hectic city where I couldn't speak the language and didn't know a single soul. I didn't even know where I was going in this taxi. How could I be sure that the driver was even taking me to my hotel? What if I was being kidnapped already? That would be a great start. It wasn't the last time I would panic unnecessarily during my time in Nepal, as my anxious brain made up stories of its own. Looking back to these initial fears years later, now that I've become so accustomed to arriving in new places alone, I can laugh at my inexperience but at the time my culture shock was very real indeed.

I took a few deep breaths and looked out of the window. There was life everywhere. People wrapped in capes were sat getting their hair cut at the side of the road, as cows meandered by and men walked past them holding hands (I later learned that it was the culture in Nepal for men to hold hands with friends). Plumes of orange clouds rose from the crumbling road, and the air was a thick haze of dust particles and car fumes. My eyes had never seen anything like it before.

Every single vehicle that had a horn was beeping it incessantly. It was a miracle that we didn't hit anybody. But, as is the way of traffic in Asia, small vehicles give way to bigger ones, everybody seems to allow an inch of space for everyone else, which is just enough to squeeze through and keep things moving, and with no white dotted lines on the road, no traffic lights nor speed cameras, it kind of works.

When I finally got to my hotel room, in the very basic Hotel Shanti, I locked the door tight shut, sat on my bed and put my head in my hands. I could still hear the traffic going crazy outside, dogs barking, people chatting and Hindi music playing somewhere. I was completely overwhelmed. At that moment, I never wanted to go back out there in my life!

I had pre-arranged a trek at STA Travel whilst back in England as a safety net. Not usually a fan of organised tours, I'd thought this one to be a good idea, as I figured I would be so out of my depth, alone here in Nepal, that I would welcome the support of a group. It would give me the chance to meet people and ease into my travels. I'd spotted a notice on the pinboard downstairs, indicating that the group would be meeting together on Friday for an introductory briefing to Nepal. It was now Monday. How the hell was I going to get through the next five days on my own? It was chaotic out there! My Primark flip-flops were already covered in dust and a nail had pierced through one of them, and I'd only been out on the streets for a few minutes. I'd have wanted to hide under the duvet, if only there had been one, call my mum, tell her it was all a big mistake and cry. Instead, I pulled myself together, put on my brand new trekking trainers and went back out there into the madness.

Hotel Shanti was located in Thamel, which is the equivalent of Khao San Road in Bangkok. It's the main tourist hub of Kathmandu and contains hundreds of trekking companies, a variety of restaurants from Nepalese to Italian to American, and shops selling hiking gear, souvenirs and countless other trinkets. You can't walk out of the door without being asked, "Madam - you want trek?" or a have a child try to sell you a bracelet - or seven. It seemed as if the touts could smell my newness, and I was particularly hopeless at getting rid of the attention.

Years later, a friend, who had been dating an Indian tour guide, told me that touts may actually be able to 'smell' a fresh new tourist.

"You mean by the way they act?" I'd asked, thinking she was speaking metaphorically.

"No," she replied. "Apparently, to the Asian nose, us Westerners can smell a bit like milk when we first arrive in Asia, due to all of the dairy products that we eat. I can only imagine it's a bit like a new-born baby smells – well, like baby sick!"

Whatever it was, on that first day in Kathmandu, either my nervous disposition or baby-sick body odour, I was definitely attracting attention!

One little girl, selling flowers, followed me for a good fifteen minutes before I had to pretend to buy a hat in a shop, just to lose her. This proved counter-productive as I ended up embroiled in a situation where I was being pressured to buy a hat, and then had to lose the pushy salesman by simply running away. It was a technique I would slowly get the hang of during my travels in Asia.

It was around 3pm and I decided to take a break from wandering and avoiding touts and get some food. Like many first time travellers, the *Lonely Planet* guide book was firmly glued to my hand and I was only willing to go into restaurants that had been recommended for fear of getting food poisoning. I found a popular rooftop café, overlooking a busy junction in downtown Thamel, and I replicated the exact same photo in my guide book of wires criss-crossing disorderly over the equally disorderly traffic below. Rickshaws rang their bells and picked up road-weary tourists whilst I eyed the menu.

One of the things you get used to fast when you are a lone traveller is going out for dinner by yourself. Whereas now this doesn't faze me in the least, at first it was a huge ordeal. "Table for one?" the waiter asked as I nodded awkwardly and scurried head down into the restaurant. Back home if you go out for a meal alone, you may get some pitying looks, and people will wonder why you have no friends to hang out with. In Asia, it is accepted that you are a solo backpacker and no one gives you a second glance. If you're lucky, you'll end up chatting with a group of travellers on the table next to you and make some new friends. It's also rather likely in Nepal that you will become the centre of attention of the waiter, who will use you to practice their English.

Sitting there on my first day, I felt so self-conscious as I tried to read my book and appear nonchalant. I'd always kept a diary from being young, and in these first few days, my diary became my saving grace as I wrote down every anxiety as a means to process and overcome it. It worked a treat as I wrote pages and pages (many of which ended up becoming the bare bones of this book), sketched scenes and people and noted down everything I found intriguing about this amazing new world.

Getting the Kathmandu Cough

After eating what I could of my strange yoghurt-rice combo, I continued to wander around Thamel, trying to get a feel for my new surroundings. Every worthy backpacker will tell you that the best way to get to know a city is to get lost in it and that is what I did, completely and utterly.

I wandered down alleyways and was met with fascinating bric-a-brac shops, shanty houses and bare-footed children flying kites. I peered into alcoves, and came across hidden Hindu shrines emitting sweet incense into the humid air and intricate temples overrun with brazen monkeys. Narrow streets opened up into courtyards with temples dedicated to various Hindu deities. Statues of gods and goddesses had been adorned with garlands of flowers, sprinkled with marigolds and dabbed with bright red or orange powder. Incense sticks burned outside the doorways of shops to tempt people inside to buy their wares. Shops were selling everything from second-hand books to pots and pans, jewellery, spices, multi-coloured tie-dye hippie clothing, knives, bags, trekking gear and any odd bits and bobs.

Compared to England's organised streets, walking through Kathmandu was a constant challenge and test of the reflexes. At the sound of a beep, a "Hello, where you from?" or the whiz of a motorbike, you had to get out of the way fast. Before long, it was getting dark and I decided to call it a day and head back to the hotel. All the way from London Heathrow to Kathmandu, I hadn't slept a wink on two separate plane journeys and the adrenalin, up until now, had been keeping me going. The jet-lag was beginning to kick in, and I felt satisfied that I had confronted my first-day travel jitters and was slowly starting to overcome my culture shock.

Before I had a chance to savour this brief moment of repose, all of a sudden, the lights went off and the city was plunged into darkness. I naturally thought that there had been a random power cut, but later I discovered that there were scheduled electricity cuts every day in Kathmandu, occurring at different times, across different parts of the city. The cuts were known as 'load shedding', and were due to the fact that the country did not have enough electricity to keep the entire capital with power all day long. You could access a schedule of the load shedding online (if the internet was working). This was just one demonstration of the extreme poverty of the country, despite revenue from around one million tourists each year, who come to see the highest mountains in the world.

I now had to find my way back to the hotel, in an unfamiliar city, in the pitch black. Nice one. Locals laughed at me as I freaked out when I came face to face with dead pigs hanging in shop fronts and stray dogs lurking in gloomy corners. Gas lamps flickered in darkened doorways as I peered in to ask faceless locals the way to Hotel Shanti. Everyone was very friendly, although I wasn't too sure about the accuracy of their directions. With a stroke of luck, I arrived at the crossroads where I'd eaten lunch and managed to carefully navigate my way back from there. Finally, heart beating, I was back safe and sound in my room that was now in complete darkness like the rest of the city. Exhausted and so relieved to be back, I collapsed onto the bed without pulling back the itchy orange sheet, a million new sights and sounds in my head.

By the time Friday came, I found myself head over heels in love with this backpacking lark. I was so enthralled by the exotic atmosphere and hectic pace that I was on a permanent high. I'd made new travel buddies who were equally enthusiastic about Nepal: a 19-year-old Dutch guy, Jasper, and a fun-loving young Irish couple, Claire and Patrick.

My life in Manchester seemed so far away, and I felt like I had experienced more in Nepal in five days than I had done in the past two years working in an office. I had ridden on the back of a motorbike through rice fields, passed by locals and children bathing in the river, witnessed a Hindu funeral and cremation, been shooed out of a sacred temple by a man whose beard touched the floor, been chased by monkeys and shared an odd conversation with a holy man who told me he hadn't eaten for ten years and was surviving on just milk. By now, I even had the famous Kathmandu cough (on account of the terrible pollution), but that didn't stop me from knowing that I was having the time of my life and I never wanted it to stop. But the best was yet to come.

The highest mountains in the world had been my biggest draw to Nepal. Walking the hills of the Lake District in England as a child and the summits of Scotland with my parents, I had been brought up with a love for high places. My bedtime reading, that my dad had chosen, was the likes of Mike Harding's *Footloose in the Himalaya*. As a child, lying in a cold bed in the Lake District in a static caravan that we owned, I had been mesmerised by the incredible stories of nature versus human endurance. Ever since the thought of taking a gap year had arisen, I knew that I had to see those mighty peaks for myself.

I had chosen to trek into the Annapurna Sanctuary; a 10-day hike through the mountains to a high-altitude basin that boasts the base camps of Annapurna South and Machupuchare peaks. The trek promised 360 degree views of incredible Himalayan scenery. My trekking buddies were John and Bob, two 40-year old IT consultants from Australia, Sarah and Dave, a newly married couple who were on the first leg of their honeymoon in Nepal followed by Thailand (a great honeymoon I thought!) and Elsa, a 50-year old, divorced Swedish woman with grown up children, who was living out a long-harboured dream to travel the world.

Coupling off for the trekking lodges, Elsa became my room-buddy, and I got to know her pretty well during the trip. I liked her a lot. There's always a reason why someone hits the road and Elsa's was one I could understand. Getting married and starting a family in her early twenties, she had suppressed a desire to travel the world in lieu of responsibilities and a life of routine for almost thirty years. With her children brought up successfully and having flown the nest to follow their own dreams, Elsa had decided that it was now or never. Like me, Elsa kept a travel diary and we wrote together every night, by candlelight, in the trekking huts. I admired her for making a brave decision that few do. She was simultaneously thrilled and terrified to be now 'living the dream'.

The group seemed to get on well together, and there was good camaraderie between us. I immediately became the naughty child of the group. I was always the last one out of bed in the morning, late for dinner, too long in the shower and so on. I was given lessons on how to treat the drinking water with iodine to purify it and given altitude sickness tablets just in case I began to feel unwell. As much as I felt I was independent and could look after myself, it was comforting to have a group of older people to look out for me at the beginning of my adventure.

After surviving a hair-raising, eight-hour bus trip from Kathmandu to Pokhara, we began our hike into the mountains. My mouth was watering at the prospect of being so close to the legendary mountains I had read so much about when I was a child. At first, I resented the regular masala chai (tea) breaks as I wanted to ascend faster. "Slow and steady steps like a shepherd," my dad had always advised when I was young. Later, as the gradient and altitude increased and my pace became slower, I was thankful for those chai breaks!

Before we were even out of the first valley, the views were already spectacular: neat rice terraces carved out of the hillside, thatched cottages stuck onto the land like magnets, and every now and again a waterfall gushing from a great height provided us with a cool way to freshen up in-between trekking. With the crisp air and clear sunshine, this was nature at its best, leaving your body feeling healthy and alive.

We awoke at 6am each morning with the rising sun, and fell fast asleep, exhausted, by 9pm after a full day of exercise. Trekking became my daily job, a far cry from my usual work day, which just weeks before had been hunched over a computer in an office or running around to stressful meeting after meeting; always in artificial lighting, stuffy rooms and air conditioning. Sleeping in basic trekking huts, on wooden planks that were surprisingly comfortable, I slept the best I had done in years. My body felt relaxed, and my mind felt calm. In a satisfying way, it felt like this activity was what my body was made to do.

It was October and the time of the Dashain Festival, one of the most auspicious events in the Nepalese calendar, which commemorates the victory of the Hindu gods and goddesses over demons. It is a time for family, community, fun and games. For the visitor, Dashain Festival means seeing hundreds of kites flying in the sky (to remind the gods not to rain anymore) and bamboo swings, known as 'ping' in Nepali, which are built all over the land for the children to enjoy. Whilst trekking, we saw families join together to slaughter animals such as buffalo, hens and goats in a ritual to give penance to the gods. For some poorer families, it is one of the few times during the year that they get to eat meat, and huge feasts are organised with great enthusiasm.

Each day, we followed an undulating path that gently led us upward towards the mountains. The path changed from cobbled steps to woodland staircases and took us over rickety bamboo bridges, before dropping us down into atmospheric misty valleys or guiding us into openings which offered vast panoramas of the Himalaya. We weaved through tiny mountain villages, passing by other smiling trekkers who would say a cheerful hello in a variety of different languages. We stepped aside to make way for Sherpas and their donkeys, laden with eggs, chickens, bread and other goods, on their way between villages.

As we got higher, the temperature fell and we were getting closer to the lofty peaks, yet still nowhere near their summits. Only serious climbers were able to attempt such a daring, and, some would say, crazy, feat of conquering the highest mountains in the world. At one point along the path, we passed by some stones that had been piled on top of each other and decorated with Tibetan prayer flags. Our guide explained that we were passing through an avalanche warning zone, and this was, in fact, the site where some trekkers had died in an avalanche just a few years ago. As much as I adored these high places, signs such as these reminded me how much respect you should pay to the mountains and the unpredictable force of nature.

On the sixth day, after a breathless climb through a mist-laden gorge full of enormous boulders, we reached Machapuchare base camp at 3,729 metres. Our guides had warned us about the effects of altitude sickness, and during the last stretch to reach the trekking lodge at Machapuchare, I had felt my body moving slower and my breath getting shorter. I was relieved to receive a hot steaming plate of the local dish, dal bhat (lentils and rice with an assortment of vegetable curries), in the cosy kerosene-heated trekking lodge. To this day, the smell of kerosene has the magical power to transport me back to those days trekking in Nepal.

That night it was a full moon, and I tried to take photos of the bright white sphere next to the impressive, jagged, double-pronged peak of Machapuchare (Fish Tail Mountain), against a navy blue sky. We drank hot chocolate, and our breath made clouds as we chatted and played backgammon in the cold night air outside the lodge and learnt the rules to a Nepalese board game called Bagh Chal (Goats and Tigers).

Our guides told us about the legend of Machapuchare. Every person who has tried to climb the mountain has failed, and has either met their fate or something has forced them back down the mountain, leaving the summit unclaimed until this day. In 1957, after a British climber came within 150 feet of the peak before turning back, it was declared a sacred mountain, and it is now forbidden to climb. Nepalese people believe that Lord Shiva lives on the peak and is angered when climbers try to reach the top. Up here, with the thin air, intense silence and awesome beauty, it was easy to understand why people, for thousands of years, have thought of mountains as a home for the gods.

The next morning at the crack of dawn, after a hearty breakfast of banana porridge, we began our final ascent to Annapurna base camp, the highest point that we would reach on this trip at 4,130 metres. Everyone was in fantastic spirits on this gloriously sunny day; hikers grinned and snapped photos whilst the porters sang a famous Nepalese trekking song, "I am a donkey, you are a monkey…" (the song refers to the load that porters carry for the trekker who is able to prance around like a monkey without any weight).

Annapurna Base Camp was the starting point for Chris Bonington's famous 1970 British expedition and the subject of the book, *Annapurna South Face: The Classic Account of Survival,* that I had been reading during the climb. Walking up to a high ridge that sunk down into an enormous canyon, I found a precarious cairn gripping to the lip of the earth. Tibetan flags fluttered in the strong, cold wind around the cairn, and I noticed the names of climbers carved into metal plates that had been nailed to the stones. I recognised the name of one of the climbers from my book. I wasn't yet up to the part where he had obviously lost his life during the climb, and I shuddered as I was confronted once again with the frightening power of nature.

Rising at dawn the next day, we were just in time for the sun to greet us with an incredible light show across the peaks. Shafts of sunshine hit the mountains at different angles causing patterns and beams of white, blue and pink across the rock. It was a five-day walk back to civilisation, and, much as I loved being so close to the peaks that I felt as if I could touch them, I was pleased to be heading down to a warmer clime and a few simple home comforts. The first hot shower I had back in Pokhara is still the best shower I have ever had to this day!

During the last week of my trip, I decided to go on a rafting expedition on the bubbling vein that runs through the heart of Nepal, the Kali Gandaki River. Rafting all day through beautiful scenery and camping on pebbly riverside beaches in the middle of nowhere by night - it was a fantastic journey. There were about thirty people on the trip, and we all became a working community as we joined together in a long line to pass water, one-by-one, from the forest to the cooking area, peeling potatoes and helping to dig the dirt toilet. Wherever we camped, seemingly miles away from civilisation, a Nepalese family would always find our location and bring whisky, beer and gin down from God knows where to sell to us foreigners after dinner. It was a testament to the tenacity of the Nepalese people to find ways to make money, and a worry for our culture at our guaranteed readiness to buy alcohol.

The rafting had been sold to us as 'the extreme, white-knuckle ride of your life' and after completing the three-day trip, I had really enjoyed the experience, but as everyone agreed, the rafting had been much more gentle than we had anticipated. What we didn't realise was that the 'white-knuckle' part was in fact the bus ride back to Pokhara. As the road twisted and turned through the mountains, our young, carefree driver navigated hair-pin bends and avoided hitting oncoming trucks without a hint of caution about the fact that our lives lay in his hands. With Hindi music blaring from the radio and a heated conversation being conducted with a friend in the seat behind, our driver didn't seem to notice that we were about one centimetre away from a 1,000 metre drop into the valley below.

At one point our vehicle actually hit one of the stone bollards that stops you from falling over the precipice, and everyone on the bus gasped. As I watched the road ahead intensely, willing the wheels to stay on the tarmac, I remembered the words from my guidebook: 'You will not pass a one mile stretch of road without seeing the carcass of a burnt-out bus crushed like tinfoil into the canyon below.' I was certain that this was the fate of the bus we were on.

Some of the cooler boys on our rafting trip had chosen to ride on the roof of the bus, a somewhat riskier version of 'getting the back seat'. Along the way, we had seen many Nepalese passengers, as well as a few startled goats doing so, and the boys had tried do encourage me that it was the 'done thing' in Nepal and a 'must-do traveller experience'. I had decided against it. Having just missed getting their heads chopped off by a low hanging telegraph wire, as well as nearly flung off the side of a mountain, they were now regretting their brave decision.

When we finally made it back, I felt like kissing the solid ground beneath my feet. The jolly, Nepalese rafting guide must have sensed my relief as he came over to me.

"Hey, you okay?" he asked.

"Not really," I replied still shaking. "I was really scared on that bus. I guess you're used to it?"

"Ha!" he laughed. "Why worry? Life is nothing!"

Even if the Nepalese people believed that they would be reincarnated, I was quite enjoying this life right now. I didn't want to enter my next life just yet. I'd experienced my first taste of Asia and completed the first leg of my adventure – but there was much, much more to come.

2

Thai Brides

I arrived in Thailand with diarrhoea to mark my 24th birthday. On the plane journey from Kathmandu to Bangkok, I had been apprehensive about arriving in a new country. Would I love it as much as Nepal? Would I make new travel buddies? Would it be safe? However, the thing that I was most apprehensive about was meeting my dad's Thai girlfriend.

When my parents got divorced over five years ago, my dad had embarked upon a few big overseas trips on his own. After a second golf trip with friends to Thailand, he'd decided to buy a house and move there permanently. When he broke the news to me over dinner at the dining room table back home, I was shocked and upset.

I was very close to my dad and had been since I was a child. I loved him to bits and could talk to him about anything and everything. For a long time as I was growing up he had been my hero and he still is in a way. To me, he had always been a pillar of logic and perspective –

the only person in the world who could give me the direction and the motivation I needed when I was feeling confused. The image that I held of my dad - guitar-playing, mountain-climbing, story-telling, teaching me about geography, history, politics and the world - somehow didn't fit with this latest decision to move to Thailand.

Like so many other people in England, despite the fact that this was my dad telling me the news, when an older man says they are moving to Thailand, in particular Pattaya, a place renowned for being a 'sexpat' destination, you begin to judge them immediately. It took me years to realise that this stereotypical view of Thailand is formed mainly by people who have never even travelled to the country. As much as I wanted to be open-minded, at the time, I was embarrassed and frustrated with my dad, and annoyed at having to put up with the predictable taunts in the office: "So has your dad got a teenage ladyboy girlfriend then?"

Oh why couldn't he have just found a nice English girlfriend? I didn't want to defend him. It was his life, not mine, and what he did had nothing to do with me, but I found myself defending him again and again and I started to resent him for it.

Now, two years after telling me the news that he had met a special someone in Thailand, I was about to meet her. I had visions of a girl my age or younger, dressed in a short skirt with high heels, and unable to speak a word of English. I was scared and nervous. Little did I know that my dad's girlfriend, Ying, would one day become my business partner and friend, and that years later we would help each other through one of the most horrifying times in all of our lives.

The first few days were a complete wipeout. I'd contracted some horrid bug from Nepal (probably due to getting drunk on the last night and forgetting to say 'no ice' in my drink), and I spent the entire week in bed or in the bathroom hugging the toilet. It was Ying who would come up to see if I was okay, give me medicine and water, and put a tender hand on my head. In my bleary, dream like state my overactive, skeptical imagination conjured up that Ying was poisoning me so that one day she could get her hands on my inheritance. After hearing so many stories of evil Thai women trapping and murdering foreigners for their money, my delirious brain was certain that this was what was happening. The sole heir to my dad's pension – I was definitely being killed off!

Thai Brides

When I finally came round from my illness, I started to get to know Ying and I found her to be kind, friendly, intelligent and caring. She was in her early 40s, very attractive, dressed in a sophisticated, stylish way and I could obviously see what my dad saw in her. Despite the fact that I really liked Ying, I still found it difficult to see my dad and her together. Part of it was because I'd never seen my dad with a woman other than my mum, but in truth, most of it was my feeling of discomfort about the 'Thai girl, Western guy' phenomenon, so common in Thailand. I just couldn't seem to shake it off.

Looking around at older Western men walking hand-in-hand with slim pretty young Thai girls, some over thirty years younger than them, I couldn't help but feel uncomfortable. Packs of white men gathered in seedy bars wearing vests emblazoned with the beer logo of the bottle that they were drinking. They seemed to be grouped by nationality, a crowd of English expats watching English football over here, a group of German expats sipping German beer over there. There were no Western women in sight and I began to feel very out of place here in Pattaya.

One afternoon I sat and watched as a group of English men flirted with Thai waitresses in a bar, and one of them slapped a girl on the bottom as she walked by. The Thai waitresses smiled and encouraged the attention. A few Thai girls sat amongst the men and I wondered if these were their girlfriends, and if so, I wondered why they chose to put up with the disrespectful behaviour of the Western men?

There's a road in Pattaya called Walking Street. It's the main tourist strip that contains all of the go-go bars and strip clubs. Elaborately dressed ladyboys and prostitutes parade the streets looking for fresh (or not so fresh) meat from which to make a fast baht. For anyone with preconceptions and stereotypical views about Thailand, they can all be met here on this one road.

In my first week in Thailand, Dad had decided to throw me in at the deep end and Ying, my dad and I went for a drink down the famous Walking Street to 'people-watch' at the weird and wonderful walks of life of tourist Pattaya. An 'eye-opener' Dad had said it would be – and it certainly was.

"Hello sexy man!" Thai women in short, tight dresses would holler to men from the bars. Some of the girls who had secured their catch sat on the men's knees at the bar with a drink in hand, yet making sure to keep an eye on any other more lucrative prey that may happen to pass by. Other girls stood front-of-shop, waving and wolf-whistling at potential clients as they walked down the street.

Here in Thailand, the women were hungry for the men and the men, regardless of their age or physical attractiveness (only the size of their wallet perhaps) had their pick of beautiful, scantily-clad females. Both Thai and foreign men walked up and down the main strip with a view to make a purchase: tattooed, body-building Americans, pony-tailed, skinny Russians in high-waisted shorts, English tourists in socks and sandals and smartly dressed Thai businessmen. Add to the mix, a good quantity of Arab men who strolled up and down as their wives, clad head to toe in burkas, followed closely behind. The whole scene seemed so sleazy and depressing to me.

Then there were the ladyboys. With their long dark shiny hair, voluptuous figures (more curvaceous than many of the women due to hormone therapy and implants) and heavily painted faces, they looked like they could be on the stage. With unshakable confidence, an exaggerated effeminate walk and incredible dance moves, you just couldn't take your eyes off these fascinating, preened creatures. Ying was having a bit of fun getting me to guess which of the women were actually ladyboys and I was flabbergasted every time!

After this initial experience of Pattaya, the new hometown of my dad, my first impressions of Thailand had left me cold. I just couldn't believe that this was the place that my dad had chosen to live! I desperately wanted to accept Thailand as a good and respectable place for my dad to retire, yet everywhere I looked, I saw examples that conformed to the stereotype that I had tried so hard to defend amongst cynical friends back home.

My dad had said I would need to be open-minded coming to visit him, but I honestly hadn't thought that my uncomfortable feelings towards Pattaya would hit me so hard. What ensued was a big argument between the two of us after dinner and a few drinks. In Thai culture, having a public disagreement is a big taboo and Dad told me afterwards that our argument had upset Ying to the point that she had cried. In Asian culture, the concept of 'saving face' means that you do not show yourself up or let anyone see you upset or out of control. To my dad and I, the argument was a kind of healthy debate, a way to work through difficult emotions and get to the bottom of what was upsetting me, but to Ying, it was an embarrassment. In a selfish way, I didn't care at the time. My emotions were overwhelming me. How could Ying possibly understand how I was feeling? How could she understand how Pattaya and the whole of Thailand were viewed in the Western world?

The next day, sat with a bit of a hangover and red-eyes on the sun lounger in my dad's garden, Ying came over to talk to me. Looking back, I imagine how difficult it must have been for her to try to understand how I may be feeling. She explained that her family had also had preconceptions about her moving to Pattaya and dating a 'farang' guy. Farang is the Thai word for 'foreigner', which is directly translated as 'French person'. When the French colonised Vietnam, Laos and Cambodia in the 1880s in what became known as Indochina, French people were the first foreigners that many Thai people had ever seen.

Coming from a traditional Thai farming family from Isaan, the rural Northeast of Thailand, Ying's parents had been concerned for the reputation of their middle daughter. Pattaya was a place where young, poor Thai girls would go to make money in the many go-go bars of the red light district. In fact, this was how Pattaya had been created in the first place. During the Vietnam War, the United States Army had a base in Pattaya, and girls would flock from all over the country to meet foreign men and make money during the soldiers' R&R. Ying tried to explain to me that there was much more to Thailand than what I'd witnessed on this one street in Pattaya. She told me that there were many parts of Thai culture that were actually very traditional and probably much more reserved than in England. I didn't respond at the time, I just listened and continued to feel confused.

It is funny now looking back at the strength of my initial negative feelings towards the country. After years of living in Thailand, I realised that Ying was right. There is much more to Thailand than meets the eye, and there are many ways of looking at a certain situation. However, I will admit that I found it difficult to come to terms with what I saw during those first few weeks in Thailand. Whether you like it or not, you are a product of your own society and it is from this platform that you form your views about the world. Travel has always been the vehicle that forces you to question these views and values, and that is exactly what it was doing to me now. As a 24-year old Western girl in Thailand, Pattaya was a confrontation of all of the values I'd been brought up with. It challenged my own dreams of meeting someone and living happily ever after, and threatened everything that I thought was wholesome and true.

I wanted to believe that relationships were based on connection, friendship and love. It made me anxious to think that the fairy-tale story of love could all be a lie. Were relationships so superficial after all? If men flocked to Thailand for beautiful women, regardless of whether they could even speak the same language as them, was it simply about sex from their point of view? And on the other hand, didn't the Thai women want to meet a like-minded partner and fall in love, rather than make an arrangement that seemed purely financial? My feelings were so much stronger because it was *my* dad who had chosen to live here - the one man who had inadvertently influenced my entire belief system about what a relationship should be.

Nothing that anybody could say, least of all my dad or Ying, could quell these feelings at the time, and any change of heart would have to come from me. In truth, even after many years living in the country, I never really felt comfortable or came to fully understand the concept of sex in Thailand. I simply avoided 'red light areas' (which were few and far between in cities), and got on with enjoying other parts of the culture which I loved so much. Prostitution and 'sex money' based relationships exist in Asia, just as they do in England and other parts of the world, and I wasn't in any position to judge each and every one of them.

I have also since met many Western men and Thai women relationships that are based on love and trust, and that are far removed from the negative stereotype set by the Western mindset. Obviously, each relationship is unique and I now realise that it was naive of me to form my entire opinion of Thai-Western relationships on just two weeks and one street in one city.

Over the next few weeks, as I recovered physically from my Nepalese bug, I slowly began to come round to the idea of my dad living in Thailand. I saw other aspects of his life; we visited the beautiful golf courses where he played golf three times a week, ate incredible seafood and drank wine at sea view restaurants, and sat and read in the tropical garden of my dad's house whilst the insects and birds chirped around me. I got to know Ying more and I could see that, as a couple, my dad and her got on really well, had good conversations and cared about each other. At the end of the day, all that mattered is that she loved my dad and I did too.

In an ironic way, the relationship that I had been so wary of at the beginning ended up changing my life in more ways than I could ever imagine. I left Pattaya with a blossoming new friendship with Ying, and although I wasn't in a position to accept all of the farang-Thai relationships in Thailand, I found that I was able to accept the only one that mattered to me.

3

The Banana Pancake Trail

After my brief interlude in Pattaya I joined what is known as the 'Banana Pancake Trail' of Southeast Asia. It didn't take me long to discover why it was called this, and to realise that this was not the untamed adventure I was looking for.

Chiang Mai was very touristy. Travel agents on every corner advertised elephant treks, overnight stays in the nearby hill tribe villages, Thai cooking classes and zip line adventures. There were trendy coffee shops, Italian restaurants, American diners, Irish pubs and, yes, breakfast bars selling banana pancakes. Travellers wandered the streets buying hill-tribe handicrafts or drinking cheap Chang beer in bars that all seemed to play reggae music, and by reggae music, I just mean Bob Marley.

Compared to the exotic, chaotic unfamiliarity of Nepal, I was a bit disappointed. I had travelled half way across the world for something different and now here I was, able to go to McDonald's for lunch and

Starbucks for a caramel latte. Everything was just too easy and lacked excitement in my eyes. To coin a phrase which has become a famous slogan of the route (used by sellers to say why the item in their shop is better than exactly the same item in the shop next door), it was all a bit 'same same, but different'.

The Banana Pancake Trail begins on the Khao San Road in Bangkok and follows a circular route clockwise, north to Chiang Mai and Pai in Thailand, east to Luang Prabang, Vang Vieng and Vientiane in Laos, further east to Vietnam, travelling from Hanoi in the North to Ho Chi Minh city in the South, west to Siem Reap and Phnom Penh in Cambodia, and then back to Bangkok before heading off to the Thai islands in the South. Following this 'golden circle', you are certain to bump into the same backpackers again and again, certain to find Western food and certain to hear Jack Johnson, Jason Mraz and Bob Marley at least 227 times.

So why were so many young people like me taking this route? Why did we come backpacking in the first place? And is this what we all expected? I discovered that there were many different answers to these questions as I met people and made friends along the way. Each person had a very different reason for why they were roaming the earth with a backpack, instead of fitting into 'normal' society back home. With a beer in hand in the THC Rooftop Bar in Chiang Mai, I began to investigate.

A young, fun-loving couple from Birmingham had rented out their house and set out on a gap year across Southeast Asia, in order to get away from a crazy social life and heavy drug scene in their hometown. They were bored with England and wanted a change, whether it was the change they were hoping for, I'm not sure. A 19-year old Swedish guy was seeking spiritual enlightenment, and had been visiting temples and going on meditation retreats in the north of Thailand. An exuberant American graduate was having a two-month 'blow-out' trip before starting three solid years of Business School in New York. A Brazilian guy in his twenties, who was coaching tennis in Chiang Mai, was trying out living in different cities before he chose which one he wanted to settle for a while.

And me? I wanted all of what they wanted and more. I wanted a change and I wanted to be changed. Although Chiang Mai wasn't rocking my boat in terms of wild adventure, I was learning more about myself and was figuring out why I had now joined the ranks of that strange species: the backpacker. So who is this character? Let me explain more.

Despite being from many different countries across the globe and having different reasons for travelling, backpackers have some surprising similarities, from minor details to major character features (at least for the short period whilst they are backpacking anyway). On the surface, the stereotypical backpacker appearance is easily discernible: early twenties, fresh-faced (some of the time), scruffy hair (perhaps dreadlocks) and tanned skin.

Moving onto the backpacker uniform. This consists of a branded vest with either a beer label on it or a symbol of a place that the backpacker has just visited, for example: 'Angkor Wat?' (the bar in Siem Reap, not the temple), Hanoi Backpacker Hostel or the Full Moon Party. The vest will be matched with either a pair of denim shorts or a pair of brightly patterned fisherman pants bought for around 150 baht on the Khao San Road, Bangkok. On the feet, Havaianas flip-flops, and around the wrist, at least a dozen coloured string bracelets, which are mementos of places that the backpacker has been.

After these similarities, I like to categorise backpackers further into the following five labels:

1. The Soul Searcher: "I'm going to travel the world to find myself!" were the parting words on the lips of this wanderer as they fled the safety of the nest in search of deeper meaning in life. Wearing hemp shirts, fisherman pants, henna tattoos, bindi spots on their foreheads and white Buddhist bracelets around their wrists, you'll find this traveller embarking upon 21-day Vipassana meditation retreats, taking yoga classes, reiki sessions, Tibetan singing bowl classes, neuro-linguistic programming sessions, emotional freedom technique classes – anything that will help in their quest for enlightenment. And, there are more than enough businesses in Southeast Asia who will cater to their quest.

2. The Beer Guzzler: When they set off on a round the world trip with STA Travel, their intentions were good; it's just that this type of backpacker can't seem to leave the bar long enough to experience the real Southeast Asia. Pale-faced through lack of daylight, the beer guzzler is commonly spotted at the local Irish pub, donning a 'SAME SAME' T-shirt or occasionally an 'In the Tubing' T-shirt from Laos (I'll explain that later), proof that they did actually make it off the Khao San Road. Unfortunately, one of the most common types of traveller in Southeast Asia. Unfortunately, usually English or Irish.

3. The Hard Corer: Likely to be found on the more remote Indonesian islands, hiking volcanoes or navigating a new river for kayaking. Many parts of Southeast Asia are far too touristy for this type of backpacker who is constantly striving to get off the beaten path. This explorer's essential items include a compass, a pair of Lowe Alpine waterproofs that detach above the knee and a roll of toilet paper for those 'caught short in the wild' moments. Preferring to go it alone rather than in packs, this backpacker is sadly, the rarest of all creatures in Southeast Asia.

4. The Flashpacker: For this new breed of young backpacker, a 'gap yah' is a must-do trend. Essential experience for all future conversations around the table at dinner parties back home which allows you to say… "This one time in Burma…" (you've all seen the videos). Southeast Asia is a playground for them to spend their (read 'Mummy and Daddy's') money and have some 'incredible life experiences' before going back home to a well-paid job, in somewhere like London.

5. Culture Vulture: Rather than going through the *Lonely Planet* and ticking off the list of must do sights, this type of traveller has a genuine interest in culture and history. Watching films about the Vietnam War before they left home, reading books about the Khmer Rouge and the political situation in Myanmar, the Culture Vulture is using Southeast Asia as a classroom for their learning. Skipping the tourist attractions, they prefer home-stays to hostels, volunteer teaching instead of partying, and working at an organic farm instead of elephant trekking - an activity which they are adamantly against.

For the record, I fancied myself as number five, with a hint of one and three, although I didn't do a bad job of fitting in with number two! Beyond these obviously exaggerated stereotypes, as a general overview, backpackers are fun-loving, a bit reckless and very friendly. Everybody chats to everybody (replace 'chats to' with 'sleeps with' in that last phrase and you're not far wrong too). Aware that this isn't ordinary life, people seem to come out of their shell more and do things that they wouldn't normally do back home.

Rather than be on your guard in a foreign country, Southeast Asia seems to do the complete opposite to people in making them over-excessive with alcohol, drugs, trusting strangers and generally being more eccentric. How many people do you know that got drunk and had a tattoo done on a night in Thailand with an attitude of 'what the hell?' I once met a guy who had two different girls' names tattooed on each foot, after 'falling in love' on consecutive nights with two different girls in Koh Phangan.

Backpacking can be the most liberating time of your life and backpackers are here to make the most of it. Every day has but one purpose: to have as much fun as possible. No responsibility, no rules, no boundaries. Signs outside street bars read 'We do not check ID cards', outside hostels 'Laundry and magic mushrooms', and outside restaurants 'Happy pizzas' (weed-laced pizzas), reiterating the sense of freedom thrown in with a touch of lawlessness. That's the attraction and the danger.

With no nine-to-five to get in the way, no routine or duties (apart from keeping hold of your passport), backpacking is a break from the strict regulation of what modern society has become. And for many people, backpacking is just that, a 'break' - an inspiring, fun-filled adventure that happens but once in a lifetime. It's a mere weekend away in the grand journey of life, something you get out your system before resuming your position in the 'real world.'

Even at this early point in my backpacking trip, I think I kind of knew that I never wanted to go back to the 'real world,' that there was so much out there to explore that a lifetime wasn't long enough, never mind shortening that with a solid block of fifty years hard work smack bang in the middle. I didn't want a gap year. I wanted a gap life! I just needed a way to earn money as I travelled, that would make a lifetime of adventure possible. I wasn't sure what that was yet.

With my mind open to new possibilities, I began to encounter people who had swapped the briefcase for the backpack permanently. For them, the 'real world' was a fluctuating string of endless travel experiences. I met a 70-year old Californian who had been on the road for 40 years and there was no sign he was about to cease roaming any time soon, funding his trip by teaching English at schools along the way. Another guy was chilling out in Chiang Mai for a few months; a 50-yr old Australian cyclist who had been journeying around the world all his life, funding his trip through travel photography and giving slide show presentations of his adventures. His mission was to visit every single country in the world, which he had amazingly achieved, with the exception of just one – the highly controversial, North Korea.

My personal favourite, who unfortunately I didn't meet but heard about through a friend, was a naturist Frenchman in his late 60s, Hugo, who has been floating around Asia for 20 years (and still is) on a boat that he built himself, occasionally picking up tourists to fund his nomadic existence. My friend had met him after replying to an innocuous flyer pinned to a palm tree in the southern beaches of Thailand that read: *'Sail the world. Live a sea gypsy naturist lifestyle'.* She hadn't realised that the requirement of being a member of the crew was that she would have to be naked on board! "You don't have to be nude," he had said, "but I much prefer it." Something to tell the grandkids.

All of these unusual stories, and many more, intrigued me and shook up my ideas about the journey of life. They went against everything that the society I'd been brought up in said you *should* do, and challenged my views on what was the correct way of living. Whilst people back home deemed a life of travel and adventure to be the stuff of fantasy, here, I was meeting people who were actually 'living the dream' on a day-to-day basis. For these people, 'settling down' and getting a real job was as bizarre and unnatural as endless roving is to most.

After just a few months away from the 'real world', after trekking in Nepal and stepping onto the backpacking trail of Thailand, I had already begun to question a future in the UK. I had originally left home to see if there was 'anything else', to make sure that I wasn't going to miss something before I resigned myself to a life of nine-to-five. Now, here before my eyes, I was discovering that there certainly was something else, and an incredible something else at that… a life of endless travel and adventure was indeed possible!

Since the hippie trail of the 60s and 70s, young people have left home in search of something more than their society could offer them at that time. Today, it seems that there is another generation who have become dissatisfied with the norm, particularly in the wake of the recent financial crises in Europe and the USA. This is a generation who have seen parents and elders have savings, that they have worked their entire lives for, taken from them in an instant, pensions that became worthless overnight and retirement dreams shattered. This is a generation who have worked hard at university and gotten themselves into heavy debt, only to come out at the other end with little chance of employment in their chosen field.

It seems that we have lost trust in the system. We don't want to dream hopelessly of a glorious retirement, when we may, or may not, be able to cash in on that lifetime of slog. And, if we *are* able to reap the financial rewards, what if we are then too old or sick to enjoy it? We have become a generation that turns to travel and other cultures for a different kind of reward. We want to live in the here and now.

I once heard a quote that said: "The only problem with the rat race is that even if you win, you're still a rat." With the recent global meltdown, it seems that the lifestyle of the rat, and indeed Western society, has been placed into question. When the office worker toils at his desk every day to pay bills to sustain a lifestyle that makes him miserable - it begs the question, what is he working for?

As Edmund Hilary said when he was asked why he wanted to climb the highest mountain in the world: "What we get from adventure is just sheer joy. And joy is, after all, the end of life. We do not live to eat and make money. We eat and make money to be able to enjoy life. That is what life means and what life is for."

4

Off the Beaten Path

After pondering the psychology of the backpacker for a week in Chiang Mai, taking in the spectacular Loi Krathong Lantern Festival, cycling around the city, chatting with a Buddhist monk and kissing the Brazilian tennis coach, I got restless. Chiang Mai had too many beer guzzlers and flashpackers for me and I wanted a taste of what I had come to Southeast Asia for. I wanted something different. As is the beauty of travelling with no set itinerary, I moved on.

I set off to the small town of Phrae, located in the rural northeast of Thailand. I had read in my guidebook that not many tourists venture here to this remote part of the country, known as Isaan, and the countryside here was beautiful and unspoiled, with traditional hill-tribe villages within easy reach. This sounded like the kind of place where I could quench my thirst for adventure. When I arrived in Phrae in the evening, after a seven-hour bus journey from Chiang Mai, I felt like I'd stepped off the bus into an entirely different country.

As I pulled on my backpack and started to walk down the street to find a hotel for the night, people, young and old, began to stare at me intently. Now this wasn't in any way hostile; on the contrary, I could clearly see that people were gazing out of pure intrigue. I heard whispers of 'farang' as I walked by, and it seemed that everybody was fascinated by the strange foreigner in town. I reacted to the uncomfortable situation by grinning at everybody, which provoked shy giggles from the adults, and children hid behind their mothers.

Looking around as I walked down the street, I just couldn't get over the huge difference to Chiang Mai. There were no travel agents, no Western restaurants and not a backpacker hostel in sight. It was becoming a very difficult task to find somewhere to stay. Nobody seemed to understand English when I spoke the word 'hotel'; I had no tourist map of the city and I was beginning to worry. After walking around for a good hour and a half, I came across a very characterless hotel that looked like it was set up for visiting businessmen rather than tourists.

I booked a bland, single room and made my way to the local night market for dinner. With Challenge Number One of finding a room, complete, Challenge Number Two, was getting fed. Two basic life necessities that you take for granted every single day at home, never giving them a second thought, become an important trial when you are placed out of your comfort zone in unfamiliar surroundings.

Everybody laughed as I tried to remember a few of the Thai words that Ying had taught me… "Goyteow moo?" (pork noodle soup), I enquired. There's nothing more baffling when trying to attempt a new language than to say the word exactly how you think it should be said and then to be subsequently misunderstood about ten times. Finally, as you are almost about to give up, there are cheers and laughter all round as granny, sister, brother, daughter and auntie (who have all come out to help decipher) say ecstatically, "Aaaah, goyteow moo!", exactly the way that you have just said it.

I received my well-earned prize, a steaming bowl of delicious smelling broth, and was then given chopsticks to eat it with. I began to wonder if I was becoming the victim of some wicked practical joke. Although I was keen to embrace cultural differences, I couldn't eat soup with chopsticks! The street vendor must have noticed my look of distress and sympathetically (and subtly) brought me a spoon.

Resorting to a game of charades in Southeast Asia when all attempts at language have failed usually achieves positive results. However, at the local corner shop after dinner, trying to act out the word 'tampons' was proving very interesting indeed. It was one of those tiny corner shops in Asia that sell everything from pet food to hair removal cream to dried mangoes; plus they'll sell you an airline ticket and fix your motorbike on the side. The girls in the shop were finding my elaborate gestures highly amusing. I'm sure they got the gist of what I wanted right away, but were finding the amateur dramatics far more entertaining than the Thai soap opera that was playing in the background, and so they allowed me to continue. I picked up a pack of tissues and decided to call it a night.

The next day I set off on my usual wanderings. The town itself was lovely; quiet with empty, tree-lined streets and hidden temples in courtyards guarded by impressive golden Buddha statues. The houses were a mishmash of white stone, corrugated iron roofs, wooden verandas in all different designs, shapes, colours and sizes - nothing like the homogeneous brickwork of regimented suburbia back home. Chickens clucked in gardens next to pigs; dogs and happy children were playing in the dirt. It was countryside living taking place right inside the town. Each street was a plethora of resourceful quirkiness – kids' toys made out of bamboo, bins recycled out of old car tyres and plant pots with exotic fruits growing out of them, fashioned out of every container from a broken Singha Beer bottle to a petrol canister. I felt happy that I was starting to see something of the real Thailand that many tourists (making a bee-line for the beach), hardly ever see.

Wandering past a school, an entire assembly stopped and about three hundred black-haired children turned their heads to look at me in amazement. Even the teacher stopped narrating, and for a split second I felt that I should bow or dance or make a speech. Slightly embarrassed at my foreign face, I shuffled on and soon found myself being followed by an extremely old man, who rode next to me on his rickety bicycle for about half an hour as I walked along the pavement. "Where you from?" was his one line.

After some effort he worked out the word 'Manchester' from my reply and kept repeating "Wayne Rooney", laughing again and again. His childish excitement amused me for a while, but soon it became rather exhausting in that I didn't share the joke and I sneakily tried to lose him by going on some rough ground. If I had a pound for every time that local people in Southeast Asia have asked me if I know Wayne Rooney, I would be as rich as him.

After walking around in the sweltering heat all day, I began to realise that there really wasn't much to do in this town apart from walk around. I got back to my hotel alone and considered what I should do next? I wondered why I always made things harder for myself? I have never been satisfied with taking the easy route, forever looking around the next corner, always going out of my way to make things more challenging, otherwise I don't feel alive or something. I could have taken a guided trekking tour in Chiang Mai: picked up in a 4X4 at 9am with other tourists, a visit to an elephant sanctuary, bamboo rafting and a stop at a hill-tribe village; all in a day's trip that included a gentle stroll to a look-out point. Instead I was in the middle of nowhere, the only farang in the village and I was starting to feel a bit lost.

If Chiang Mai was one extreme, packed with tourists and flashpackers, Phrae was the complete opposite. I needed to find an in-between. I set off to the small town of Pai, a bohemian hangout that lies three hours west of Chiang Mai, in a luscious mountain valley. As well as beautiful mountain scenery, waterfalls and canyons, the town was renowned for its long-term resident hippies and great live music scene. I had found what I was looking for.

Even though the small town itself was quite touristy, it was easy to get off the beaten path and into lovely Thai countryside of lush rice fields and blue, misty mountains. There were gushing waterfalls, canyons, hot springs and abundant fresh air - Thailand was showing its glorious, diverse self to me, and I was starting to love the many facets of its personality. I hired a motorbike for a few days to explore the surroundings. To this day, it never ceases to amaze me that many tourists stick like glue to their designated areas, and even just twenty minutes away from the main drag locals will stare at you as if to say "What are you doing here? The sandwich shops and tourist offices are that way!"

I met a few like-minded travel buddies to share beers with over a campfire at night and enjoy the town's vibrant live music scene. The most memorable was a rather interesting Swedish guy, Erik, who, after reading Neil Strauss's famous 'pick-up artist' book, *The Game*, had set up a unique dating agency in Sweden that had proved very successful. Over a weekend-period, he gave lectures on how to dress, how to approach and chat up the opposite sex in a nightclub and how to secure a phone number. Men who were living at home in their 40s and had never had a girlfriend were claiming life-changing results! It had become so popular that Erik had recently appeared on Swedish television. He was taking a few months out to travel and ponder other business ideas. Erik and I had some very interesting chats over log fires in the mountains, and we discussed life, starting a business, building things and, of course, relationships and love. Interestingly, three years later, the same Erik wandered, by chance, past the SEA Backpacker office in Chiang Mai whilst on holiday and recognised me as the same ambitious girl who had looked up to him and talked about doing something different with her life.

I could have stayed in Pai a lot longer, living the laid-back, countryside lifestyle and chatting with hippie folks about fate and the universe. Yet, as is the bane of all backpackers' lives in Southeast Asia - my visa was running out. It was time to take the two-day slow boat to Laos.

5

In The Tubing, Vang Vieng

Vang Vieng in northern Laos was notorious on the Southeast Asian backpacker trail for one thing. Tubing. A single idea that had completely transformed a sleepy riverside town into a 24-hour party zone that rivalled Thailand's famous Full Moon Parties. As soon as you arrive in Southeast Asia you'll see people wearing vests that read 'In the Tubing, Vang Vieng' - a sign that they'd survived the wet and wild dangers of Laos (the phrase never quite made sense to me, surely it should be 'In the Tube?').

For those of you who have never heard of tubing, the concept is quite simple. Step one: give a backpacker an inflatable rubber ring (tube), and charge him a considerable fee for rental. Step two: point him in the direction of the river and tell him to set afloat. Step three: hook him in with a fishing rod at various points along the river where bars have conveniently been set up for said backpacker to get a beverage when he is thirsty (which is every few metres). Step four: watch and laugh as he attempts precarious zip lines, slides and other forms of entertainment that are totally unsuitable for a backpacker under the influence of an incredible amount of alcohol. And that, my friends, is tubing in a nutshell.

In November 2012, due to an increasing number of injuries and even deaths attributed to 'Tubing in Vang Vieng', the Australian government pressured the Laotian authorities to do something about the dangerous activity. Buying alcohol at bars along the river was consequently banned, and Vang Vieng is now re-inventing itself as an ecotourism destination. Back then, however, the town was total mayhem.

Rumour has it that tubing was invented by the charismatic Mr. T, of Mr. T's Organic Mulberry Farm, who would rent out rubber inner tubes to tourists to float down the river from his small riverside café. What began as a relaxing pastime ironically became the most notorious tourist activity in Southeast Asia. At the time, many travellers would tell you, particularly the Culture Vulture types, that the village was an example of how tourism could completely ravage and ruin a place. As you glanced down at tacky pizza and burger joints and cheap souvenir stalls and see young foreigners in the middle of the day blind drunk falling down in the street, you couldn't help but cringe. It was hard to believe that just ten years prior, this little countryside town, nestled amongst limestone karsts along the beautiful Nam Song River, had no electricity or paved roads.

In a country such as Laos, which is extremely poor, particularly in rural areas, tubing was certainly an interesting way for the locals to generate money. There are various debates surrounding the question of how tourism can positively or negatively affect a place, and like so many arguments, nothing is black or white. On the one hand, many people loathe the development of villages and the introduction of fast food restaurants and television in remote areas all over the world, believing it to be a loss of culture and a demonstration of the negative effects of globalisation. On the other hand, it is worth turning this argument on its head and asking the local people - what do they want?

Looking at tourist development from a privileged Western standpoint, perhaps our view of a rural, self-sustaining existence is romanticised. Westerners would like to keep certain parts of the world seemingly 'untouched', so that we can witness the novelty of a village that has remained unchanged for hundred of years. After 'oohs' and 'aahs' and claims of 'wouldn't the world be a better place if we all lived such uncomplicated lives that are so in touch with nature?', we then return to a modern, comfortable Western life with every amenity and technological gadget to hand. With over 75% of the population of Laos working in agriculture and an average yearly income of US$1,500 per year, perhaps the local people of Vang Vieng enthusiastically welcomed development. Despite outcry from concerned Westerners, the tourist dollar that tubing generated for the small town may have helped Laotian people to advance their futures.

Years later, I would get the opportunity to interview Joe Cummings, one of the original writers for *Lonely Planet,* who wrote their first ever travel guide to Thailand, and ask him about his opinion of such places deemed as 'over-touristy'. How did they reach such a level of popularity that caused them to change so rapidly and who was to blame for the negative affects to the environment and the loss of culture?

Joe believed that whilst fast tourist development is a major threat to the environment, on some occasions tourism could be a force for good. For example, before Thailand's mega-destination Phuket relied on tourism, the main industry was tin mining, which was ravaging the island's environment much worse than tourism is doing now. There are also examples of dynamite fishing destroying coral, and other bad practices taking place in celebrated 'beauty spots' way before tourism arrived, many of which have been stopped now, as the environment becomes protected to 'show off' to tourists. Sometimes, tourism can help to preserve a place, for example, locals becoming proud to display their culture and traditions, once they notice that foreigners are interested. But as Joe suggested, this still remains a double-edged sword.

When you travel in many parts of the developing world, you discover that Western culture, in particular the USA, is very much idealised. It makes travellers sad when they see locals in remote parts of the world coveting the music, film and TV culture of the West and being less proud of their own heritage. Yet who are we to tell people what they should and shouldn't yearn for? Who are we to tell people to not crave the things that money can buy: mobile phones, laptops, designer fashion? All we can do is to point out the negative effects of fast development and a greedy consumer culture that idolises wealth, and suggest to locals that Western culture is not all it is cracked up to be.

All these ideas are ones that I pondered a few years after my initial visit to Vang Vieng and a debate that is still current in my mind, as I continue to travel the world and see places that I love change and develop for better or for worse. However, back then as a gung-ho backpacker, up for pretty much anything, I embraced the shenanigans of tubing as a 'must-do' backpacker rite of passage. On my first morning in the town, I set out to get a number written on my hand with magic marker pen (the number was around 300 which signified the number of tubers who had gone out that day) and went out to join the rest of them.

Starting at the top of the river, at Mr. T's Organic Mulberry Farm, I began to get into the swing of things with my first drink of the day (and definitely the most sophisticated), an organic mulberry mojito. Looking around at the colourful and scantily dressed backpackers, paint on their body in various places, it was clear that everyone was up for a good time. The place was swarming with people who were learning much more about each other than anything about the culture of the country they were in. English and Irish made up a lot of the party crowd, plus Americans, Aussies (a large group in fancy dress), Israelis, French and many others.

By early afternoon I had successfully completed a treacherous zip line, partaken in an enormous mud fight and belly-flopped off a high slide into the river, which had given me an enormous bruise on my stomach. Dancing to cheesy tunes in the hot Laotian sun, with a drink in hand, I had completely lost track of time. A few of my new tubing companions and I underestimated the length of time it would take us to float back to our hotel, and ended up trying to navigate the river in the pitch black.

Other stragglers, who were passed out drunk and had been caught like river debris in the bushes, awoke to our shouts as we floated down the river. We all joined together, holding hands like a safety convoy going down the last stretch towards the main village. As we were beginning to panic slightly about never finding our way back to civilisation, we spotted some canoes coming upstream. Our rescuers! They tied up our tubes and lifted our shivering, drunk, mosquito bitten, bruised bodies into the canoes and took us safely home. We weren't the first tubers to get stranded and there are many stories of drunken backpackers lying out there on the river all night. Can you imagine the health and safety outcries back in England?

It was here in Vang Vieng where I encountered my first brief backpacking relationship in the romantically named 'Bucket Bar'. For those of you who don't know, a 'bucket' is a coloured beach toy filled with a cocktail of extremely poor quality and incredibly strong alcohol with about ten straws poking out. It's the most famous and popular drink for backpackers in Southeast Asia. I was with a group of people that I'd just met discussing the crazy tubing adventures of the day when I met Jimmy.

Jimmy was full of cheesy lines. "You can kiss me, but be warned… you'll want to marry me." He was a right laugh and we spent the next few days tubing on the river or lounging around in rustic backpacker bars. Lying next to Jimmy, watching crap films in bars that catered to hungover backpackers, it was hard to believe I was in Laos or even in Southeast Asia at all. *Friends* and *Family Guy* were the solid favourites, and as you walked past bar after bar, you could catch an entire series on repeat day after day. If backpackers weren't tubing, they mooched around the town like zombies, recovering from the day before. In a paradisiacal mountain village in the middle of Laos, many backpackers didn't see beyond this strip of bars or the nearby river.

In The Tubing, Vang Vieng

Jimmy and I didn't really have anything in common, but we had good fun together and that was all that mattered at the time. When you are backpacking, relationships are so transient that it isn't a big issue that the two of you aren't really compatible. All that matters is that you may enhance each other's travel experience for a few days. Back home, you tend to analyse the person you are dating constantly, rather than just going with the flow. Is this person right for me? Would he make a good father one day? Can I cope with the fact he leaves the lid off the toothpaste every day for the rest of my life? When you are travelling, none of these things apply. After all, you often don't know if you'll even be in the same country tomorrow night to go out for dinner together.

Instead of that awkward 'let's just be friends' conversation, when you are backpacking, you have a multitude of excuses to end the relationship: 'I have to catch a plane to Kuala Lumpur tomorrow', 'I have to meet a friend in Vientiane', ' I left my laundry in Hanoi!', 'I HAVE TO GO!' Anything will do.

So, all of this means that, when choosing partners for a short while, you are much less picky. You end up having brief relationships with people who normally wouldn't be your type and, for a while, it can be great fun! It's a bit like travel speed dating. One night I had dinner with a French, pony-tailed artist, the next day lunch with an English, law graduate, followed by drinks and dancing with a hunky, rock-climbing Canadian! Anyone getting a bit too close for comfort? "Hey this is great, but I left my bag in Bangkok!"

One day, during the five days we were together, I left Jimmy's side to explore the countryside of Vang Vieng. Just ten minutes away from the dusty town, rice fields opened up into vast plains with huge limestone karsts jutting out from the luscious green earth. Farmers laboured in the fields using traditional farming tools, and children played in schoolyards next to ramshackle school buildings. It was incredibly beautiful and picturesque.

Again, it was so easy to get off the beaten track that I just couldn't understand why more backpackers weren't out here cycling in the sunshine. A Dutch travel buddy and I explored an amazing cave, waterfalls, an incredible lagoon, and even stopped to give an English lesson to some very enthusiastic local children. To those people who said that Vang Vieng was ruined, stepping away from the main town you could see a thriving farming community that had remained the same for centuries.

When the time came to leave Jimmy, I didn't make any excuses. It was just time to move on and that was that. Much as I was having fun here in Vang Vieng, I knew I wasn't going to find out the answer to the meaning of life floating on a tube with a bucket in hand.

6

Job Prospects in Vietnam

Getting from Laos to Vietnam overland is easier said than done. It's a tough decision that many a backpacker is faced with when taking the popular clockwise route around Southeast Asia; whether to bus it from Vientiane to Hanoi, or fly. One journey taking a potential 30 hours, but costing just US$18; the other taking a cool 40 minutes, accompanied with a soft drink and a packet of peanuts. However, the latter will set you back around US$150. You only need to glance at a few of the horror stories in travel forums online to be totally put off opting for the bus: 'It took 30 unbearable hours!', 'We were dropped off in the middle of nowhere in the dark!' As a backpacker yet to earn my stripes, I decided it was just one of those journeys that had to be done.

Leaving from Vientiane to Hanoi around 7pm in the evening, the rather unprofessional-looking staff on the bus told us that it would take 24 hours to reach Hanoi. It actually took 27 gruelling hours. Of course, I was sat next to the largest man on the bus, who managed to sleep for the entire length of the journey. I resented his contented snoring so much, as my eyes refused to close, and no amount of snacks, books or iPod tunes could appease my boredom.

I had already sung to myself every song that I knew in my head, tested myself on how long I could hold my breath for, given fellow passengers marks out of ten for cleanliness, attractiveness and hair style, and gone through the alphabet reciting girls and boys names beginning with the letter A, B, C and so on… *Am I the only one who does these things?* This part of the world can certainly teach you a thing or two when it comes to the art of patience.

I have never been very good at just sitting still. It's something that people in Southeast Asia seem to be a lot better at than Westerners. Coming from a 24/7, business-driven culture with deadlines and timetables and WiFi and entertainment on tap, there is no reason to miss a single second in which something, anything, could be 'getting done'. In the Western world, we spend very little time just doing nothing, and hardly ever allow a moment for our brains to not be stimulated. In Southeast Asia, particularly in rural areas, time just seems to float by without a care. Buses, trains and boats are delayed for hours and nobody really cares, or complains. You hardly ever see someone rushing down the street, late for a meeting, barging passed people in a queue or checking their watch agitatedly. "Mai pen rai" (it doesn't matter) as the Thai people often say (or 'bor pen yang' in Laotion).

The bus was bursting to the seams and there were not enough seats for everyone. Much as I felt sorry for myself, I was glad that I wasn't one of the unlucky backpackers who ended up sitting on a tiny plastic chair down the aisle for 27 hours! There were not only people on the bus, but rice and other food bags too – upon which mounds of luggage were piled, and more rice bags on top of that. Getting off the bus included a challenging obstacle course for passengers. Apart from a frustrating and confusing three hours at the Laos-Vietnam border, the *last* three hours (that they hadn't warned us about) were definitely the most difficult. I sat impatiently watching the kilometres on the road signs count down to our final destination.

Despite the arduous journey to get there, arriving in Hanoi at night was a magical experience. I instantly fell in love with the city. It was such a drastic contrast to peaceful, laid-back Laos where I'd stepped onto the bus the day before. This place was lively and atmospheric, and felt so different to anywhere that I had ever been before. The city had its own unique smell that I found strangely alluring; a concoction of traffic fumes mingled with clove cigarettes and the aroma of the boiling beefy broth, Pho Bo, the most popular breakfast dish in Hanoi.

I loved the higgledy-piggledy architecture, the criss-crossing wires, the outdoor cafés with coloured plastic stools and the buzzing streets of the Old Quarter that were each named after a different trade that had first been established there during the 13th century: Silk Street, Woodworking Street, Silver Street. There was life on every corner and down every dark alleyway: families cooking their dinner on the floor in the ubiquitous Vietnamese squat position, mothers tending to babies, artisans making bamboo baskets, street vendors selling flowers and fruit, all amidst a million beeping motorbikes. It seemed that everything was transported on a motorbike: a family of five along with their pet pig, a washing machine, a dozen geese, a six-foot mirror, a precious toddler teetering on the back seat wearing a horse riding helmet and a wicked grin. So many things made my mouth drop open in amazement.

I spent a lot of the time wandering the intricate streets taking, what I thought were, 'arty' photographs of the fascinating street life. In the day, I sat around Hoan Kiem Lake drinking strong Vietnamese drip coffee, reading the Hanoi Expat Newspaper and writing in my diary. At night, I sat at the legendary Bia Hoi (fresh beer) Junction, where litre jugs of beer cost just under a dollar. I loved the spontaneity and vibrancy of the city. Hanoi was never boring - you never quite knew what was going to happen next. With so many different vehicles and few pedestrian crossings, navigating your way across the road was entertainment in itself.

Hanoi was the first place that I visited where I actually thought, *I could live here*. It was the first place that I seriously started to think about jobs that would allow me to stay in Southeast Asia and lead an exotic expat lifestyle. The more I thought about it, the more I bumped into a variety of foreigners who were actually living and working here. I quizzed them about every aspect of their lives.

Most of the expats in Hanoi were English teachers, earning around US$20 per hour teaching English to children and adults. With the low cost of living in Vietnam, they could afford to only work around eight hours per week, with the rest of the time dedicated to leisure or pursuing their own interests or entrepreneurial ideas on the side. One girl that I met was editor of one of the expat newspapers in Hanoi; another girl was working for a travel and adventure company. All of the young expats seemed motivated, empowered and thrilled to be living in exotic, exciting Asia. I marvelled at their quirky, interesting lifestyles, in comparison to my stressful, predictable work life back home.

Whilst discovering Hanoi on a permanent high and wanting every single day to last longer than 24 hours, I was fortunate enough to meet a girl who was to become a great travel buddy for the rest of my trip in Southeast Asia. Daisy and I would share experiences, memories and a lot of cheap beer.

When you travel as a lone backpacker in Southeast Asia, or indeed anywhere else, it is very easy to make friends. Thrown into close proximity on tightly-packed buses and in backpacker dorms, you end up sharing a lot of things. You find that you get close to other people very quickly, telling someone you have just met on the train your deepest, darkest secrets. Daisy and I talked about the past, our jobs, relationships and family, and our hopes and dreams for the future. We became 'wing-women' for one another as we flirted with boys from all different nationalities.

We travelled to the northern hill town of Sapa together, trekked through rice terraces, drank tea and ate boiled eggs with hill-tribes, washed our hair in hot springs, sang Vietnamese karaoke and drank Vietnamese rice wine at a home stay in one of the misty villages. We went on a tour of the UNESCO World Heritage site, Halong Bay, kayaked around sea caves, snapped photos of floating villages, visited deserted beaches and kissed a French boy called Pierre (oh, that was just me). When exploring the incredibly beautiful surrounding area of Hanoi, I almost had it in my mind that these places could be weekend trips when I lived in the city. My brain was racing with ideas and possibilities of a different life.

At the end of almost two weeks of non-stop fun, Daisy set off by bus towards Vientiane, Laos. She was taking the anti-clockwise route around Southeast Asia, which meant that we had to part ways. Watching the bus depart, I sat in a little café in Hanoi, tears welling up in the corners of my eyes. I was sad to leave Daisy and close the chapter on all of the fun we'd had together in Vietnam. Yet, as is the way with transient travelling relationships, there is always another potential best friend to meet just around the corner!

My own bus, destined for Hoi An, a colonial coastal town 17 hours south of Hanoi, would be leaving in a few hours. Despite the fact that I was sad to leave Daisy, for some reason I didn't feel sad to leave Hanoi, a city I had come to love in such a short amount of time. I just *knew* that I would be back here one day.

Travelling the length of Vietnam, you can buy an open bus ticket that costs around US$50, taking you all the way from Hanoi in the North to Ho Chi Minh City (Saigon) in the South, getting on and off where you like. This is a really cheap way to travel over 1,600 kilometres. Along the way, I was able to appreciate the great diversity of Vietnam: buzzing cities, rice fields, endless beaches, ancient cultural towns, windsurfing spots, sand dunes and green mountains. No two places felt the same, yet everywhere had that addictive Vietnamese pace. I had handmade clothes tailored for next to nothing in the lovely town of Hoi An, visited mud baths in Nha Trang and trekked the red and white sand dunes in the small fishing town of Mui Ne.

Whilst exploring Mui Ne, I visited an interesting red canyon where the 'Fairy River' flows through the middle. Tripping up, face first, into the slouchy, sandy river, to my horror, my beloved camera fell deep into the soup. I had become quite obsessed with taking photographs during my trip, and I panicked at the thought of losing precious shots of the Himalaya in Nepal, beautiful days in Pai, boats in Halong Bay and temples in Laos - memories of friends I may never meet again and photos of places I would likely not return to. Any backpacker will tell you that losing your camera is one of the worst things that can happen. Steal my money, okay, but leave my camera! I'd even heard of backpackers having their cameras stolen at hostels, but the sympathetic thieves had removed the memory card and left it in their bag for them.

I retrieved my camera from the muddy water, cut my day-trip short and grabbed a motorbike to take me back to town to see if I could find a camera repair shop. I remember repeatedly saying to myself in my head on the way back, *Please don't be broken. I promise to myself that if you aren't broken I will do something creative with all of the photos – I don't know what yet, but I will!* It turned out that my camera was utterly ruined, but my memory card and all the photos were safe. (Starting a Southeast Asia-based travel magazine without a good bank of travel photography would have been impossible. I just didn't know yet that this is what I wanted to do!)

My last stop in Vietnam was Ho Chi Minh City, formerly Saigon, and I spent a few pleasant days here with an American traveller, Mike. Hanging out at bia hoi junctions, eating dried squid and crab from the street vendors, visiting the shocking American-Vietnam War Museum, walking around the Chinese markets - we had a lot of fun together.

After three weeks travelling the length of the country, I was totally set that Vietnam was the place that I wanted to live. I paced around the city in the heat, with a crumpled copy of my CV, approaching language schools to ask them the requirements of becoming an English teacher. It seemed that with my English degree, I could pretty much step into a job here and earn US$17 per hour right away!

My plan was to find work as an English teacher to fund my existence, and then with little time spent in the classroom, I would have the time to explore other pursuits that I enjoyed. The main problem with my job in advertising in the UK was that I was overworked and didn't have time for any hobbies. I decided that this could be the opportunity for me to rekindle some of my forgotten creative passions: writing, painting, singing, playing the guitar – and see if I could make a career out of doing something that I loved. As the saying goes – then I wouldn't have to work a day of my life. I think that so many people have hidden talents and passions that they cast aside due to stressful, demanding careers in the West. I felt grateful now, to have this chance to dedicate time to some of these lost loves.

After living the best, most varied, most colourful three months of my life, I felt that there were now so many possibilities to live an exciting life here in Southeast Asia. Despite not having much money in the bank at that point, I felt like I could do anything. Cut loose from the nine-to-five, I was now free to explore whatever path I desired. I felt a release of stress to be away from the pressure of a competitive career path in the UK. Southeast Asia was a land of opportunity where anything could happen. You didn't need reams of qualifications, certificates or money. If you had a skill to share – you just did it and you got paid for it. I had no desire to go back home and hop back on the career ladder. I had seen that there was a different way - a way that was much more fun and interesting, and filled my heart with excitement. Life was here for the taking.

7

New Year in Isaan

I'd flown from Ho Chi Minh City to Bangkok on Christmas Eve to be with Dad and Ying for Christmas. On Boxing Day, we'd be travelling to spend New Year at Ying's home village in Isaan, northeastern Thailand, where she is originally from. I was very much looking forward to the experience, seeing more of Isaan and staying with a local family who could teach me more about the rural Thai way of life.

The night before we set off for Ying's village, I lay in bed at 4am unable to sleep. I've never been a good sleeper at the best of times and now, with all the stimulus I'd experienced over the past three months and all the ideas I had for my future, it was even worse. That night, my mind was whirring with a thousand thoughts and possibilities. My future lay before me like the unwritten pages of a diary, and I wondered what adventures they would be filled with.

With my original STA Travel itinerary, I had a flight booked to

Perth, Australia in the first week of January that I hadn't yet put back or cancelled; yet I now knew that I wanted to remain in Southeast Asia for a longer period of time. There was so much that I hadn't explored in this region, I didn't want to go back to the Western world just yet. Plus, with the new discovery that I could earn money in Southeast Asia, there was no need to go to Australia to pick fruit or work on a farm in the Outback, like so many backpackers did to make money to continue their travels.

Yet another reason to keep me in Asia was the economic crisis, which had hit the West with disastrous consequences in December 2009. Particularly for young, inexperienced people, jobs were now hard to come by and, some of those people who did have jobs, had wages cut, hours cut or were made redundant. Facebook messages from travel buddies I'd met who had just made the leap to Australia to find work, were telling me that it was becoming more and more difficult to find a job in a restaurant or café. Just a few months prior to this there had been endless opportunities in Australia or New Zealand. The traditional backpacker plan of making money Down Under, to fund further travels in cheaper destinations, seemed no longer an option.

Before coming to Asia, I had thought about applying for a job at the Sydney or Melbourne branches of the advertising agency that I worked for in the UK. One thought had been to wing my way into the HQ of *Lonely Planet* (based in Melbourne), and pitch myself as a travel writer! It was an unlikely dream I'd cradled every day whilst working at my desk in England, looking at vacancies on their website.

However, after travelling for three months in Southeast Asia, my feelings had changed. I just didn't feel ready to fly to a Western country yet, get back into the rat race and go through all of the stress that came with trying to get a 'proper' job. Even in this short space of time, Asia had changed me and my view of the world. Everything, all of a sudden, didn't have to be so ordered and regimented anymore. I wasn't worried about an unexplained gap on my CV or what Western society would think about my travels. I felt an overwhelming sense of freedom to do whatever I liked with my life.

I turned on the light and jumped up to write a list, one of my favourite things to do when I can't sleep. It helps me to figure everything out in my head, and once the thoughts are down on paper, I can, usually, let them lie for the night. I pondered the serious option of working as a teacher in Hanoi and started to write a list of all of the lost passions I would be able to explore once I had the time.

I was so excited as I scribbled down ideas in a stream of consciousness. My pen seemed to have a life of its own. Perhaps I would use my spare time to become a novelist? Maybe I would write songs and form a band? Perhaps I would write for a local newspaper and then once I had some experience, submit articles to international travel magazines? Hey, maybe I'd even start my own travel magazine?

Point four on my list, 'set up a magazine for backpackers in Southeast Asia', had my heart beating fast. I wanted to wake my dad up immediately and tell him I had just had an idea that would change my life. At 4.30am *that* wasn't a good idea, but I couldn't possibly go to sleep now with the excitement of my new venture brewing.

Along the backpacker trail in Southeast Asia, I had been picking up hundreds of free magazines in hotels and cafés, looking for something interesting to read, but nothing spoke to travellers like me. Most of the magazines were for wealthy tourists and advertised spa hotels and fancy restaurants. There were no magazines about adventure, backpacking the Southeast Asian circuit, or getting off the beaten track. Topics that I, and many others, would have loved to read about! There was such a huge audience - I just knew it would work!

I envisaged a kind of *Viz Comic* (a student rag that I used to buy for about 30p as a teenager): quirky, rough-edged and full of personality. The magazine would be funded by advertising and be free for backpackers to pick up in hostels, cafés and bars all across the Southeast Asian backpacker trail. I already had loads of stories of my own that I had written down in my diary, plus thousands of photos (thanks to that camera repair man in Mui Ne!). I would also ask friends and people I had met along the way to chip in with their travel tales. Eventually, I would ask other backpackers to send in their stories through the magazine.

The concept would be 'a travel diary for everyone'. Almost everybody that I had met on the trail was keeping a travel journal anyway, and everyone loved to share their travel stories with others. One of the best things about travelling was comparing your crazy experiences with others, and discussing new opinions and emotions that were arising directly because of the wacky word of backpacking. There were so many brilliant stories left untold. The magazine could become an outlet for people to share their travel tips, get inspiration for destinations to go and reminisce about places they had been. That night I pretty much wrote the introduction to my very first issue:

Welcome to the very first issue of the brand new Southeast Asia Backpacker Magazine. The first and only one of its kind in Southeast Asia, this magazine is dedicated to the art of backpacking through this intoxicating part of the world. From the dusty streets of Cambodia to the pristine white beaches of Thailand, we bring news from travellers far and wide. No stone shall be left unturned as we delve into every nook and cranny of the backpacking experience.

This is a high-energy fusion of the thoughts, feelings and stories of messy-haired, bracelet-clad travellers from all over the world, journeying through Southeast Asia right now. Every article is written by adventure-loving, inquisitive travellers - just like you.

As you well know, travelling is as much about meeting interesting people and exchanging stories as it is about visiting the country you're in and it's a wonderful thing that no two people have the same experience of a place they visit. Travellers of all ages, from all different backgrounds choose Southeast Asia as their classroom and their playground. SEA Backpacker Magazine aims to unite independent travellers in celebration of this incredible time of life.

From relaxing two-day slow-boat trips along the Mekong in Laos to exhilarating 10-minute motorbike taxi rides in Ho Chi Minh City, each journey is an exciting adventure. Live your unique adventure to the full and appreciate every moment with Southeast Asia Backpacker Magazine!

I spent the whole of the rest of the night scrawling down ideas: thoughts for feature articles, regular columns and spotlights. I sketched out layouts, and remembered interesting quotes and anecdotes that I thought other backpackers may like to hear. After all, when I had related stories to fellow travellers over a drink they had found them amusing / interesting / shocking, so why would it be any different if they were reading them in a magazine? Rather than worry about being too clever when you write, I always think that the best way to tell a tale is to think about how you would relate it to a friend over dinner. If you can make your friend smile, then why can't you make a complete stranger smile? The magazine would give backpackers a voice and a place to share their stories with a wider audience.

I impatiently waited for it to get light so that I could tell someone my idea. We were leaving early in the morning around 8am as it was a 10-hour drive to Udon Thani, the nearest main town to Ying's tiny village of Ban Lek. As soon as it got light, I finished packing in my room, went downstairs to make a cup of tea and waited for movement to suggest that someone was up. The minute we were all settled and sat in the car ready to depart, I told my dad about my idea and asked him what he thought.

"That is golden," Dad said. Never someone to give a compliment when it wasn't due, I felt that I was onto something. I was so happy that he believed in my big idea.

Arriving in Ban Lek in the evening was like stepping back in time. We drove the car onto a narrow, unpaved road, lined with houses on stilts and chickens and goats running around wild. We were greeted by dozens of barefooted children who ran out of their houses to see the strange new farangs in town. That night, exhausted from the journey, I slept soundly on the floor of Ying's mum's house. We were awoken at 4.30am by the loud countryside alarm clock, "Cock-a-doodle-doo!". Shortly afterwards, it seemed that everyone was up and about their daily business.

Bleary-eyed, I crawled out of bed around 5.30am to see Ying sat with her mum and sisters cooking Isaan's famous sticky rice over a hot flame. A funny conversation ensued with some of the children of the village as I tried to explain my abrupt awakening by the 4.30am natural alarm clock. In Thai language, the sound that a rooster makes is 'ek-eey-ek-eey-ek!' and they found my 'cock-a-doodle-doo' absolutely hilarious. This soon led into a discussion, with Ying translating, about the different sounds that animals make in Thai language, compared to in English. Apparently a dog in Thailand goes 'raw raw', a cow goes 'aaaar' and a pig goes 'poo', rather confusing as the actual Thai word for a pig is 'moo'. That means a cow should be an 'oink' right? Anything that I said had the local kids falling about laughing, and it was a lovely way to break the ice and bridge our very different cultures and upbringings.

After breakfast, my dad and I borrowed the village motorbike to explore the local area. What is very interesting in Thailand is that many local people don't seem to have that same exploring itch as us Westerners do. After asking Ying and her family if there were any places of interest nearby, what was down this road and the next, it was clear that many of them had not travelled much further than their own village and the main town.

"Every village is the same as the next, why you want to go?" Ying said with a puzzled look, and added, "Crazy farang out in the sun getting brownie!".

'Brownie' was the word Ying used to mean tanned, which she and most of the other Thai women absolutely hated! They wanted to be as pale as possible, and many of them actually used whitening moisturising creams and bleaching shower gels to achieve whiter skin to make them look more Western. It's a crazy world.

After an embarrassing ten minutes to get the bike started, and even more laughter from the kids, we set off to explore. Just out of the village, the rice fields seemed to go on forever in this pancake flat, arable landscape. Buffaloes munched through the rough grass at the side of the road and farmers, driving beat up old tractors, stared in disbelief at the two farangs on an unlikely holiday in Isaan. There wasn't a 7-11 convenience shop, travel agent or internet café in sight.

Isaan was, in fact, joined with Laos until twenty years ago and retains a lot of the culture and traditions of Laos: ceremonies, songs and extremely spicy food such as the beloved somtam (papaya salad) and larb moo (spicy pork salad), plus a very laid-back way of life to boot. People from Isaan are sometimes called the derogatory term 'banork', which probably means something like 'country bumpkin'. Nowadays, a lot of 'banorks' leave Isaan to go and live in big cities such as Bangkok to earn money as a taxi driver, waiter or waitress, massage therapist or work in a clothes factory.

There wasn't much to do in Ban Lek and that was just fine by me. I wanted time to ponder my exciting new project. In the heat of the day, I sat in the shade at the side of the house and wrote ideas for articles, going through photos on my laptop that would make good front covers and double page spreads for feature articles in the magazine. Occasionally, some of the younger children would come and sit by me as I worked, marvelling at my photos of Nepal: the high snowy mountains and sadhus (holy men) with colourful painted bodies and beards down to the floor.

Some of the kids had never even seen a laptop, never mind the photos of these bizarre new worlds that I was showing them. What a different upbringing I had to these children, and how fortunate I was, to have the opportunity to travel the world and experience such different cultures. Taking a gap year to Nepal and Southeast Asia would have been a ridiculous notion in their world. However, I would certainly not call the village poor in terms of the quality of life. We ate so much amazing fresh food while we were there! The children here in Isaan grow up with good nutrition as the families grow most of the vegetables in an organic way, right there in the back garden. Playing in the streets every day and exercising amidst the fresh, unpolluted air, I would say that these kids were healthier than most of the children back home playing computer games indoors.

One morning, Ying woke me up at 6am and asked me if I'd like to go 'lat' hunting with her brother.

"What's a lat?" I asked, thinking it could be a strange exotic bird.

"A lat. A lat. A lice field lat!" she said. It clicked, and I decided that I certainly didn't want to get out of my bed when it was still dark to go hunting rats! I really hoped that rat wasn't on the menu for tonight's dinner.

By night, we sat around an open fire, cooked and ate sticky rice and talked until late. My dad and I were clueless about what was being said half the time and Ying explained the odd joke or funny story, which was somehow not so funny once it had been translated. Every night, the children tried to stay up to join in the fun, yet fell fast asleep in blankets on their parent's knees around 10pm.

I noticed how close the children were to the adults; there was almost no separation in the daily tasks that they did together, with the kids helping their parents without complaint. In turn, the parents didn't have to say, "Right, get to bed now, stop messing around!" There were no tantrums and no disciplinary measures involved at all. The kids were so well behaved and polite: tidying up, doing chores with a smile and giggling shyly at my dad and I as we ate our food.

I asked Ying more about her upbringing and she told me how life had changed so much in Isaan since she was a little girl. They now had a TV in the house, which the youngsters were becoming addicted to, and images of Bangkok, city-life and American pop culture were seen as desirable and something to aspire to. Four out of five of Ying's siblings had left Ban Lek village to go and work in cities, in factories or in offices in and around Bangkok. Only Noo, Ying's oldest sister, stayed back home to look after the family's rice fields, tend to buffaloes and take care of other farming duties. Noo's children went to the local village school, and her husband was working away in construction in Saudi Arabia and sending money back to the family. Both of Ying's parents, now well into their sixties, still worked in the fields every day.

Out of the six grandchildren, all had aspirations to work in Bangkok or abroad, which initiated the question - who would carry on the traditional farming life in another twenty years? Was this a culture and community on the verge of extinction? Ying told me wonderful stories of making homemade, herbal shampoo and toothpaste and making meals out of things she had found in the garden or picked off the trees. I found it strange that rather than being proud, Ying was almost embarrassed as she retold these facts about her childhood. It seemed that this self-sustainable life was not something to be proud of in Thailand, as it meant that you were poor.

I thought about how ironic it is that these things would be considered so hip and trendy in middle-class areas of England today, where farmers markets are cool, second-hand clothes are vintage and having an allotment is 'hipster'. Whereas Western culture had begun to look to a more simple 'real' way of life, the Thai countryside people desperately wanted to become more sophisticated, "more civilise", as Ying called it, and emulate a money-orientated Western culture.

One of my favourite characters in the village was Ying's dad, a gentle man, who was well known in the village for being a very stoic, religious person. Some people even thought that he had special magical powers, bestowed through years and years of meditation and adhering to the Thai Buddhist way of life. Ying told us a story about how a local family had been working on a building site in the main town of Udon Thani, an hour away from the village, and their little girl had been playing around amongst the bricks and construction equipment. By accident, she had sat down in a steaming cement mixer and had badly burnt the skin of her bottom and legs. Mistrustful of contemporary medicine, the family had rushed the little girl to see Ying's dad, who had, reportedly, miraculously healed her. What should have been a very bad burn did not develop into a blister and the little girl's skin did not scar.

Ying also recounted a very strange period in her life when she was a little girl of about six or seven. Her family had been involved in a local dispute with another family about who had the ownership rights to a certain piece of land, not far from their house. With both families adamant that the land belonged to them, the dispute had become nasty and the other family apparently put a curse on Ying's home. All of a sudden, Ying's mum, usually a very quiet, pious lady, began acting totally erratic, saying crazy things and becoming violent towards the children. Ying's dad, who had heard of things like this happen before, suggested that an evil spirit had possessed her. The situation got so bad, and Ying's mum was behaving so out of character, that her dad decided that the children should go and live with their auntie for a while.

With the children safely out of the home, Ying's dad went to speak to a monk at the nearby temple and begged him to come to the house to help with the unusual situation. After some discussion, prayer and meditation, the monk concluded that they had, indeed, been cursed. He pointed to an area in the garden and they began digging. Not far beneath the surface of the earth, they found old bones – a sure sign of black magic! The monk immediately performed a Buddhist ritual, which acted like an exorcism, and the curse was lifted. Ying's mum returned to normal, and the family were able to live together again. I listened with a skeptical ear, my mouth wide open. It seemed an incredible, impossible story and I found it hard to believe. Yet I wondered why Ying would fabricate a story like this?

After more than five years living in Southeast Asia, I had heard many stories about magic and bizarre occurrences. Some of the stories I heard about black magic (particularly in Indonesia and Cambodia where animism is still very much alive) made me shiver. At the time, I had no desire to explore it too much as frankly, it scared me a little! This part of the world is certainly filled with 'magic' and unexplained phenomena that perhaps us cynical Westerners will never truly understand.

On New Year's Eve, we had a Buddhist ceremony in the house and all of the monks from the temple were invited. In Thai, it was known as a 'tam boon' (merit-making) ceremony, and it was performed to create good fortune for the coming year. My dad and I had white bracelets tied around our wrists; "For lucky", Ying said, and we were told that we had to keep them on for at least three days, or, until they fell off completely. It was a lovely ceremony with the whole family involved, and I felt honoured to be included in this unique tradition. The ceremony was an example of how much of an important part religion played in the lives of the people in the village. Everything centred on Buddhism, a religion, or rather in my mind, a philosophy, that I would grow to have a lot of respect for over the coming years, and that would actually help me a lot in my own times of need.

After the ceremony, in true Thai style, it was time to party. We had heard that one of the houses down the road had a large karaoke machine and that there was a party in full swing to celebrate the New Year. If there is one thing that Thai people love, it's karaoke, and so off we went! Copious amounts of rice wine and SangSom (cheap Thai whisky) were consumed at the party and people were literally queuing up - men, women, children, grannies and grandads - to have a dance with either me or my dad. It was hilarious and exhausting to say the least. Falling into bed, tipsy and with a smile on my face around 4am, I remembered that the rooster would soon be 'ek-eey-ek-eey-ekking' (it still doesn't sound right to me). It had been the strangest New Year's Eve I'd ever had.

I loved this quirky part of the world, and felt so excited about my upcoming new business idea that could hopefully keep me here a little longer, and give me the chance to explore more.

8

The Full Moon Party & Beyond

After New Year, I set off on my travels again, meeting Daisy at the Full Moon Party on the Thai island of Koh Phangan. There are various stories about the origin of the legendary Full Moon Party, but so one rumour goes, it all started with a group of hippies over thirty years ago, playing guitars on the beach on the night of the full moon to celebrate someone's birthday. The birthday party was so much fun that they decided to repeat the party in the same spot the following month (although people argue about the original venue, it is believed to be on the beach outside Paradise Bungalows in Haad Rin). What a legacy that birthday party created! Today, up to 30,000 people congregate on Haad Rin sands, glow-in-the-dark paint on their bodies and buckets in hand, to dance to a variety of different sound systems pumping out music until dawn.

I had no idea at the time that two years down the line I would be living on this party island, running my own magazine, often getting the boat to the neighbouring islands of Koh Samui and Koh Tao for business meetings, and living a very bizarre lifestyle compared to many of my friends back home. When I actually lived in Koh Phangan, however, it would be on the quieter west coast, in Haad Yao, far away from Haad Rin and the site of the Full Moon Party. You see, the best thing about Koh Phangan is that people stereotype it as a party island and stay clear, leaving parts of the island untouched with beautiful deserted beaches and national parks. It is still one of my favourite places in all of Southeast Asia to this day.

After a very drunken Full Moon Party, Daisy and I parted ways and I felt down for a few days as I always did when I said goodbye to a travel buddy on the road. Living and travelling in Southeast Asia, transience was something that I never enjoyed and never really got used to. When you are travelling alone especially, you constantly have to readjust and gear yourself up to make new friends again and again. It can be very tiring, when all you want is a familiar face. I caught the boat from Koh Phangan to the mainland with tears in my eyes, sad to be on my own again. The backpackers around me were all in a daze after days of hard-core partying and no one bothered to make small talk. "Where are you from?", "How long have you been travelling for?" I was pleased to have a rest from the predictable questions for a while. I sat on the boat and started to write an article in my diary about the ups and downs of backpacking life that would later appear in the printed magazine.

I had decided to check out the beautiful Andaman Coast of Thailand and was heading to Krabi and the hotspot for rock climbing in Southeast Asia, Railay. The area is a spectacular peninsular that is cut off from the rest of the mainland by jagged limestone karsts, making you feel like you are on an island. It is only accessible by a twenty-minute long tail boat from the mainland and has no roads, nor cars. Before I could wallow in my loneliness, everything turned around - rather spectacularly! I met three gorgeous Chilean boys and from then on, life seemed so much better again (it didn't take much).

When we arrived in Railay during a busy period, and there was not a room to be found on the entire peninsula, the four of us ended up sharing one cramped room. There are things that you do when you are backpacking that you would never consider doing in any city back home. All thrown into the same boat, you tend to trust people more out here. Imagine calling my mum (and I did, my poor mother), telling her that I was sharing a hotel room with three random boys from South America that I had just met on the boat a few hours ago! Of course, the guys turned out to be great friends and we spent an incredible week rock climbing in beautiful Railay and neighbouring Tonsai. It was an absolutely magical place.

One day, Diego, one of the boys, and I trekked over the cliff from Railay beach to Tonsai Bay where the other two boys had been looking for a hostel. After a tough climb with four big rucksacks, we sat down on the beach and waited for the others to appear. Diego found an old, battered guitar in a beach bar, and we sat in hammocks for about half an hour strumming and singing in the sun. The next day, we all took a boat trip to snorkel near some outlying islands. A barbecue on a beach, followed by an amazing sunset and night-time swimming as phosphorous plankton twinkled around our bodies in the dark sea. Everything was just perfect.

These unforgettable moments seem to occur more when you are travelling than at home, not just because you are doing some pretty amazing things (which you are every day!), but for another reason. When you are travelling, you are constantly aware that the moment is about to end. That the people you're with will carry on down their own path in a few days, and that you cannot stay in the same place doing the same thing forever. The doctrine of Buddhism 'nothing lasts' is played out so formidably when travelling that it can be hard to deal with. Constant goodbyes to people and places make you sad. There are a hundred highs and lows, a hundred lifetimes jam-packed into a few months. From suffering uncomfortable, sleepless bus journeys that seem to never end, to watching a beautiful sunset over the ocean whilst eating the best food you've ever had in your life, it's the stark contrasts that make backpacking the rich experience it is. You can't have one without the other. The bad times make the good times seem all the better.

The next day my Chilean buddies were leaving for Bangkok. I said my goodbyes and prepared to suffer from the inevitable in-between backpacker blues. I took a boat to Koh Phi Phi and met some lovely English girls along the way. Together we took boat trips, snorkelled, partied and explored the castaway island of Koh Lanta by motorbike. All the time, the idea of starting the magazine was gathering force in the back of my mind and I wondered if I should just settle somewhere for a while and get to work. But was it really possible?

"I'm almost out of money," typed Daisy over Facebook chat, "but how about one last adventure? It's Chinese New Year and Malaysia is meant to be the place to be!"

I flew from Krabi to a very rainy Kuala Lumpur and met Daisy in the atmospheric China Town, which was full of cheap hotels, knock-off goods and some enormous rats. The word 'multicultural' doesn't even begin to sum up Malaysia's capital. Just 150 years old, it's a remarkable melting pot of cultures, religions and architecture. We crammed as much as we could into two days in the city. We ate lots of spicy Malaysian street food, visited the sacred Hindu site, the Batu Caves, dressed head to toe in a purple burka and visited the national mosque, Masjid Negara, before heading to the Chinese temple for midnight to experience the Eve of the Rabbit!

At 11.45pm, it was all happening in the temple. You could hardly see for the smoke coming from hundreds of incense sticks. As the only foreigners here, everyone was really keen to show us a special part of their culture on this important night. We were ushered over to the front of the temple by a very wrinkly old woman, who gave us a pot full of sticks and motioned for us to shake it. Each of the sticks had a number on and the idea was to shake the pot hard, with your eyes closed, until one of the sticks fell out. That number depicts significant meaning for you. After a lot of shaking, I got number 23. Lucky? It would seem not.

The old woman ushered us over to an even older, even wrinklier woman, head down eating noodles in the corner of the temple. She took our sticks, rooted around in a few secret drawers and gave us two pieces of paper. Then, without looking up from her noodles, in broken English, she foretells the future for the both of us.

She tells me that I should be more careful with money and that my love life is basically doomed. Whereas Daisy shall have good luck in finding the love of her life in August this year, my romantic destiny is going to be, and I quote 'very very slow.' Great. After this revelation we crawl under a long red table to make the fortunes come true. Why I wanted it to come true I don't know, but you find yourself doing these things. Leaving the temple that night with a dozen lucky nectarines and our fate laid out, my friend quietly satisfied, me slightly concerned, we decided to go for a beer.

With only one week left travelling in Southeast Asia, before heading to Australia, Daisy wanted to get out of the city for some real adventure. With the idea that this too could be my final adventure before starting work on the magazine, I told Daisy I was up for it. We leafed through a guidebook and our attention stopped on what sounded like a dream isle only a three-hour ferry ride from Penang in Malaysia. Daisy was talking about Sumatra, Indonesia. As she read out the blurb, this place sounded too good to be true. Amazing scenery, volcanoes, surfing beaches, rainforests, enormous lakes, friendly locals and dirt-cheap accommodation.

"Just one thing," my friend said after she'd finished reading, "it mentions there are quite a lot of earthquakes, erm… and volcanic eruptions, and flash floods, oh and the transport is really dangerous. Also, we should be careful of terrorism when we're there, other than that it really does sound awesome!"

"Okay," I said. "Let's do it."

Early the next morning we caught the ferry from Georgetown in Penang to Indonesia's third largest city, Medan. Daisy slept the whole way, but I was restless after a local had told us that swashbuckling pirates roam the Indonesian seas, so I'd been looking for sightings of the Black Pearl on the horizon all the way there. Having resigned ourselves to each other's company for the next seven days, thinking we wouldn't meet many others coming this way, we were surprised to see quite a few backpackers on the ferry, and before we knew it there were five of us travelling together.

After a crazy ride from Medan port on a clapped out, durian-smelling bus, filled with betel-nut chewing locals, we arrived at our first destination, Berestagi. Berestagi is a small town surrounded by volcanoes and hot springs that has very little in the way of tourism. We booked ourselves into Hotel Ginsata and then headed to the nearest bar. We ended up in a friendly little place called Raymond's, chatting with some very interesting, intelligent locals who all spoke excellent English. They were very eager to talk to us, and soon we got chatting about the decline in tourism in Sumatra over the past 15 years.

They attributed the decline to recent terrorist activity, some in Aceh, north of Berestagi, a few years ago, but in particular, the Bali bombing of 2004, which they say greatly affected the number of visitors to Indonesia as a whole.

"People are scared to come here," they said, "just because of the actions of a minority."

It occurred to me the immense power that the media has on influencing small towns that rely on tourism. Negative TV and newspaper coverage of a place can seriously damage the livelihood of small, local-run businesses that depend on overseas visitors. It seemed ridiculous to me, sat in this lovely bar feeling totally at ease with welcoming locals, that an isolated incident more than 1,500 kilometres away could deter so many people from visiting this place.

The next day, we climbed the volcano, Gunung Sibayak, from the town, which took us about three hours through jungle paths to reach the top; a steaming, egg-smelling crater, alive with the sound of gases rushing out of holes in the earth's surface. Wonderfully atmospheric and even though it last exploded over 4,000 years ago, you couldn't help but feel a little nervous that it may erupt again at any moment. The views from the top were fantastic and after a day climbing, soaking in the hot springs at the bottom of the volcano was heaven.

Our next destination was Lake Toba, a one-day, bumpy, chicken bus ride from Berestagi, on various buses with various drivers, all of whom had clearly had dreams of becoming Formula One racing drivers in their youth. With a bit of luck we made it there safe, and we knew at once we were in for a treat. Lake Toba is the biggest volcanic crater lake in the world, and we'd heard great things about it from everyone we'd met. As the steamy rainforest began to thin, the bus turned the corner and the lake came into view. A beautiful silver sheen sparkled on the horizon, in-between luscious green mountains, as monkeys played at the side of the road.

We'd heard of an island in the middle of the lake, Palau Samosir, and decided to settle ourselves there for the next few days. We stayed at the only resort on the island, Tuk Tuk, a spot which apparently once played host to its own Full Moon Party when the hippie trail was at its height in the 60s and 70s. Nowadays it's hard to imagine lots of drunk party people disturbing the lovely peaceful streets.

Rows and rows of cute little restaurants and bars, bookshops and cafés were devoid of people. We had the place to ourselves, and everywhere we went people were excited to see us, going out of their way to make us feel welcome. I couldn't help but feel a little sad that this wonderful place, that had once enjoyed an abundance of cash-carrying foreign visitors, had become a ghost town. We booked into Samosir Cottages in Tuk Tuk and paid a meagre US$5 per night for a brilliant room with hot shower and a bath (yes, a bath!). We were so close to the lake that you could hear the sound of the water lapping against the shore as you lay in bed.

The next couple of days were spent relaxing by the lake, attempting a bit of fishing, exploring the island, having some pretty heated table tennis tournaments and swimming in the lake at sunrise. Oh, and eating far too much of the amazing local curry, chicken rendang!

One day we hired a motorbike and travelled around the island, visiting some ancient tribal sites where gruesome deeds such as cannibalism once took place. Above all, we were astounded by the natural beauty of the island. Bright green rice fields, mountains, waterfalls, unusual ancient Batak houses, buffalo roaming the land and the metallic sheen of Lake Toba always in view. It was extraordinary to see quaint little churches dotted here and there, a throwback to the Dutch colonisation of the island 300 years ago. It seemed an incongruous sight after reading that Indonesia is 88% Muslim.

After four days at the lake, we just didn't want to leave. So much so, that we ended up staying an extra day and having to pay a fine on our visa as we left the country from Duran port back to Melaka in Malaysia. After reading about all the things that could have gone wrong on our trip before we came, upon leaving Sumatra we had experienced nothing but friendliness. Sumatra really was a fantastic destination, and a wonderful finale to the first stint of my travels in Southeast Asia.

By now, my funds were dangerously low and it was time to make a decision about my next step.

Should I fly to Perth Australia as planned and try to get a job? Or should I give this magazine idea a go? I made it back to Bangkok and walked around the city in a strange daze, pondering what to do next.

Looking back, it is incredible to think of those small decisions that you make that change the path of the rest of your life.

I decided to give it a go. What did I have to lose?

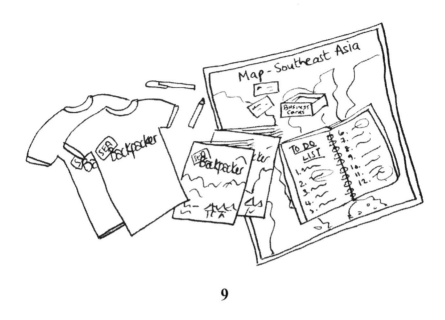

9

Getting Down to Business

I made it back to my dad's house in Pattaya in a taxi from Bangkok, and I was so broke that I had to get my dad to pay the money for the taxi when I arrived. I unpacked, had a good sleep in a comfortable bed, and wasted no time in getting to work on my idea. I stole my dad's laptop day and night, and would be up until daybreak writing articles, sketching layouts and attempting to design pages using the ever-sophisticated Microsoft Paint and Publisher. I laugh looking back at my first childish attempts!

One night, Dad came home from a game of golf and a few drinks with his friends, and I had transformed his downstairs bedroom into an office. All across the floor I had laid out pieces of A4 paper with various ideas for articles and photos, and was trying to get an idea of what would become the layout of the magazine. An events and festivals section, an arts section, photography, traveller stories, book reviews, games section, favourite travel quotes etc. I had scraped every story out of my little pocket diaries that I had been carrying around with me and had been emailing friends for their input, encouraging them to have a go at writing a travel article for the very first issue of *SEA Backpacker Magazine!*

Staring into the room, my dad could now see that I was really serious about starting this magazine. He looked at the rough design of the front cover and my illustration idea for the logo, and we both smiled seeing that it was really coming to life. There was no going back now. As I spoke at a hundred miles an hour about all of my ideas, my dad began to get as excited as I was, and even though it was already 2am we made a cup of coffee and spent the next few hours talking more about the business side of things and how I could really make this work financially. It was clear that the creative side was coming along nicely, as I was so passionate about that side of things, but would this magazine really make any money? How do you even open a business in Thailand? My dad was always the one to bring me back down to earth and make me think practically.

In Thailand, in order to protect the Thai people, a foreigner cannot own 100% of a business or land. If you want to enter into business or buy land, you must find a Thai business partner (or partners) and the most that you can own, as a foreigner, is 49%. Naturally, this deters many entrepreneurs from choosing Thailand as their location to start a business, as they must be sure that they have a local partner that they can trust.

There are, of course, ways around this. One option is that you can choose a number of 'shareholders' for your business, each owning a smaller percentage of shares – so that you become the major shareholder and therefore, the major decision maker. Another common way around this is for the Thai 'shareholders' to sign over their 'veto' rights to the foreign owner – meaning that although they have an ownership in the business, they have no decision making rights and could never sell their shares of the business. All of these rules, of course, have their own intricacies and from the very beginning, I could see that in Thailand, nothing was going to be black and white.

In the next few days, my dad, Ying and I made an appointment with a local lawyer to discuss my options. It was decided that Ying would become my silent business partner, owning 51% of the new company, yet, all of the decision-making rights would be signed over to me. I was nervous about this, yet, as I trusted my dad with my life, and he trusted Ying, I decided to go ahead. After all, there was really no other way of starting the magazine here. From Ying's side of things, she actually had experience working in a newspaper in Bangkok and had sold advertising to local businesses. She had kindly offered to help with the sales and marketing side of things, which was great, as I would certainly need someone who could speak the language, knew how things were done and could help me connect with Thai businesses.

The female Thai lawyer spoke very good English and explained the important facts to me, answering my long list of questions as best she could. Intermittently, Ying would ask a question and the two of them would spin off into a long conversation in Thai. Of course, my dad and I no clue about what they were discussing. I had only just begun to pick up a few odd words in Thai like 'dog' and 'no thank you' and this was way beyond my capabilities. When the dialogue was over, I would ask them to explain what they had been discussing and I was often given a short, one sentence answer. I was flummoxed as to why it had taken so long to debate. My dad and I looked at each other and shrugged – this was their country, not ours – and if I wanted to start a business here, I was going to have to learn about the nuances of the culture and the way Thai people did business. Indeed there were many things to learn.

Having never run a business in England, never mind in Thailand, I was concerned about doing things 'by the book' and correctly. Of course, my dad being with me made things a lot easier as I trusted his judgment having run a successful engineering business himself back in England. In this case, however, I think that both of us realised that we were treading on unfamiliar ground. Things seemed to work very differently here in Thailand. I didn't want to get in trouble for making a mistake unknowingly that went against Thai law and custom. I wanted to do things properly with the business from day one. I soon learnt that acts like giving the Head of Police a basket of fruit might get your work permit through faster, but I didn't want to get involved. I left the cultural side of things to Ying, and tried my best to do things correctly. I also hired a Thai designer, Jeb, who agreed to design the magazine to print-ready for around 25,000 baht (around US$700).

In addition, I took time to research Thai culture to make sure that I wasn't going to unknowingly commit a crime or say something utterly taboo in an article that may get me in trouble. The most memorable point to remember was that anyone who insults the King could be imprisoned under the 'lèse-majesté' law immediately. I'd heard the story about the foreign writer who had written a satirical book about the Thai royal family and had landed himself seventeen years in prison! I certainly wasn't going to use my magazine to make any political statements, and would steer away from serious and controversial issues. In just a few weeks, I had gone from carefree backpacker to responsible business owner, and I wanted to make sure that I was not foolish in my new role.

Over the next few weeks, I worked with our designer, Jeb, to create a suitable mock-up of what the magazine would look like. I would show him what I wanted by sketching the design on a piece of paper and he would create the page with Adobe InDesign. It was more difficult than working with an English designer, as I had done back in the advertising agency in Manchester. Unable to read English, Jeb had no real concept of what the article was about, and so it was tricky for him to come up with an idea for the design. Even when I explained the article to him (with Ying translating), Jeb had little concept of backpacking in the first place and so it was difficult to inspire him. I did learn certain Thai design rules from Jeb, like you cannot put a picture of a monk or the King below anything else on the page; they must be top right on the page in order to demonstrate respect.

Over four years later, when we were designing Issue 25, I shot out of bed, bolt upright, at 3am in horror. I had just dispatched a PDF of the magazine to the print shop with a cartoon of a monk and a pair of feet above it on the same page! The article was about holistic therapy and the cartoon of the monk was to depict meditation, whilst the feet where to depict reflexology. I alerted the print shop (via Ying) to explain my terrible error, in the middle of the night, and luckily they hadn't started to print yet. This would have been such a tiny, seemingly innocent error that could have been extremely serious for the magazine. Whatever made me wake up that night meant that I never had to discover the consequences of making such a cultural faux pas!

After a few weeks of working with Jeb, the design of the first issue of the magazine was complete except for white spaces with 'YOUR AD HERE' amongst each of the feature articles. I was proud and happy with the result. We got a quote from a local print shop to print five mock-ups, and I felt exhilarated and simultaneously sick with nerves, finally holding the fresh-smelling paper, stapled together with two staples along the spine, in my hands. We also got a quote for printing 5,000, 15,000 and 25,000 copies of the magazine and the costs were much more than I had expected.

I had taken the risk of setting up the company, to make everything legitimate, before I began telling backpacker-related businesses about my idea. Was this going to be something that I would regret? The hard task now in front of us, was to get out there on the backpacking trail and win some support (and much-needed hard cash) to pay for the printing of the magazine.

I had 300 snazzy business cards produced at the print shop, four white polo t-shirts printed at the local market with the SEA Backpacker logo across the front, and I printed 500 sales leaflets which contained prices for advertising. If I was going to make this work, I needed to look and act the part.

10

Door-to-door Sales

It was our seventh day out on the road trying to sell advertising space in the magazine. Dad had driven the car down south to Surat Thani, the jumping off point for the islands in the Gulf of Thailand, and the three of us had taken the car ferry over to the islands of Koh Samui, Koh Phangan and Koh Tao. After that, we headed over to the Andaman coast on the west, to visit Krabi, Phuket and the island of Koh Phi Phi. It was so strange to be out on the backpacking trail with my dad and his girlfriend! Just months before, I had been here rock climbing with Chilean boys and having the time of my life! However, this time I was able to enjoy the experience in a completely different way. Dad and Ying were as excited as I was about the magazine, and the three of us made a good team.

Although we received a lot of encouragement about the magazine from the start, with a few companies saying that they would likely be on board within the next six months, we still hadn't got anyone to commit to an advertising contract. I was getting worried. I had told everybody, confidently, that the magazine would be out on 1st June 2009. However, if I didn't manage to get any sponsors and find money to fund the printing, the whole thing was off. Despite the immense hard work that had gone into creating my five glorious mock-ups, I wouldn't be able to afford to print more magazines without advertisers.

For the whole week Ying had been by my side every day, helping me to introduce the concept of the magazine to potential customers. Whilst on the island of Koh Phi Phi, I'd encouraged her to take the day off with my dad and take a boat to Koh Phi Phi Leh. This island was home to a beautiful National Marine Park, famous for having featured in the Hollywood version of *The Beach*. With impossibly turquoise waters and limestone karsts surrounding a pristine white beach, it was undeniably stunning. However, the tourist boats and crowds somewhat ruined the image of perfection. Although this was Ying's home country, I had evidently seen a lot more of it than she had, and she was fascinated by this completely new scene and the cult of 'backpacking'.

Dad and Ying were just tucking into their breakfast at the hotel before jumping aboard the tourist boat to Maya Bay, as I set off around the island in an attempt to draw in customers. In the main Phi Phi village, I sat down with an English guy, Phil, who was the owner of one of the biggest and most respected dive schools on the island, Viking Divers. I began my sales pitch. Newly printed SEA Backpacker black T-shirt and white shorts (to match the logo) I tried to seem as professional as possible in appearance and manner.

Before I'd even finished extolling the benefits of advertising in the "brand new, unique, never been done before, bound to be a success, first and only *Southeast Asia Backpacker Magazine*", Phil uttered a cool, "Yep. I'm in. Put me down for six months." My hands were shaking as I wrote out the very first contract and asked Phil to sign it.

Literally sprinting back through the streets, I caught Dad and Ying who had just finished their breakfast and were about to set off to catch the boat. I sat down, heart beating fast, and placed almost 16,000 baht (US$450) on the table. Phil had paid me in advance! All of our eyes lit up with excitement and a sense of achievement. It was the most significant moment in the life of the magazine so far, as it now meant that there was no turning back. Whatever happened from now on, I had one customer who had paid me already, and I couldn't let him down. Even if we didn't get enough money to fund the printing, I had committed and would somehow have to cover the bill myself. It was an incredible moment, but also a nerve-racking one.

After the first sign-up, other companies seemed to jump on board more easily. I returned to my dad's house after the three-week trip and started to make phone calls to all those who had shown interest or encouragement. (I estimated that we must have seen over a thousand companies in all!)

The friendly Australian rock climber, Tim, from Goodtime Adventures in Koh Tao: "Yeah sure, I'll take a one year contract. Sounds like a great idea!"

The lovely Fiona from Mai Pen Rai Bungalows in Koh Phangan: "Sounds like something I'd like to be a part of. I'll go for six months!"

Isaac from Deep Blue Dive School in Koh Tao: "A half page will do us. Thanks!"

It was thrilling to have people email me the artwork for their advertisements, and as the printing deadline approached, the magazine was filling up and more importantly, the funds were adding up. Yet, we still needed a lot more if we were going to be able to cover the expensive printing bill.

As I called customer after customer, Ying called the business owners who preferred to liaise in Thai. It was clear from the start that the Thai customers needed different treatment than the Western ones. Whereas I had a 30 second phone call, ending with "Yeah sounds good, but I'm busy right now, can you email me?", Ying would be on the phone for hours. She would be getting to know the person who would be advertising with us, learning about the nature and history of their business and finding out their marketing needs. At first, I found it frustrating coming from a Western mindset where efficiency was of paramount importance. At work, I had been taught not to waste anybody's time, especially not my own. Straightforward yes or no answers were what I wanted so that I could move on quickly. However, I respected the contrasting ways that different cultures conduct business. It was clear that Ying knew what she was doing with the Thais, much more than I did. She was signing up customers and building relationships that would last the lifetime of the magazine.

This was just another lesson in discovering how things were done so differently in Asia. From small negotiations to large business deals, building relationships is the key. Developing trust and slowly nurturing a business connection is something that us Westerners often do not have the patience for in such a fast-paced business world.

Other cultural differences left me in amazement. Every day with a long 'to-do' list, I would work my way through the tasks one by one. I felt a sense of achievement as I ticked things off and signed up advertisers, and I felt disappointed if I hadn't achieved as much as I had wanted to that day. On the other hand, Ying believed that there were other variables involved in achieving success - a little extra was needed to bestow good fortune. She would enter our homemade office in the mornings, light an incense stick and pray to the statue of Buddha that she had placed on the top of the filing cabinet. She believed that he would bring us customers and money. Although at the time, I would have much preferred for her to do something more practical to help us get sales, who was I to question Thai culture and beliefs? Anyhow, whatever it was, my determination or Ying's 'lucky', between the two of us, it was working!

The laid-back 'mai pen rai' (no worries) attitude is something that many Westerners fall in love with when they first arrive in Thailand. It represents a refreshing change from our stressful society and our constant desire to achieve things. The phrase seems to suggest 'whatever is going to happen, will happen - so why concern yourself?' Whilst you are on holiday in Thailand this sentiment fits perfectly with your desire to enter 'de-stress mode', but it can be very frustrating when trying to do business and get things done.

To me, it seemed that the entire concept of time was different in Southeast Asia. Whereas I wanted things to be done *now*, the Thai attitude towards me tended to be 'what's the rush?' If you completed a job it only meant that there would be another one waiting, so why not just take your time? And, more importantly, enjoy yourself while you're doing it. I thought back to my days in the advertising agency in Manchester, where I would sit at my desk at lunch time, shoving a sandwich in my mouth, not even tasting it, trying to carry on with all the work I had to do.

In my new 'job', Ying would always make sure that we stopped to cook a big Thai lunch and eat it outside on the table in the garden, away from the office. With precious days going by until the launch of the magazine, I didn't want to waste even a moment, but I look back and appreciate those special moments where I took a break. Today, they are vivid memories pitted in-between a period of very hard work.

Later, after many years of working and living in Thailand, I pondered that the different ways in which the East and the West think about time could be an ingrained cultural difference that dated back thousands of years.

To Westerners, the concept of time is a linear process. Time is like a river flowing from a source to the delta – once elapsed, time cannot be retrieved. No wonder we consider it so precious, so important to use it wisely. Once it has gone, we can't get it back. In Southeast Asia, on the other hand, time seems to be viewed differently. Concepts such as karma, reincarnation and the influence of Buddhist, Hindu, Tao and Confucian philosophy mean that time is not viewed as something which has a start and finish, but something which is a circular process. Just like the river flowing into the sea and evaporating into the sky, only to fall again onto the earth; time renews itself again and again. Time doesn't run out. It doesn't fly or go anywhere. There is always enough time.

For example, the Chinese calendar is cyclical and the years are dated using the signs of the zodiac, which repeat every 12 years. The Buddhist notion of karma is an endless cycle whereby the deeds you do in life will come back to you in this life, or the next. Even some Asian languages do not have tenses, perhaps reiterating the focus on the present, rather than past or future. Just like the tides and sunrises, time is continuous and well… timeless.

No matter how long I lived in Southeast Asia, it is a concept that I don't think I could ever get used to. A list-maker and a planner, I feel that time creeps up on me with a sense of panic. I rush to fill my life with all of the things that I want to do, terrified that I will miss out on something if I don't move fast enough. I'm not saying for one second that this is the best way to be.

On our second marketing trip, we set off up north to Chiang Mai and Pai to speak to hostels, trekking companies, mountain biking companies, zip line adventure companies, elephant sanctuaries and a huge number of cafés and restaurants. The response was, again, favourable, but we still weren't getting enough people to commit. In the North, we also came across quite a few cynical sorts, mainly older Western men, expats who had lived in Thailand over ten years or more, who spoke to me in a patronising manner.

"Aren't you a bit young to be embarking upon something like this with so little experience of Thailand?" They would make sexist comments and ask me particularly tricky questions to try to catch me out and make me look like I didn't know what I was doing.

One worry that had been niggling me ever since we had set out on the marketing trips, was distribution. I had been telling everyone that the magazine would be available all along the backpacker trail, in hostels, travel agents, guesthouses, adventure centres and cafés in Thailand, Laos, Vietnam and Cambodia. In truth, apart from using the postal service to send out the magazines in Thailand, I had no idea how I was going to get so many copies to the neighbouring Southeast Asian countries. If I were to post 5,000 copies of the magazine to Hanoi, for example, it would cost something like three times the amount of money that it cost to print the magazine in the first place!

There had to be another way. Yet, without speaking the language or knowing the ins and outs of doing business here, I had no idea if distribution companies like UPS or TNT existed, and I didn't have the first clue where to look. What was even more baffling, was that some places didn't even have proper addresses:

Banana Guest House
Down the Temple Road, left at the school. Next to the 7-11

How was a post deliverer supposed to find this?

It turned out that I was addressing the problem all wrong. I was coming at it from a very Western perspective, trying to organise everything all in one go. I needed to think on a smaller scale, more local, break things up. In a land where pigs, dogs, five children, cabbages, microwaves and TVs are carried around on the back of a motorbike, I needed to look at how the local systems worked in each area.

Everywhere that we travelled, Ying would chat to local people and tell them what we were trying to do with the magazine. I explained to her my worry about distribution, wondering if she had any good ideas.

"I make friend on the boats who has cousin looking for job and he have brother who live in Nong Khai on Laos border. He can delivery our magazine for us. No problem!"

I raised my eyebrows. "How much?" I asked.

"A few thousand baht maybe," she replied, "let me ask him." (A thousand baht in Thai money is 20 English pounds).

What followed was (of course) a lengthy conversation to the cousin's brother in Laos, whilst I hovered over Ying's shoulder desperately trying to understand any word. She put the phone down and sighed.

"600 baht," she said sadly and dropped her head. "I wanted to get him down to 500."

"What?" I screamed. It would cost us all of twelve pounds to have the magazine distributed around the whole of Laos! This was unbelievable. Ying started to explain how it would work. We would pack a cardboard box full of magazines and label it with the delivery guy's name (Khun (Mr.) Kye) and his phone number. Then, we would drop the package onto the bus in Bangkok and Mr. Kye would pick it up at the other end in Vientiane, the capital of Laos. We would give him a clear list of places where we wanted the magazines to be left, and Mr. Kye would distribute the magazines around the city according to the list. When the job was finished we would transfer the money to Mr Kye's account.

"It'll never work," I told Ying naively. "How can we possibly find people to do this all over Southeast Asia?"

"Khun Kye have auntie on Cambodia border who looking for work," she replied.

And for five years it worked just like this. Every issue, I would pack up my beloved magazines in a cardboard box with a name scrawled on the top in Thai handwriting, and place it on a rickety old bus with rice bags and chickens and wave it on its way. Each time I did this, I felt nervous thinking that the precious load wouldn't reach its destination. Not only were the magazines my thoughts, designs, photos and ideas – it was expensive to print and I would have hated to have them go missing and all that money go to waste.

The organised Westerner in me wanted a signed, stamped recorded delivery, a piece of paper saying exactly what time it would arrive at the destination, and a way to check online that someone had collected it. Doing things the Thai way, I just had to trust that it had got there safely. At the bus station, I often had to hide as Ying negotiated a price with the driver for delivering my parcel. If the bus drivers saw a farang they would naturally charge double price for the service.

So off the magazines went. And most of the time, it worked pretty well. All over Southeast Asia, the magazines travelled by various means: buses, long-tail boats, motorbikes, across borders and over seas; always arriving in the right place, although not always at the right time. It's a miracle really! I'll bet there are still a few piles lying around in bus stops, to be discovered in years to come, the thought of which makes me smile. Doing business in Southeast Asia was proving to be an eye-opening experience, and a lesson not only in business, but in life. Patience and trust. I was learning so much.

After distribution was potentially solved, we set off in the car again - this time to tackle a different country. I felt more confident now, knowing that we had a cost-efficient way of delivering the magazines to Laos, Vietnam and Cambodia. So, we could now focus on getting some advertising revenue from these places. Laid-back Laos was first on the list.

It was just one month away from launch date and despite a good number of sign ups, we still didn't have enough customers to cover the cost of printing. My dad was very supportive.

"Well Nikki," he would say, "if it was easy, everyone would be doing it!" And so, as a formidable team, Ying and I battled on, with our T-shirts ironed and our smiles and sales pitches *almost* perfected.

Not a natural salesperson (I actually don't like selling that much at all!), I think what spurred me on in those first few months, and throughout the lifetime of the magazine, is that I truly believed in what I was selling. As a backpacker prior to my business idea, I had felt the need for a magazine like this myself. They say that the best business ideas are when you create something that you want that doesn't already exist. So, I just knew there was a gap for it in the market as I was speaking from genuine experience. My only task was to convince the business owners of this and get them to believe in me. I think that my determination was evident, despite not having the answer to every difficult question. 'Mai pen rai'. I was getting the hang of it.

In Laos, we started the sales trip in the sleepy capital of Vientiane, followed by the party town of Vang Vieng and then finally, the pretty colonial city of Luang Prabang. It was in Vang Vieng, where I had been tubing just months before. For anyone who has ever been to Vang Vieng, you will know that this is not a place that you take your dad and his girlfriend! It is like taking your grandmother to Ibiza.

In terms of sales, Laos was a completely different ball game. If we thought Thailand was laid back and fostered a 'no worries' attitude about growing your business, Laos was asleep. Literally.

"Sabaidee. My name is Nikki from *Southeast Asia Backpacker Magazine* and I would like to talk to the owner of the hostel about advertising."

"Owner asleep in back" was the common answer at backpacker hostels at any time of the day. "You want me wake him? It important?" Well yes, I thought, it is important. Moments later, a guy in a dirty vest appeared, bleary-eyed, stretching and scratching his bum. I guess it was more important to me than it was to him.

"You could make lots more money with your business, attracting backpackers from all over Southeast Asia!" I would say. "When a backpacker picks up a magazine in a travel agency in Bangkok, they will read it on the bus on the way to Laos and they will see your hostel as they are travelling," I said. "Reach backpackers before they reach you!" It had become my slogan for the sales pitch.

I looked around at the shabby house that had been turned into a makeshift backpacker hostel, the hammocks lining the porch, the barefooted children laughing and chasing the chickens around the garden. The owner would look at me and contemplate my words carefully. *Maybe he didn't want to make any more money.* I thought. *Maybe he was happy with things just exactly the way they were.* This was a rather groundbreaking thought that I was confronted with during that week in Laos.

When do you stop trying to achieve, trying to make more money? In the East and the West the concept of work and lifestyle can be quite different. Do you work to live or live to work? Ambition, achievement, the constant improving of oneself, seems to be something that we are so preoccupied with in Western culture, not always with a beneficial outcome. After all, the most important thing that we have, is the time that we spend on this earth, rather than the possessions or accolades that we accumulate during that time. I loved the way that Southeast Asia made me question my own culture and the values I had grown up with.

After those initial marketing trips, over a period of four months, we managed to get a solid 18 customers to advertise in the very first issue of *SEA Backpacker Magazine*. An incredible result, and I would like to say thank you to all of the people who saw the passion in my eyes and believed in my idea. Thank you for trusting that I would print a magazine, rather than running off with the money to Australia and getting drunk like the backpacker I still was at heart!

11

The Khao San Road Launch

It was the big day of the launch and I was feeling extremely nervous. On the 1st June, Ying and I stood on Khao San Road in Bangkok, wearing our SEA Backpacker t-shirts, with 3,000 magazines wrapped in brown paper at our side. My 'new-born baby' was ready for its first outing, and I was terrified to show it off to the world! Would people laugh at my writing? Would they find the stories childish and boring? Would they want to share their own stories in the magazine and help to continue this 'travel diary for everyone?'

The Khao San Road is the backpacker hub of Southeast Asia. It's a place once described by a Thai poet as 'the shortest road with the longest dream in the world'. With backpackers coming here from all over the world, to embark upon their once-in-a-lifetime adventure, you can understand why this road is so significant to so many people. Love it or hate it, there's a special energy in the air on any given night down that road - a sense of escape, excitement and a loss of control, even.

The Khao San Road Launch

The strong smells, the noise, the hustle, the purchases, people from all different walks of life - all create a kind of sensory overload. Every hunger can be gratified on that road, if only for a very short while. For sale, there's cheap clothing, t-shirts, flip flops, DVDs, CDs, fake IDs, bags, belts, books, jewellery and ornaments. To eat, there are noodles, Pad Thai, pizza, curries, falafel, spring rolls, fruit, crickets, beetles, cockroaches, as well as McDonald's and Burger King. In a matter of minutes you can get a tattoo, a massage, dreadlocks - all "Cheap, cheap for you my friend!" For what the road lacks in quality, it definitely makes up for in quantity.

I had heard a lot about this famous road before I came to Thailand, and during my own backpacking adventure I had chosen to miss it out. Yet here I was now, about to start a new adventure and a new chapter of my life. Just like all of the other backpackers on the Khao San Road that day, I was starting to live my dream. So, like the opening to Alex Garland's *The Beach*, like the beginning of the Thailand travel section in the *Lonely Planet* and like the beginning of almost every backpacker's journey in Southeast Asia, the story began on the Khao San Road in Bangkok.

My dad wasn't able to make it for the big launch. It was the time of the economic crisis in the UK, and he had been forced to go back home to England to pick up the pieces of what was left of his manufacturing business. He had retired early, at age 56, and he took a yearly income from his business that enabled him to live a great quality of life in a country that was much cheaper than Europe. In Thailand, your money could go a lot further than in England. He could have carried on working longer and retired a wealthier man. Yet at that time of life, or at any time of life for that matter, what is more important in the end – time or money?

So it was just Ying and I that day, and she was finding it hard to understand my apparent anxiety. She handed the magazines out to people sat in bars, who would begin to flick through the pages, and I would sit behind them looking to see if they were laughing in the right places. I felt embarrassed that people would be reading the words that were so personal to me. It felt like backpackers were sat in a bar, in the light of day, reading my diary! I think that there is a similar feeling with any kind of personal creativity that you share with other people. Whether you are singing a song you have written in front of an audience, showing a painting you have drawn, or allowing somebody to read the first rough draft of your book – you are exposing another side of yourself, a more vulnerable side than you show day-to-day. At least that's how I felt that day, as the backpackers, unaware, held my dream in their hands.

When starting to write this very book I had remarked to a fellow travel writer. "What about all of the really personal things? People will discover what I'm *actually* like – warts and all."

"Get naked," she replied. And that's exactly what you are doing when you write a book, a song or a personal article. Getting naked gets easier the more you do it. You soon realise that everyone is pretty much the same, with niggling anxieties and insecurities, and there's nothing whatsoever to be embarrassed about, least of all something that could shock people. Everything in this world has pretty much been done before.

So people seemed to laugh in the right places, and after a few weeks I had emails in my inbox from backpackers offering to write articles. Others had sent me links to their personal travel blogs and given me permission to use their stories in the magazine. Furthermore, I had been sent at least three actual, well-written, full-feature articles with good quality travel photos that were starting to become Issue Two of *Southeast Asia Backpacker Magazine*. I was more than delighted with the initial response!

Advertisers called me to say that they loved the magazine and had seen a good response from placing their adverts. I also had interest from those businesses that had been reluctant at first about advertising. Having seen the magazine in print, they were now interested to jump on board. They had witnessed people reading the magazine in hostels all across Southeast Asia and had started to think that we were all onto a good thing!

After getting back to my dad's and relaxing for a few days to get over the busy and emotional launch, I began work on Issue Two. Jeb came to the house most nights, and I sat by his side watching his computer screen. I began to learn how to use the program InDesign, so that one day I may be able to do the design of the magazine myself. I bought a pirate copy of the program for the equivalent of about US$5 at the local IT store and started to practise, and pick up a few skills from Jeb. Back in the UK, this software would have been too expensive for me to purchase at that time – just one of the examples of how things can be easier and more accessible in Southeast Asia. Even if things weren't always done 'by the book'.

I called some more of the sales leads that we had made during our first marketing trip. These were the ones that had said "Maybe" or "We'll see how it goes", and I spoke to them about signing a six month or one year contract. In two months, we managed to increase our customer list to a grand total of 24 companies, many of whom had decided on the longer, one year contract. I was so pleased that the businesses were starting to place trust in me and believe that I was in it for the long haul. I certainly was!

Ying and I also took a trip to Cambodia to approach businesses about advertising in the magazine. Ying had never been to Cambodia before, and I discovered that she had an irrational fear about travelling there. She had heard all her life, from other Thai people, that Cambodia was a dangerous place.

"The people there are thieves and they practice black magic!" she declared. Having already been to Cambodia I knew that this wasn't true at all, and I was shocked at her racist attitude towards a neighbouring country.

I guessed that such ridiculous stereotypes came from old folk tales. If Thai people didn't travel much or mingle with people from different races then, sadly, the stereotypes would remain in place. After living in Thailand for almost five years, unfortunately, I did encounter quite a lot of ethnocentric behaviour amongst Thai people, in general. It seemed that many Thais believed that they were superior to Laos, Burmese and Cambodian people, particular people from countries that were not as developed as Thailand.

Like all stereotypes and bigoted opinions, the problem came from lack of education. The Thai education system is notorious for teaching solely about Thai history, and not much else about the rest of the world. Much later, when I began to make friends with Westerners who were teaching English in Thai schools, I found out that ethnocentricity and racial problems ran deep. I heard horror stories of Thai teachers who would arrange their class by 'shades of colour', the whiter children (who looked more Chinese) were regarded as more intelligent than the darker children (who looked more like farm workers according to the teachers).

I also heard a story from my black, American friend, who had applied for a job at a school in Bangkok. The Thai head teacher had said to him in all seriousness, "So your credentials are great, but I think the way you look would scare the children." I was utterly shocked and appalled at this racism, and sadly it exists ferociously in Thailand today. When I helped to advertise TEFL schools and jobs for English teachers in Thailand, I would be forced to tell people of ethnicity about the racism that existed in the Thai school system, so that they would have realistic expectations of getting a job. Thai schools would always prefer the whitest skin and the lightest hair and eyes. Thai people are also unafraid to speak their mind, and will point out how they feel about other races quite openly and unabashed. Political correctness does not exist in Thailand as it does in the UK.

One unbelievable example of cultural insensitivity happened when a friend of mine, who was working in a school in Chiang Mai, was asked to monitor Sports Day. There were four teams of children across the school (red, blue, yellow and green), and each of the teams had to come up with a theme to denote their colour. For example, the blue team chose 'underwater' as their theme and had planned to dress as sea creatures, fish and mermaids. No problem. The red team, however, decided to keep their theme a surprise until the last day.

To the utter shock and horror of the three foreign teachers working at the school, the red team marched out on Sports Day dressed head to toe in Nazi uniforms, waving swastika flags the size of houses. They marched throughout the town in the school parade, passed the local synagogue, and the teachers did nothing to not stop them. My English teacher friends had run into the school panicking, and urged the head teacher to stop the proceedings immediately. The head teacher had replied, "Mai pen rai, not our culture."

Someone tried to put it into Thai context: "You must realise how serious this is - it's like the children dressing up as Pol Pot and the Khmer Rouge, and marching through the streets!"

The head teacher of the school replied, "Who is Pol Pot?"

Despite Western media being up in arms about the event, Thai authorities dismissed it with a 'mai pen rai', and, miraculously, they seemed to get away with the whole affair, with foreign tourists still choosing to come in droves to Thailand's shores, despite bad publicity.

So, after reassuring Ying that we would not be robbed or killed or become victims of black magic in Cambodia, we travelled across the border to Siem Reap. Siem Reap is the backpacker hotspot of Cambodia and a purpose built city for tourists visiting the spectacular ancient Khmer temples of Angkor Wat. The Angkor temples are a UNESCO World Heritage Site dating back to the 12th century, famous more recently for being the ruins that Angelina Jolie bounded through in the film *Tomb Raider*. It's also the place from where she adopted her Cambodian son, Maddox Chivan. Far from being the most spectacular things about the country, these are the facts that backpackers would remember.

We didn't manage to get any more advertising that week in lively Siem Reap, but we did find new ways to expand distribution, and introduced our magazine to a lot of new people. The aptly named 'Pub Street', that runs through the middle of Siem Reap, became the hub for the distribution of *SEA Backpacker Magazine*. We'd be back here in a few years to get more advertisers on board. In the beginning, it was all about taking little steps that would open up doors later on.

When we returned from Cambodia and were just about to produce the next issue of the magazine, another fortuitous thing happened. A professional writer and photographer who went by the pseudonym, Flash Parker, contacted me. He had worked for the big names like *Lonely Planet* and *GQ Magazine,* and now he wanted to write for *SEA Backpacker Magazine!* I was star-struck.

Flash sent a proposal entitled 'Dear Editor...' (which of course was me, as well as Deputy Editor, Designer, Distributer, Accountant and Tea Maker) with an absolutely riveting adventure story about an off-the-beaten-track motorbike trip through Vietnam and Cambodia. It was entitled *Cola Bottle Gasoline.*

The photos, particularly of the sun setting over the sand dunes in Mui Ne, Vietnam, were incredibly professional and beautiful, and this guy was clearly out of our league! I replied with a polite, 'We would be honoured to print your amazing photographs and story, but I'm afraid we are a free magazine with absolutely no funds to pay professional travel writers. All submissions are voluntary. Thank you so much for your time and in the future... well you never know!'

The next day I received a reply from Shawn, AKA, Flash Parker: 'I thought you might say that! Well, anyway, I loved your magazine so much during my trip that you can use the article for free - and there are more articles where that came from.'

I was overawed. Things were looking up! And, once we were able to get some professional photography printed in the magazine, the quality seemed to just get better and better. After Issue Two, Three and Four were printed, we were receiving more and more excellent articles, humorous travel tales and beautiful photographs. Advertisers were coming in fast and steady, and we were breaking even on the cash front, with a little extra to pay for business trips to nearby countries to accumulate more advertising. Business was going well, but personally, I was feeling a bit down in the dumps.

12

Back in Nam

I had been living at my dad's for about eight months whilst the magazine was getting off the ground. After the initial excitement of the launch and the business trips, I started to get a bit down. Apart from Dad and Ying, I had no friends in Pattaya, and there were no young people nearby to go out and socialise with. Dad was becoming a bit pissed off that I was taking his girlfriend away from him and keeping her up all hours of the night to work on the magazine. We argued a lot during this time, as he was also coping with the fact that he had just shut the doors on his own business back in England. He wasn't really in a position to be positive and inspirational about my venture.

The truth was, I was feeling lonely and just needed to go out for a drink with a friend that I could talk things through with.

"Go for a Thai massage?" Dad suggested. What I really wanted was a night of fun and laughs, and to blow off steam with a good group of friends, but there was no one around. I couldn't afford a flight back home to England to achieve this. My fun and fancy-free backpacking days felt very far away.

I spoke to my mum and friends back home daily over Skype and Facebook. As much as I couldn't live without this contact, chatting online is just not the same as real personal interaction. I was beginning to doubt my initial reasons for starting the magazine. Was all the hard work worth it if I had no social life and wasn't enjoying or exploring the country I had chosen to live in?

The purpose of starting the magazine had been to allow me to live a life of excitement and adventure in another country. The plan had not been to move back in with my dad, in a retirement community in Thailand! Every two months, I made just enough money to pay off the print bill. I was not in a position to look for a place of my own to live. Where on earth would I begin to look anyway? I didn't know anything about expat life for young people in Thailand.

At that point, Bangkok seemed like the logical place to be based for travel throughout the rest of Southeast Asia, but how would I find an apartment? Would I make any Thai friends? Would there be other expats living there? I was confused and overwhelmed by my future. My mum decided to come for a visit, as I hadn't seen her now for over a year and a half. My mum and I had always been very close, and I know that she missed me terribly. In some ways, I felt guilty for starting a business in Thailand and a life that was so far away from her. However, she always supported my decisions, and encouraged me every step along the way.

During the years I have lived abroad, I don't think I would have coped if it wasn't for Skype (thank you Skype!). Some days, when I was feeling lonely, my Mum would turn on Skype in her kitchen and I would listen to her as she went about her day. I loved to hear her normal day-to-day activity: chatting to my uncle on the phone, washing the dishes and helping me to proofread articles for the magazine. I missed her just being next to me, rather than on a screen in front of me, and it made me lonely to think that she, like so many of my good friends, people who really knew me, were so far away.

I was very excited to see her, but it was her first trip to Southeast Asia, and I wasn't sure that she was prepared for the culture shock of what my new life was like. I met her at the airport in Bangkok, and we decided to go the tropical island of Koh Tao in southern Thailand for a week to relax. 'Relaxing' isn't something that I have ever been very good at, and at such an early stage of the magazine, I couldn't help myself from wandering off to try to find customers, or speak to backpackers in bars about the magazine. I think I must have been really annoying to spend time with at that point, but as ever, my mum was behind me all the way.

I talked to her about my feelings of loneliness, and discussed how I was going to move on from living at my dad's house and find more balance in my life. We sat on the beach and discussed everything, from what I wanted to achieve with the magazine, thoughts of giving up and coming home, things that I enjoyed and didn't enjoy, the worry about if I could ever make good friends or meet a potential life partner out here, and basically - was it all worth it? I've always believed that mums use that clever tactic that psychologists use, where rather than dishing out advice, ask you questions and make you come up with the answers yourself. Answers that you knew already, deep in your heart, but were perhaps just too frightened to admit.

After our beach trip to Koh Tao, I persuaded my mum to tag along on my next ambitious mission. I was going to Vietnam to speak to the government.

So far, I had managed to sort out distribution in Thailand, Laos and Cambodia, but Vietnam was my next challenge. Apart from the fact that Vietnam was so far away, in terms of distance, from where we were printing in Bangkok, there was also the teeny weeny problem that Vietnam was a communist country and had restrictions on foreign media. We had figured out a way (using the rather handy Mr. Kye who was now distributing for us in Laos) of getting the magazines on that famous 27-hour bus journey from Vientiane to Hanoi. It was funny to think that my magazines would now be taking that test of endurance that I had undertaken a year ago as a wide-eyed backpacker!

Remembering the unbelievable palaver of getting an actual person, with a valid passport, across the border between Laos and Vietnam, I had no faith that a box of magazines could get across without a problem. Being the worrier that I am, I was terrified that the magazines would be stopped by Immigration Control and I would be slung into a Vietnamese prison for smuggling foreign media across borders. I know it was far-fetched and dramatic (as Mum repeated), but how did

I know that I wasn't going to break any rules, if I didn't know what the rules were in the first place? What if my magazines were seen as revolutionary pamphlets? Weirder things have happened.

During the time of my paranoia, there was a story in the news about a young, reportedly innocent, English backpacker who was imprisoned in Laos for trying to smuggle drugs across the border. She was awaiting the death penalty in a Laotion prison, but rumour had it that she was about to be spared from capital punishment because she had fallen pregnant. Whether she had become pregnant on purpose in order to delay the charge, or whether she was already pregnant before she went into prison, nobody seemed to know. Whether she had been set up and was innocent, or whether she was guilty, no one seemed to know either. The case was confusing and the facts blurred. There were reminders all of the time that in this part of the world, the law doesn't protect you in the same way as it can back in England.

Before I set off to see the Vietnamese government (Department of Travel and Tourism), I decided to contact an English-speaking law firm operating in Vietnam.

It turned out that they were actually an American company specialising in Vietnamese law, residing in the capital, Hanoi, where we were heading next week. Perfect, I thought. They would be able to speak English, and give me details about the laws that I needed to be careful of in Vietnam. I wrote out three clearly defined questions and sent it in an email to them. The very next day, I received an enthusiastic email from them saying that they were extremely interested in my project, and that they were eager and willing to help. However, they wanted US$4,000 just to answer my questions!

There was no way that I could afford that amount of money! So what should I do? Should I forget about distributing in Vietnam altogether? It was only one country in Southeast Asia, so perhaps it didn't matter that much. Yet I knew in my heart that it did. Vietnam was a very up-and-coming backpacker destination that was only going to get more popular as the country opened up and its riches became more accessible to tourists.

Vietnam is a country abounding in natural wonders. Just recently, a couple of amateur cavers from the UK had discovered a cave that would easily become the world's biggest cave, beating Malaysia's Sarawak Chamber by considerable height and depth. This was one of the many attractions that would draw adventurous backpackers to its diverse shores in the years to come. On top of that, there was rock climbing, kayaking, trekking, mountain biking, diving and more outdoor adventures. But more than all of this, I loved Vietnam. My time backpacking there had been exhilarating. Some of the highlights of my trip had taken place there, amongst great friends. I didn't want to leave Vietnam off my distribution list, simply because it was personally so important to me. So what should I do?

My mum and I arranged our visas through a travel agent in Bangkok and booked a flight to Vietnam. If my mum had experienced culture shock in Thailand, it was about to get ten times worse. When she was dropped onto the streets of crazy Hanoi, she had to learn how to cross the road all over again. People cooked their dinner on the streets as she walked by in her best shoes. And, being far too friendly and polite, she was hopeless at getting rid of the many salespeople that pestered her incessantly. She was coping well, and certainly being a good sport. However, when I suggested hiring a motorbike so that we could get around more easily, and find the government offices, her eyes widened.

To add to that, it was pouring it down. I hadn't realised that it was monsoon season in Hanoi. No problem! I would not be deterred. I picked us up a couple of bright blue ponchos from a streetside vendor, and drove up to the hotel holding two (what appeared to be) World War II helmets.

"Jump on!" I said. "We have a meeting with the Vietnamese tourist department at 3pm!"

Wearing a skirt and heels (she'd dressed nice for her daughter's meeting with the government), Mum came down the steps of the hotel and saw that the road was beginning to flood. Her face was a picture. She hopped onto the back of my motorbike, and we navigated our way around the hair-raising roundabout that hugs Hoan Kiem Lake in the centre of Hanoi's Old Quarter. Mum turned the map every which way but the right way, as we tried to find the tourist department for 3pm.

We arrived at the austere offices soaking wet. Nevertheless, we were smiling after our exhilarating journey. The head honcho in the Vietnamese Department of Tourism was very interested to see us. To our surprise, she actually knew all about the concept of backpacking and was eager to attract more of their kind to Vietnam! She thanked me

for creating such a magazine and for showcasing her beautiful country, of which she was very proud. She gave me her blessing to distribute the magazine in any hostel, restaurant or travel agency that we liked. In fact, could they have a copy sent to the tourism department as well? And also, could she have an advertising rate card? I was amazed by such a positive response from a country that had a reputation for being somewhat closed to new ideas.

Six months later, the Vietnamese Tourist Board became the first tourist board to advertise in the magazine and support us financially. After all of the worries about Vietnam rejecting my magazine, this was the best possible result. I was so pleased that I hadn't shelled out US$4,000 for 'legal expertise' to get answers to the questions that I could easily ask myself. I had just needed to get in front of the right person.

I realised, after that experience, that when you are trying to do something that hasn't been done before, you are in all senses, the 'expert' in this case. Expertise is just experience, and I was getting heaps of that as I was going along. Of course, 'middle men' will very willingly take your money in return for their opinion. What really matters, however, is that you will be the one risking everything, not them. Your venture isn't as important to anyone else as it is to you.

Again, this was another lesson about doing business in Asia. The lesson was this: don't be afraid to give it a go. Goals that had seemed unreachable were achieved one by one, as we slowly knocked down each wall that was in our way. In a communist country where Facebook was officially banned and foreign press was highly monitored, *SEA Backpacker Magazine* was freely distributed with the backing of the official tourist board. It was a triumphant moment for the magazine. As well as a great relationship forged with the Authority of Tourism, I met another character that would become a good friend and a huge support to the magazine along the way.

My mum and I walked into Hanoi Backpackers Hostel on Ngo Huyen Street, behind the rather incongruous St. James Church in the Old Quarter. I knew that the hostel was legendary on the Southeast Asian backpacker trail, famous for its wild parties and booze cruises to Halong Bay and their own private island, Castaways. The hostel was founded by a couple of Aussie guys who knew exactly what backpackers wanted. I asked the good-looking English guy at reception, who was chatting up some young backpacker girls in hot pants and vest tops, if I could speak to the owners.

Long-haired, smiley-faced Max walked out of the kitchen, wiping his hands on his jeans, and shook my hand firmly. Intimidated by his cool and confident demeanour, and his obvious experience and success with running a backpacker-related business in Southeast Asia, I was very nervous as I told him about my project. As we weren't yet distributing in Vietnam, he had not heard of the magazine, but I could instantly tell that he thought it was a good idea. He was excited and eager to get involved.

I had asked my mum to keep a low profile around the hostel while I conducted my 'official business'. There amongst the crowd of 18-25 year old backpackers she looked a little out of place, and Max noticed her sat awkwardly in the corner. I explained that my mum was on holiday with me at the moment, and she had been roped into coming along on my marketing rounds. He called her over for free gin and tonics and we all got to know each other better.

I really liked Max, and have always admired his fun-loving, laid-back approach to doing business. He told me a story about the launch day of the very first Vietnam Backpacker Hostel. Max and his business partner, Mick, had walked around the traffic-clogged city of Hanoi in board shorts and surf boards, approaching backpackers to ask where the beach was. Of course everyone knows that Hanoi is nowhere near the sea and the nearest beach was a five hour journey away. The quirky marketing stunt made backpackers laugh, and the dorm beds started to fill up.

Despite being professional, Max always remembered to have a laugh when doing business. Nothing was too serious, and everything was about enjoying the ride and making good decisions that benefited *people*, rather than profits. He was definitely one of the good guys, and it was the perfect time for me to meet such an inspirational entrepreneur in Southeast Asia.

Max called his business partner over. Mick was another friendly enthusiastic Aussie, who mentioned that he had a similar idea for starting a backpacker magazine a few years ago, but hadn't yet got round to it. They both seemed very interested in the magazine and wanted lots of copies at their hostel. Plus, they were opening a new hostel on Ma May Street in Hanoi and another further south of the country, in Hue. They wanted copies of the magazine in those locations too.

Mum and I spent the rest of our time in Vietnam doing day trips, riding our rental motorbike round the city and stopping for delicious street food in atmospheric corners of the city. Mum was starting to get used to the hectic pace of Vietnam, and it was great to be showing her new sights and sounds that would give her awesome stories to tell to her friends back home.

After the trip, Vietnam Backpacker Hostels became the official back page advert on *SEA Backpacker Magazine*. Over the years, Max became a good friend who I bounced ideas off and asked for business advice. In turn, I helped to promote their backpacker trips and tours. It is still a great relationship to this day and Vietnam Backpacker Hostels, as well as Vietnam as a backpacker destination, is booming.

13

Bangkok Expat

When my mum left to go back to Europe, I was devastated. I didn't know when I would see her again, and I didn't want to go back to living at my dad's house in Pattaya, with no prospect of making friends. It was time for a change. I got back to my dad's and worked on getting the next issue of the magazine out as fast as I could. I had decided that I would go and try to forge a life for myself in the weird and wonderful metropolis of Bangkok. I packed my backpack and left for the only place I knew – the notorious Khao San Road.

The next few days were a complete disaster. Trying to start my life in Bangkok, here on the most transient road in the whole of Thailand, was very naive. It was like trying to make friends with people who were just about to get on the plane in an airport.

People linger on the Khao San Road only for a few days. If you buy a CD it will play okay for the first couple of tracks, just long enough for you to feel confident that it works, before purchasing nine more. Rest assured, when you get home, it will break completely. The jewellery will fall apart. The stitching will come undone on all of those new clothes that you bought. On the Khao San Road, a massage lasts an hour, relationships last one day, Pad Thai lasts ten minutes and the incredibly 'orange' orange juice, lasts two minutes. Transience is played out so strongly here, in the capital of travel of Southeast Asia, that it can make you feel unstable. I should have got out sooner. I didn't. I lingered and made absolutely no real friends or connections that would help me in my life as a new 'expat' in Bangkok.

If it wasn't for Skype (and the entire series of *Flight of the Conchords* on DVD), during a very extreme case of homesickness that week in Bangkok, I think I would have given it all up there and then. I was exhausted after a year of working hard on the magazine alone, and I was at breaking point. I didn't have any friends who could understand or encourage me at this time. I wasn't sure if I wanted to put this much effort into a life in Southeast Asia, when I wasn't even making enough money to enjoy it. Should I go back home, treat all this as good experience under my belt, and get a *real job?*

My dad was only a few hours away from Bangkok, but it was my loving, caring mum that I needed now. Dad was there for logical, practical advice, and to give me a kick up the bum when I needed (and deserved) it. At the time, I just wanted a hug and to be told that everything was going to be okay. After a dramatic failure to start a new life in Bangkok, I went back to Pattaya and began to regroup. I got the hug I needed from my dad, as well as a kick up the bum.

So, in a city of over six million people, where you can't speak the language and don't understand the culture, how do you begin to carve out a life for yourself as an expat? In today's technology-driven world, the best place to start looking for fellow expats is, of course, the Internet. As I began to research, I found so many Facebook groups committed to connecting people: 'Expats in Bangkok', 'Young Entrepreneurs in Bangkok', even 'Farang Girls in Bangkok'. I started to cheer up as I saw that lots of people were in exactly my situation - in need of friends.

It appeared to be even easier than it would be at home to make friends in this new city. Expats seemed to stick together and make an effort to support each other in an unfamiliar country. Lots of people had posted in forums and Facebook groups: 'Hi I'm new to Bangkok and have no friends at the moment. I'm desperate to meet people!' I felt that it would be much harder, as an English person, to admit this so blatantly in an English city. I found a cheerful advert on 'Farang Girls in Bangkok' from an American girl called Monica, who was looking for a housemate pretty much immediately. We arranged to meet under the clock at Siam Square sky train station in Bangkok. In a much better position mentally than I had been the first time I set off to live in Bangkok, I caught the minibus from Pattaya and went to meet my potential new housemate.

After realising that we got on well enough to share the same apartment, we got down to business straight away. Monica was an ex-lawyer from New York who had decided to give up her job and change the direction of her life. She was now working for VSO (Voluntary Service Overseas), based in Bangkok, and her role was helping to support a shift to democracy in Myanmar. I admired her for making such a drastic change to her life. It was obvious from what she told me that she came from a family of high-achievers in the USA. Her family didn't quite understand her latest decision to go against the grain and earn a pittance of the money that she used to earn as a lawyer in the Big Apple.

Over three days, we looked around a variety of apartments in Bangkok, and were pleasantly surprised at what we could get for our money. For 23,000 Thai baht (about US$640) between the two of us, we secured ourselves an absolutely beautiful, two-bedroom apartment in the Victory Monument area of Bangkok. The luxurious apartment was on the 23rd floor of a swish skyscraper, on a lively street of bars, restaurants and shops called Soi Rangnam. The skytrain station of Victory Monument was just a five-minute walk away. Within minutes you could be at Thai markets, shopping malls, trendy bars and clubs. The apartment itself had two bedrooms, *three* bathrooms and two balconies offering up incredible views across the city. Plus, there was a gymnasium and a large swimming pool that residents could use. If this was expat life in Bangkok - things were definitely on the up!

Almost immediately, I started to settle into life in Bangkok. I began to really enjoy it. I was working on the magazine from trendy little cafés around the city, and meeting other interesting expats who were living in Bangkok doing a variety of different things. The city was buzzing by day and night, and it seemed that there was so much opportunity for young expats at that time. I met foreign correspondents, nightclub owners, journalists, radio presenters and TV stars. I would never expect to hang out with these types of people back in England. Here, however, we all seemed to stick together under that great big umbrella of 'expat'. Life was varied and colourful.

Without a nine-to-five restriction on my job, I could choose my own working hours. I was able to enjoy the city at any time of day or night I liked. Every day, I stumbled upon charming new places to eat lunch and dinner. Sat on a plastic chair right in the middle of the street, I would sample a variety of delicious Thai street food, as people, cars and motorbikes whizzed by. I bought exotic fruits from street vendors. Ripe, fresh mangoes and sweet pineapples in bite size chunks made perfect poolside snacks. I attended random street shows in sprawling Lumphini Park, and shopped for vintage bargains at the enormous Chatuchak Weekend Market. Every other day, I treated myself to heavenly foot and body massages. At just 150 Thai baht (US$5) a pop, it was hardly splashing out!

By night, I explored interesting bars and nightclubs with new friends. We went to the famous Thai student nightspot, RCA, the more mature Q Bar, Iron Fairies and The Nest, and Bed Supperclub, a rather lavish nightclub on the rowdy Soi 11. Bangkok's nightlife is notorious all over the world. However, I was finding out that it wasn't just go-go bars and strip clubs. There were huge clubs with international DJs, sophisticated wine bars and some spectacular rooftop cocktail bars. After all the bars closed in the city around 2am, many expats seemed to end up in a late-night dive called Chai's Bar. It had become a kind of Bangkok institution. Inside the dingy, poorly lit bar there were dog-eared photos of all the expats over the years that had attended the bar to sing drunken karaoke after hours. It stayed open until the last customer finished their drink.

I was enjoying my newly regained freedom, and once again understood the reason why I had started the magazine. I was giving myself the opportunity to experience a different, perhaps more interesting kind of life than I could have back home. The magazine continued to grow and flourish, as my life in Bangkok became more stable and I became happier in myself.

What made this period an even happier time for me was that one of my best friends from university, Pearl, had decided to move to

Bangkok and teach English.

Before heading off to travel around Southeast Asia herself, Pearl had taken a CELTA course (Certificate in English Language Teaching to Adults) back in England. Pearl was now qualified to teach English as a second language anywhere in the world. After a few months of backpacking, she now wanted to stay in one place and earn some money. She found herself a really good job in a Thai primary school teaching children of three and four years old.

Pearl and I explored the city together, and she helped me with aspects of the magazine from time to time. Pearl is a fantastic writer and eternal adventurer, and she wrote some of the best, most hilarious articles that we ever printed in the magazine. This was the girl on the boat with the naked Frenchman, the girl who went through a 'hitch-hiking' phase and refused to take buses. She was the girl who was the only stowaway on a cargo boat on the Mekong River from Laos to China. Her spirit of adventure in these stories made some backpackers look like they were on a package holiday!

One particularly hot day, Pearl was kindly helping me to distribute the magazine around some hostels in the Khao San Road area. After running around to various backpacker hotspots all day, we returned to the spot where the magazines had originally been unloaded from the taxi - on the pavement outside Vieng Thai Hotel, Soi Rambuttri. We'd nearly finished for the day. We were sweaty and tired, and looking forward to finishing distributing the last 1,000 copies so that we could go for a well-earned drink. Things didn't go entirely to plan. As experience was already teaching me in this part of the world, things rarely did.

We walked up and down Soi Rambuttri thinking we'd gone crazy, as the remaining magazines were nowhere to be found. They had seemingly vanished into thin air. It's no small feat to transport a thousand magazines in such a short space of time, leaving absolutely no trace, and we were utterly bewildered. It was a mystery.

I began asking every person on the road if they'd seen my beloved magazines. In my best 'Thinglish' (a mixture of basic Thai and English) I tried to explain what had happened. "Before. Magazine. Here. Now. No have!" I made the action with my arms of a shooting star to signify a mysterious disappearance. Naturally, I didn't get the answer I was after.

I ran up and down the street harassing people for information. An old woman down an alley way muttered a word none of us could understand…'leesykel'. What the hell did that mean? Was it the name of a person? Lee Sykell. If so, who is this Lee guy and what did he have to do with the theft? It was a wild goose chase. Who on earth would bother stealing 1,000 *free* magazines? Did one of the famous frog ladies of the Khao San Road have it in for us for printing an unflattering photo of her? (The frog ladies are women who sell wooden frog-shaped ornaments on the Khao San Road that make the sound of a frog in the wild.) I began to suspect everyone.

After noticing the kerfuffle outside his hotel, a member of staff from Vieng Thai Hotel came out to inquire about the antics. He had the ingenious idea of checking out the events on the hotel's CCTV. We felt like the FBI as we nervously waited, expecting to see two villains, in black jump suits with stockings over their faces, spring into view and commit daylight robbery. 'There they are, the perpetrators!' I would cry. 'Send them down!' Instead, it turned out that the CCTV didn't cover the scene of the crime. Our hopes were dashed. So, what were we to do?

Just as I was about to start crying and Pearl was combing the area for fingerprints, a little old man came shuffling along next to me picking up bits of old cardboard and paper cartons off the floor. He looked up at me and smiled. All of a sudden, it dawned on me what had happened. I nearly kissed his dirty face!

"Hey everybody! It's Mr. Lee Sykell," I screamed! Or more revealingly, 'Mr. Recycle!' The mystery was solved.

If you have ever wondered what happens to the rubbish under the cover of darkness in Bangkok, now you know. For some Thai people recycling is an important source of income. They clear the streets of everything that can be recycled: tin cans, paper, plastic bottles, glass bottles. They take them to the local refuse dump where the recycled goods can be exchanged for a small payment. With a huge wad of magazines, Lee Sykell must have been well chuffed with his pickings that evening! After a lot of explaining and help from Mr. Vieng Thai, we were led down a dark alley way with the little old guy, to his 'hoard'. This was his secret place where he had been storing the magazines, along with a load of other cardboard boxes and paper waste. I was so relieved and happy to see them safe and sound.

Lee Sykell wouldn't allow me to help as he picked up each bundle, gently brushed the dust off each one and, without a hint of reluctance, gave them back to us. I thanked the man and tried to give him 100 Thai baht for helping us, a compensatory offering after making him out of pocket that evening. After all, like us, the man was only going about his daily grind in the way he always did. He wouldn't take the 100 Thai baht; he wouldn't even consider it.

This was just another unexpected evening in Thailand that challenged my assumptions, and made me realise, not for the first time, why I loved living here in Bangkok. My life was, indeed, unpredictable and messy, but never, *ever* boring.

14

The Digital Nomads

After about two months of living in Bangkok, I came across a very interesting subculture known as the 'Digital Nomads'. I discovered this group after my housemate, Monica, attended a 'Tweet up' in Bangkok, while I had been visiting Dad and Ying in Pattaya for the weekend.

"What on earth is a Tweet Up?" I asked, unaware even of Twitter at the time.

"It's where all the people you've met on Twitter meet up! IRL – In Real Life!" she replied. At that time in my life, I wasn't Internet savvy at all. I hadn't realised that Twitter was such a huge resource that like-minded expats used to meet each other. I started to investigate.

A digital nomad is basically someone who works from their laptop from anywhere in the world. They do not have a permanent office, and pride themselves on being able to 'lifestyle design'. This means that they can work in their underpants in bed, or from a beach bar, any hours they like and they have no boss to answer to. Sounds pretty good doesn't it? Many of the digital nomads that were living in Bangkok at the time were also of that strange group known as 'Travel Bloggers'. Up until this point, I had thought that the purpose of a travel blog was just to keep your family and friends back home updated with your travels. I hadn't realised that it is possible to make a lucrative career out of travel blogging!

Many of the digital nomads that I met had begun with a personal blog through which, over time, they had built up quite an impressive following. With regular high numbers of traffic, they could now make money in various ways. They could sell banner adverts on their website, sell ad space through Google Adsense, make money through affiliate marketing (selling travel insurance or flights on a commission basis), or sell eBooks on Amazon related to the topic of their blog. At the time, it seemed to me that the travel blogger group was like some kind of cult. They all seemed to share similar values and ideas about how to live your life, helped each other out by promoting each others' websites or eBooks, and met up regularly, on and off-line, to discuss business and lifestyle ideas. It was a whole new world to me and I wondered if I was a digital nomad and a travel blogger too?

The big guy that many digital nomads worship is an author, lifestyle designer and digital nomad on an epic scale - Tim Ferris. He had written a groundbreaking bestseller called *The Four Hour Work Week,* which encouraged people to think radically different about their working lives. Written mainly for an American audience, Tim disparages the concept of working your entire life with only three weeks holiday a year, for what many call the 'American Dream'. Tim sees something very wrong with the nine-to-five society that values work over quality of life, leisure time and the pursuit of pleasure. Throughout a powerful, some would say, life-changing book, Tim demonstrates ways in which you can break free from the chains of your cubicle (office) and lead a life of awesome adventure. Through automation and efficiency, in a 'work smarter, not harder' approach, the ultimate goal is, as stated,

to only work four hours a week. Reading the book, after getting my hands on it from one of my new blogger friends, I found that many of his ideas resonated with me.

I started meeting up to 'co-work' with some of my new digital nomad friends at a place for freelance workers in Bangkok called Third Place. There was Sean Ogle, who ran the blog *Location 180* with the slogan 'Build a business. Live anywhere. Achieve freedom!' He was originally from Portland in the USA, and had won a competition through another lifestyle designer, Dan Andrews of *Tropical MBA*. Sean had been their first applicant in Manila to learn about building a 'location-independent enterprise', and since then he'd been living in Thailand and building his blog.

There was Cody McKibben who ran the lifestyle design blog, *Thrilling Heroics*. The aim of his blog was to encourage people to step outside the nine-to-five and start to live a life of adventure and freedom on their own terms. His writing was powerful and motivating and I was inspired by his unconventional ideas about how to make a living. Then there was David Walsh, also from the USA, who had written an eBook called *Source Control*, explaining the advantages of hiring 'virtual assistants' in countries such as India and the Philippines to help you build your business cost-efficiently.

As I was just finding out, there were huge 'virtual staff' centres all across Asia, where you could hire your own personal assistant for as little as US$3 per hour, to help you build your location-independent lifestyle. It seemed that the digital nomad was encouraged to make the most of the way that the world and certain systems worked. This process, popularised by Tim Ferris, was called geo-arbitrage. Some people had a problem with it as they felt like it was taking advantage of people with unfairly low wages, in countries like the Philippines. However, looking through websites where you could hire personal assistants, such as oDesk and Elance (now both under the name of Upwork), it seemed that local people were very much jumping on board with a new way to make money independently with just their laptops.

Another guy I met online, Chris Ducker, who was based in Cebu in the Philippines, had a business called *Virtual Staff Finder*. He was originally from the UK, and now ran a team of Filipinos, in an office space, who all worked for different businesses or individual entrepreneurs. At that time, I discovered that it was possible to hire a personal assistant for less than US$300 per month. Some of the digital nomads believed that you should hire an assistant, even if you didn't really feel like you needed one. It would force you to find them jobs to do, and therefore make your business grow at a faster pace.

There were other bloggers as well that made up part of the gang. Canadian, Jodi Ettenberg was a former New York lawyer who ran a popular travel blog called *Legal Nomads*. She had become so famous in blogging circles that she was being quoted in the likes of the *New York Times* and *BBC Travel*. I was very impressed. I also met 'Benny the Irish Polyglot', who ran a website called *Fluent in 3 Months*. Benny was making a living selling eBooks that taught people how to learn languages fast. His method was total immersion, and it certainly seemed to be working for him as he listed 13 languages that he could speak fluently.

I finally met the King of travel bloggers, Nomadic Matt, who has recently brought out a book called *How to Travel the World on $50 a Day!* With over 95,000 Twitter followers, Nomadic Matt is considered a celebrity VIP in the travel blogger world, as well as another American blogger and photographer, Gary Arndt, who runs the *Everything Everywhere Travel Blog* with over 160,000 Twitter followers.

I found the achievements and independent, quick rise to fame of the digital nomads incredible. It was a whole new world to me, and I was motivated and excited about the new possibilities for the magazine. It seemed that if I wanted to become famous in the 'blogosphere' then I was hanging out with exactly the right crowd! It was strange during this time that we called each other by our Twitter handles, rather than our real names, and I became simply 'Nikki Backpacker'.

I began dating one of these travel bloggers, Jake, and I became a real part of the digital nomad gang in Bangkok. I would go out with the group to fancy night clubs and attend networking parties, and they would introduce me to lots of interesting people. Hanging out with that crowd, you just never knew when you would be photographed for a blog post, quoted in an article or interviewed for a digital nomad YouTube video! There is certainly some dodgy footage of me out there at a few of these parties, if you look hard enough!

Although I learned an awful lot from the digital nomads, and this time in my life definitely helped me to grow the magazine, I never really felt that I had what it took to become a real 'digital nomad'. I much preferred to be out in the open air, wandering the streets and getting lost in villages, mountains and cities, chatting to real people, rather than sat at my laptop networking all day. However, I knew that growing my online following was an important means to help my business grow.

Despite spending more and more time on social media, privately I nurtured a kind of aversion to Facebook and Twitter, and only posted about things that were relevant to the magazine. I didn't want every photo of my personal life out in the open for everyone to see, and I felt embarrassed about showing off and trying to make other people back home jealous. This was not the reason that I had gone travelling in the first place. In today's world, I often wonder if an event has actually happened if it hasn't been photographed and documented on Facebook for the whole world to see. I just didn't feel comfortable announcing my feelings online to wait for comments and 'likes'. I felt that my everyday feelings were personal to me, and I only wanted to share them with people who really knew me. Somehow sharing them online made them less authentic and left me feeling empty inside.

Can't you just go for a drink with your friend down the pub and tell them your personal feelings, instead of posting it to the world and waiting for sympathetic comments? I just didn't get it. *How are you feeling today Nikki?* 'Hey Facebook, I have diarrhoea and have been on the toilet all day. I also have a spot on my chin and have been stalking my ex-boyfriend on Facebook.' Post! People never really write the truth online.

I also wondered about this strong desire to live a 'different life' and 'think outside the box' of normal society. Once you start to follow the mantra of the *Four Hour Work Week*, aren't you, once again, following suit and conforming to a different kind of lifestyle, one that is already laid out for you? I certainly didn't fit into the nine-to-five work ethic back home, but I'm really not sure I wanted to become a disciple of the *Four Hour Work Week* either. I didn't want to live my life by any blueprint; I just wanted to do what made me happy.

15

Not a Beach Holiday

I managed to escape the intensity of Bangkok quite a bit during the year that I lived there. Marketing the magazine and selling advertising space was an ongoing task. Due to the fluctuating nature of businesses in Southeast Asia, you couldn't just rely on getting advertising contracts renewed year after year. Marketing departments changed, businesses changed ownership or the owners just shut up shop and moved on. There were also new backpacker-related businesses springing up all the time in this thriving part of the world. If I wanted the magazine to be a success, it was my job to get out there and meet people, in order to keep spreading the word about the new brand I had created.

Off their own back, Dad and Ying were also helping to build the brand. They took trips all over Thailand and Southeast Asia, visiting places that neither of them had ever been to before. Whilst Ying went around chatting to businesses, my dad would take the chance to rent a mountain bike and head off into the mountains exploring. Dad often said what a happy time this was for the two of them, and how they would never have actively done this if it weren't for the excuse of the magazine. I was pleased that I had inadvertently opened up new opportunities for them. And, they were helping me immensely!

The island of Koh Samet is only three hours away from the city of Bangkok, and I met friends from back home there for a week's holiday. Standing on the white sandy beach, looking out at the clear turquoise waters, it was hard to believe I was only a few hours away from the polluted, crowded capital where I lived. Although meeting up with friends from back home always roused homesick feelings, I had to remind myself that this was just a holiday for them, but for me, it was my life. I could do this any weekend that I wanted. What I realised though, time after time, was that the people you share your life with are the most important thing. More important than any gorgeous beach or any paradise location. More important than money. People are the most important thing.

I travelled to the backpacker hotspot of Koh Chang, the second biggest island in Thailand, for a fun-filled New Year's Eve 2010, with my best friend Pearl, my housemate Monica, and some other expat girls we'd become friends with in Bangkok. Pearl, Monica and I also took a fantastic trip to the beautiful Khao Sok National Park in the south of Thailand, where we went jungle trekking, spotted the world's biggest flower, the rafflesia, and hired a boat to explore the amazing Ratchaprapha Dam with its strange limestone formations. From bustling city, to lonely beach and dense rainforest, Thailand is such a diverse country. With tourism well established and VIP bus routes that led pretty much everywhere, it's clear to see why the country attracts the highest number of tourists in Southeast Asia.

I travelled alone to the Krabi area of south Thailand (Railay, Koh Phi Phi and Phuket) to gain marketing support. The entire trip was a succession of disastrous events and a comedy of errors, which was enough to make me call the whole thing off! On the overnight bus on the way down to Krabi, I was sat quite comfortably for once, looking out the window, excited to be on the road again. Suddenly, there was a cough and a splutter from the seat behind me, and I felt a spray of liquid all over my head. To my horror, I realised that the hungover backpacker behind me had projectile vomited on my head. I started to pick out pieces of carrot from my hair. For anyone who thinks that travel is glamorous and that I have 'the best job in the world', as I am so frequently told, I like to remind them of incidents like this. The bus journey was another five hours and I spent it trying not to gag at the smell of my own hair.

"It always happens to me," the backpacker behind me said ironically, as I stared back at him with a puzzled look, vomit dripping down my forehead.

After I arrived in Krabi and caught the two-hoar boat that would take me to Koh Phi Phi, the bad luck continued. Head down, reading my book, trying to forget about the night before, I began to smell smoke. All of a sudden, there were screams that the engine of the boat had spontaneously caught fire. All of the passengers' rucksacks had been stacked up against the engine, which had become so hot that it had ignited. We were rescued by a passing boat, and everyone was safe, except for the fact that a few rucksacks had been completely incinerated in the inferno. At this point, you don't even need to ask if one of the rucksacks that had gone up in flames (out of about 100 bags) belonged to me. Of course it did! I walked off the boat, past the charred remains of my knickers and bras, as people sympathised, "Ah, look at that poor girl's clothes."

Therefore, my sophisticated marketing trip began with me carrying around a black bin bag containing the odd bits of burnt clothes that I had managed to salvage from the boat. Trying to keep up the image (like I ever had it in the first place) of clued-up businesswoman, motivated entrepreneur and magazine editor was not easy when you were really just a backpacker in Southeast Asia, just like everyone else.

I still had my sales sheets in their clear plastic folders, business cards and magazine samples, so I set off around the town to speak to businesses about advertising. Koh Phi Phi is a tiny island with no cars or paved roads, and I walked up and down the beach, from dive shop to beach bar, to try to talk to the decision makers. Looking around at colourful longtail boats bobbing in the gorgeous bay, or people sat having sunset drinks in beach bars lit by candles, I had to pinch myself to realise what I was doing. It was so weird to be here, on this paradise island, working to earn my daily bread, while other people were on a two-week holiday from their own jobs and daily life back home.

After getting rejected from most of the businesses that day, I sat my folder and myself down on the sand and reflected on how strange my life had become. I felt so different now to the average backpacker, as I now had a means to make money in Southeast Asia. I wore a uniform and I held a folder in hand, rather than wearing a bikini and holding a beer. I found it very difficult, in those early days, to strike a balance between work and pleasure. When I spent my whole day working hard, I would think to myself, *Hadn't I started this magazine in order to enjoy my natural surroundings more? Here I am not giving myself a moment to relax!* Yet when I spent my time exploring or partying, I felt guilty that I should be working and growing the magazine that was allowing me such freedom in the first place. Many times, I desperately craved a work colleague and someone to share the highs and lows with.

After a particularly difficult day in Railay, just as the rainy season had begun to kick in, I was feeling exhausted and defeated as none of the rock climbing schools had been interested in advertising. The cheap, bamboo bungalow that I was staying in smelt damp, and felt dark and depressing. All I wanted to do was to have dinner with a friend and talk about my bad day, as perhaps you would back home in the pub on a Friday, after a bad week at work.

As a travelling business owner, and no longer a 'backpacker', I felt so different and removed from everybody else. My goals and desires had changed. I found it hard to continuously make the effort to go out and talk to people after a day at work. The regular backpacker questions: "Where are you from?", "How long have you been travelling?" had started to drain me, and I would hear the same response again and again as I told them about the magazine. "Oh my god, that's amazing!", "I would love to do that!", "You have the dream job!" I felt that no one understood what it was really like and so sometimes I just avoided talking to people altogether. Or, I lied, "Yeah I'm on a two week holiday! Cool. Wooh. Yeah!"

The remarks of backpackers made me feel guilty about not being constantly inspired and appreciative of my work and my amazing surroundings. I felt like I should always be on a permanent high; after all wasn't this a lifestyle that I had dreamed of myself back home? I felt, on the one hand, lucky and elated, yet on the other hand, lonely and out of my depth. Even though I was working in, what many people would call 'paradise', the ups and downs and roller coaster of emotions that make up 'normal life' didn't disappear.

Whilst in Railay, I heard that there was a local concert of the Thai reggae band *Job 2 Do* on Tonsai Beach one evening, and I decided to go along to cheer myself up. "Doo doo doo doo ter tam…" was the most played song in the entire Krabi area, and Job, the Thai lead singer, was somewhat of a celebrity and local hero, having originated from Krabi himself.

I spent the night with a group of Swedish girls and their hunky rock-climbing instructor, Thai boyfriends, drinking beer and dancing to the music. It seemed to me that these type of guys were the Thai guys that Western girls found most attractive. The guys were rough around the edges, tattooed, long hair and promoted a bit of a bad-boy image. A few of them adopted a kind of pirate look, modelling themselves on the handsome Johnny Depp as Captain Jack Sparrow. One even wore guy-liner! Here in the islands, I encountered quite a few Western girl (very often Scandinavian or German) / Thai guy relationships, much more than in the cities, where the total opposite was much more common.

When I retired back to my damp bungalow in the middle of the jungle around 1am, a little tipsy, I fell fast asleep right away, but was awoken abruptly an hour later by a stranger trying to break into my room! There was a dark shadow at the window that was clearly a man, who was wearing no shirt and had big curly hair. I jumped out of bed terrified, wearing only knickers and a vest, and hid behind the door, holding a long glass bottle of perfume that had been in my daypack - as a weapon to protect me against the intruder. My heart was beating fast. The lock wasn't even attached properly to the door of the straw hut, and so if this guy wanted to enter the room it was as easy as giving the door a little push. Would people hear me scream out here in the jungle at night?

I heard a kerfuffle next door and, luckily, a couple were returning from the concert and drunkenly trying to open the door to their bungalow. The guy must have heard them and scurried off. I walked out in a panic and told the couple what had happened. After calming down, and coming to the conclusion that this guy was probably just drunk and trying to find his own bungalow, I went back inside and sat on the bed. A solitary bulb hung from the ceiling and lit up a room full of spiders and a dirty adjoined bathroom with nothing but a cold hosepipe for a shower. I had a little cry, and wondered if I could keep up this turbulent lifestyle long-term or would I get fed up of it eventually?

The next day, I pulled myself together, had a big breakfast and set off to the large, touristy island of Phuket, where I had a meeting with a TEFL school about helping them to attract students to their courses. Arriving at the pier, I'd been thinking along the way that it was my mum's birthday in less than two weeks and I hadn't sent her a card or present yet. I decided to buy her a souvenir in Phuket and post it, there and then, so I wouldn't forget. After purchasing some tasteful cushion covers and incense sticks, I set off to find the nearby post office.

It was pouring down with monsoon rain and I was trying not to get my purchases soaking wet, as well as asking directions to the post office. I was also still carrying around that black bin bag as my backpack, which was cumbersome, and becoming sticky and dirty! Deep down, I was still in a bit of a mood about the unsuccessful trip, and was feeling a bit sorry for myself about the events of the night before. When I finally found the post office and tried to pay for the stamps, I realised that I couldn't find my purse. In a panic, I ran outside to retrace my steps, not quite believing that this trip could get any worse! There was a little tap on my shoulder.

In my rush to get into the post office, I had stepped over a very old, homeless woman, who was sat on the steps, wearing a ragged dress and holding a walking stick. She smiled at me and handed me my purse back, which she must have seen me drop across the road at the souvenir shop. My eyes filled up with tears as she touched my hand with a gesture as if to say 'stop worrying – everything is okay.' Mai pen rai.

I felt ashamed at myself for being so selfish these last couple of weeks, and getting myself in such a stress and upset about minor setbacks. Here was a woman, who had the equivalent of around two months' wages in her hand, who could have quite easily kept the purse for herself. She smiled and sat back down on the steps, making me remember all of the moments in Southeast Asia where I had been made to appreciate what I did have. There were always people much worse off than you, that were getting through their day with a smile on their face and a sense of purpose. It was a humbling realisation and again and again, Southeast Asia forced me to confront my own self-absorbed problems.

16

Thailand Coup

It was a normal afternoon in Bangkok and I had spent the morning at my boyfriend Jake's apartment. I arrived home around 2pm and went downstairs to fill up the large bottles of water in the dispenser in the reception. I spoke to Jake on the phone, deciding whether or not we were going to take our laptops to the co-working space across town that day. For some reason we decided not to go. As I walked back to my room, I thought I heard gunshots. Monica was home for the day as her office was closed due to the 'Red Shirts' being present in her area. The Red Shirts are not football hooligans, as you may have thought, but anti-government protesters who had been causing chaos in the city for months.

The Red Shirt and Yellow Shirt clash was an ongoing drama that seemingly had no end. As far as I could gather, the Thai political system goes through a series of coups every two or three years. I had heard that passionate protesters throw out a corrupt government and replace it with another one, who turn out to be equally as corrupt as the government before. At the time, the Yellow Shirts represented those who were in favour of the King, the Royal Family and Prime Minister Abhisit Vejjajiva, who held office whilst I was living there. The Red Shirts, on the other hand, were followers of the notorious politician, ex-Prime Minister Thaksin Shinawatra, who had been thrown out of the government years before on suspected money laundering charges.

Over the months that I had been living in Bangkok, there was always some kind of protest here, or riot there, as the Red Shirts showed their dislike of the current government. During his time in office, Thaksin Shinawatra (Red Shirt hero) had, supposedly, passed legislation to help working class farming communities in Thailand's rural areas. Since then, Thaksin had been banned from the country for his corrupt antics, and prohibited from entering Thailand ever again. People said that he wanted back in.

Although some cynics claimed that Thaksin had done nothing but bribe the poorest people of the country by 'buying votes', there was certainly a lot of support for Thaksin from small countryside villages, particularly villages in Isaan. Big families would drive down to Bangkok in pick-up trucks for the weekend, and drive around the city wearing red shirts and hats, shaking rattles and chanting. I couldn't help wonder at times if the children, grannies, grandads, mums and dads actually understood what they were protesting about, or, indeed, if they really knew anything about the complicated game of Thai politics (do any of us really know what is going on in the world of politics?). From the outside, the protests appeared like a jovial weekend outing to the big city!

Over a period of about six months, the protests were becoming increasingly heated, with larger crowds assembling and some vandalism of government buildings taking place. The Thai Army had been sent to the streets, with tanks and tear gas, to disperse the protesters, and people began to whisper about possible civil war. My mum was worried. She had been on the phone every day asking me if it was safe in the capital, after watching reports on the BBC suggesting that things were at breaking point. I tried to calm her down by telling her that everything appeared a lot more exaggerated on the TV than it was in real life.

This had certainly been the truth from my point of view so far.

Despite increasingly bad TV reports, on the ground in Bangkok, life had been going on as normal. Living in Victory Monument, I was a good distance away from the main protest area of Ratchadamnoen Avenue, and I hadn't seen anything that had alarmed or concerned me. Although my mum and I would both watch the same events unfold on TV on the same channel, myself twenty minutes away from the violence and my mum a 14-hour flight away, it still felt so distant to me. Daily life in the market, shopping, restaurants and nightlife all went on as usual whilst the events occurred elsewhere.

But on this day, something was different. After hearing what I thought were gunshots outside, I went upstairs to see if Monica had heard the same noises. We went out onto the balcony of our apartment to have a look if we could see anything. The road below our apartment block (23 storeys high) seemed to be getting blocked with traffic, and people were gathering on the street. There were Red Shirts, Yellow Shirts, Black Shirts and every other colour shirts! Were the protests moving into our part of the city for the day? A little later we saw a plume of black smoke coming from one of the buildings in the not so distant vicinity. Was this a bomb? A grenade? We looked at each other, and after being in good spirits and nervously laughing about the whole thing, finally it sunk in that we could be in danger here. Our apartment building was becoming the centre of a volatile protest and what could potentially become a war zone!

We walked to the slightly higher central balcony that we shared with other apartments, to see if we could see what was happening on our nearest road of Soi Rangnam. This time, the noises that we heard were most definitely gunshots, and instinctively, we ran back into the building. Simultaneously, a Thai woman shouted from the apartment above that it was not safe to stand on the balcony. We ran back into the apartment, closed all of the doors and windows, and positioned ourselves in the middle of the hallway. We figured that here, we would be the furthest away from any ricocheting bullet, should this become a danger. I called my dad who told us to stay calm and stay put. I called Jake, who was bewildered that just five minutes away at his apartment it was Bangkok life as normal.

"I'll come over," he said, disbelieving that it could be that dangerous just a short distance away. From the hallway, I could just about see through the bedroom window and I could see the agitated crowd down below, and I could still hear gunshots. I persuaded him not to come over. Who knew what was going to happen in the next five minutes? I did not want him to be in the wrong place at the wrong time.

From 2pm in the afternoon, gunshots pretty much continued until about 4am. Not only that, but we heard really loud bangs frequently, and we couldn't figure out what they were caused by. Grenades? Petrol bombs? It was getting scary. It was all so surreal. We went downstairs to get some food supplies from the little shop on the basement floor of our building, which was selling out pretty fast. All of the dried noodles, eggs, cereal and crisps had gone, so we bought a few chocolate bars and took them back to our apartment. How long did people think that this was going to continue? Did we have enough food in case we were forced to stay cooped up in our apartment for days? The shopkeeper told us in broken English that we must go back to our room, and under no circumstances should we try to leave the building.

A few hours later, we heard a voice-over in our apartment building, and, being in Thai, we couldn't understand a word. We went downstairs to the lobby to find someone who could translate for us. Was the voice telling us to stay or to leave the building? It provoked even more fear, as we were left guessing about what was the correct thing to do in this abnormal situation. There were two paramedics and another farang downstairs. We learned that someone had been shot and killed just in front of our building, and the body was being dragged into the lobby. I'm not sure whether the poor person had been directly involved in the protest or was just an innocent passer-by. Apparently, the paramedics were not here to assist the person who'd been shot, as we had originally thought, but were trying to go to work! We were again told by security guards not to leave the building, and went back upstairs, shocked and bewildered.

As the gunshots continued and became even more frequent, we decided that it wasn't safe to be near any window at all. We placed a mattress in the middle of the corridor where we could sit away from any potential shattering glass. We made some toast and a cup of tea, and tried to chat about normal things to take our mind off what was happening. During the 'sit-in' in the apartment, I had been trying to distract myself and was writing an article for my website, ironically entitled 'Top 10 guide for things to do in Thailand'. Under the circumstances, I began to wonder whether I would even be able to carry on the magazine. Backpackers didn't travel to war zones.

Occasionally getting up from the mattress and looking out of the small window in the bathroom, we could actually see the fire of bullets coming out of guns. It seemed like there was a group of protesters hiding underneath our building and others, hiding in phone boxes opposite, shooting and throwing grenades at the army. It was impossible to understand who was the Army and who were the protesters, and impossible to understand who were the good guys or the bad guys. If indeed it was that simple. It all seemed to me such a big unnecessary mess, I guess that's my opinion of all wars and needless violence. What was really scary was that the building directly below us was on fire and emitting thick, black smoke. Would that fire spread to our building? Would we all be evacuated? We heard no more voice-overs, and had no other option other than to sit tight in our apartment and wait out the night.

We tried to watch a bit of TV. *Everybody loves Raymond* was on one of the English speaking channels, but it wasn't even making us chuckle. I tried to go back to my 'Top 10 things to do…'; I could write a good list about 'Top 10 things *not* to do in Bangkok right now' – and that was get yourself caught up in the middle of a civil war!

I spoke to Jake again around 3am. He told me that the Red Shirts had made a barricade underneath the window of his apartment block to ward off the Thai Army. He was filming the scene hanging out of his bathroom window, and I shouted at him for risking his own personal safety! I told him to get back inside and as far away as possible from the action, but he was eager for footage for his website. He told me that the rioters were smashing bottles, throwing grenades and going absolutely crazy.

Around 4am, the gunfire was getting more sporadic and quieter, and it seemed as though things were calming down and going further away from us. I tried to switch off and get a few hours sleep during this time, but I wasn't able to drift off after what we'd just been through. Then around 5am, once again, the gunfire and bomb noises started getting much louder, and seemed closer than ever before. Huge booms echoed around the apartment building, and my eyes widened. Monica had somehow managed to drift off to sleep with her earplugs in and I wondered whether or not to wake her up. I think for the first time since the day began, I was actually really, really scared. For a long time, everything had just seemed so surreal, and perhaps my adrenalin was preventing me from feeling fear. Now, tired and worried, everything felt very real. How on earth were we going to get out of the building?

I woke Monica up just as a huge explosion went off, and we both ran to look out of the window to see if anyone was trying to escape the building. People (who looked like civilians) were now sprinting down the street. The situation was definitely getting worse, not better. We ran to the window in my room and saw people escaping over the wall at the back of the apartment building. We heard the Thai voice-over again and decided that whatever it was saying, we would pack and get ready to leave. Before we went down the stairs, we knocked on the apartment next-door to check what our neighbours were doing. Next door to us lived a young couple and a grandma, who looked after their gorgeous little baby girl called Fasai (which meant blue sky in Thai language) while they worked in the day. There was no answer at the door meaning that they had left already. I was glad for them.

Downstairs, the main door to our apartment was completely blocked off. We walked through the underground corridor, which connected our building to another apartment block and went into the other building to see if the Juristic Office was open. It was closed. We met a French guy living in the apartment block, who said that people were lying dead at the end of the street. He warned us, seriously, not to go out onto the road. Soi Rangnam, where I ate breakfast every day and went for massages, was a complete open fire zone!

We went back upstairs to collect our bags, and decided for sure we should leave, any way we could, right now. This situation could get much worse. We went out the back door and followed the crowd of people who seemed to be escaping over the back of the garden via a ladder over the wall. We ran through the garden towards two members of the Thai army who were helping people over the wall and onto the quiet soi (lane) behind the back of the apartment, which ran adjacent to the now impassable Thanon Rangam. We ran down the road, with our backpacks on our back, and caught a taxi to the other side of the city.

We went to the house of a colleague of Monica, who lived in the Phra Ram 9 area, just a ten-minute taxi ride away. Here, it was a completely different city. I couldn't believe the difference, and Monica and I were jumpy and nervous while everybody else was calm, laughing and going about their normal day. We decided to go for a Thai massage and try to relax as we had hardly slept the night before. We felt shook up and nervous, and kept listening for gun shots during our massage, but this side of the city was uneventful. It was truly incredible.

That evening I received a call from Jake, who suggested getting out of the city and heading to the town of Kanchanaburi in the countryside, two hours away from Bangkok. He reckoned that there were more road blockades being erected across the city and that the situation looked to be getting worse. If we were going to escape, we should leave now. That same day, Monica flew to Myanmar with her friend from work, and we heard news that all of our other friends were doing the same and getting out. Jake and I met at the Khao San Road and left on the 6'o clock backpacker bus out of Bangkok.

When we were finally safely out of the city, the exhaustion began to hit me. On the first night, staying in our 200 baht per night room at the Jelly Frog Backpackers Hostel, I had dreams about getting shot and woke up screaming. Growing up in a very calm, predictable area of suburban northern England, you never expect to even hear a gunshot in your life. I felt as if I had dreamt the whole thing and I tried to put it out of my mind. Although I was now safe, I still felt incredibly anxious, almost worse than I felt when I had been smack bang in the middle of it. With worried family members at home, my whole life now felt unsettled here. It made me wonder if I should really be living in such an unpredictable, volatile country at all?

Jake and I sat in the Jelly Frog, watching more events unfold on the Thai news on the TV. Although we couldn't understand the words, the images told a story of a city that had completely lost control. Apparently, the army had divided, and the Red Shirts were now also split into factions of opposing fighters. Buses were being blown up and more buildings were on fire.

There was also another mysterious group of snipers that had appeared, known as the 'Black Shirts', who were turning up in random areas of the city and shooting civilians. Nobody knew whose side the Black Shirts were on or where they had come from. Was this the Thai Army trying to kill off the ringleaders? Or was it, as some rumours implied, snipers employed by Thaksin to cause as much mayhem in the city as possible so that it looked like the government had completely lost control? Nothing seemed clear. The Thai TV said something different to British or American News, and neither the Thai people nor the expats knew what to think. We heard that somebody had been shot on the 27th floor of our apartment block, and I breathed a sigh of relief that Monica and I had managed to escape when we did.

By now, the whole area where our apartment block stood, had been declared a war zone. A photo on the front cover of the *Bangkok Post* Newspaper showed a cardboard sign upon which someone had scrawled the misspelt words, 'LIFE FIRING ZONE'. I was praying that my mum hadn't remembered the name of my road, as journalists were now repeatedly saying it on the BBC. Soi Rangnam. Ratchapraprop Road.

Unable to trust the news reports, Twitter became the best source of accurate information as real people, who had not been able to get out of the city, tweeted what they were witnessing. We followed the tweets of one Bangkok expat who was trapped with his wife and child in one of the tall apartment buildings, watching the horrors unfold below in the street.

My friend Alicia, who was a foreign correspondent living in Bangkok, asked me if I would be interviewed for Channel 4 News about my experience. I realised that it wouldn't exactly be good for business. I ran a magazine that was trying to encourage backpackers to come to Thailand's shores! Not only that, my mum would never let me live in the city again if I told her the truth. We had expected to be able to return to Bangkok after a few days, once everything had calmed down, yet, as we watched the main shopping mall, the beloved 'Central World' burn down before our eyes on Thai TV, we knew that things were not getting any better. Being the digital nomads that we were, Jake and I decided to take the opportunity for a trip to Bali, a place that I had always wanted to go, and get as far away as possible from whatever was happening to our so called 'home'. Would we ever be able to return?

Three weeks later, the ordeal had calmed down. The Thai Army had regained control and the Red Shirts had left the city. It seemed that nothing concrete had been resolved, and it was only a matter of time before something similar happened again. Journalists on the BBC and CNN were talking about democracy and how the Thai people were fed up of the wealth of the country being in the hands of an elite few.

They wanted reform and a new government that stood up for their rights. But was Thaksin the one to provide this? Hadn't he already been found guilty of, basically, stealing from his own people? It seemed that whatever government was in power, nothing changed.

In addition, no journalist seemed to mention the strong rumour that the Red Shirts were actually being paid a daily rate to protest. We had heard that there were tables set up amidst the Red Shirt camp, where people from the countryside were queuing to get their promised 1,000 baht a day for protesting. If you were a Red Shirt leader, rumour had it that you received a hefty wage. Did anyone care that these so-called democracy freedom fighters were being blatantly bribed and used as pawns in a much larger political game? Nothing was as it seemed.

After my brush with the Red Shirts, Bangkok never felt the same to me. When we returned to our apartment building, there were bullet holes in the sign over the door, and I couldn't get the image out of my head of the dead body being dragged into the building. The little Japanese restaurant at the end of the road, where I used to eat amazing food, drink Japanese tea and play board games with their cute little boy, had been burnt to the ground. I wondered where the family had gone? I didn't think that such a thing like house insurance existed in this area. I hoped the family were safe and okay.

Over the next few weeks, Bangkok returned back to normal. In fact, it was just like nothing had ever happened, and nobody really spoke of the terrible violence that had occurred in the city. I was shocked at how easily the local people seemed to move on and get over things so quickly. I can imagine people in England analysing such an event for decades afterwards, centuries even. Weekend markets down our road sold things that had been looted out of the shops when Central World had been burnt down, and nobody batted an eye-lid. Perhaps it was time for a move. Why was I working in a polluted city anyway when I could take my laptop to the beach?

17

Healing Hippie Island

I arrived in Koh Phangan in need of a break. I was fed up of the pollution and stresses of life in volatile Bangkok. It was the perfect time for a visit from my mum. For the first time in two years I put an 'out of office' on my emails, sat on the beach for a week, and talked and talked and talked. I told my mum about everything that had happened since I'd been away from home: the trauma of the protests in Bangkok, my doubts about the magazine, the challenges of life as an expat in Thailand, even as far back as worries I had before leaving England. I talked about things that I had no idea were on my mind or concerning me, things just came out in one big splurge. She said to me "Let Mother Nature take her course." I didn't really understand what she meant until months later.

Sometimes, you can keep powering on and forget why you started doing something in the first place. You cannot underestimate the power of taking a break, stepping back and reviewing the direction in which you are heading. After that one-week holiday in Koh Phangan with my mum, I made the decision to leave Bangkok. Why was I living in a dirty city, when I could be swimming in the sea and running on the beach in the fresh air every day? Hadn't that been the reason that I had left England and started the magazine in the first place? Somehow, along the way, I'd got lost in growing the business, 'networking' and rushing towards a goal, maybe a goal that I didn't really want after all. I would always remember this quiet time on the beach, relaxing and eating good food with Mum, and discovering that the world didn't end when I didn't reply to an email. Life was about having fun, and as soon as it stopped being fun, there was something wrong.

I won't talk about the time I was with Jake in Koh Phangan. There isn't much point going into detail about how we split up after living together on the island for just one month. Away from the distractions of a big city and away from the digital nomad community, it was now just the two of us on a chilled-out tropical island. We argued like crazy until, finally, Jake caught the boat to Koh Samui and went his own way. The most important time in Koh Phangan for me, was the six months I spent there living on my own. During this time I rediscovered a side of myself that had been pushed aside, and remembered all the reasons I had started the magazine in the first place.

Koh Phangan is a truly magical place. It may be the gorgeous white beaches, palm trees, green mountains and turquoise sea, or perhaps it is the incredible sunsets that change with every moment, deep shades of red and crimson. The fresh air and beautiful nature inspired me, and I was able to write pages and pages and wake up feeling motivated and alive. Koh Phangan was to become a kind of retreat during my time living in Southeast Asia. It was for me, a spiritual place, which calmed my mind and relaxed my body.

Despite the notorious party reputation of the island, Koh Phangan has become a spiritual haven for many people over the years. It had been monks that first discovered the paradise island, way before the Full Moon Party escapades began. They built a Buddhist temple, upon which grew the main town of the island, Thongsala. The hippies will tell you that the high concentration of quartz in the rock underneath the earth in Koh Phangan has a lot to do with attracting spiritual people to the island.

I'd never had a religious upbringing or a spiritual awakening in my life, and in an *Eat Pray Love* kind of way, I suppose Koh Phangan was this time for me. I began to learn more about the Buddhist philosophy of living in the moment and appreciating nature. I witnessed the benefits of meditation and yoga, and realised that my physical and mental health were totally connected. As I ate healthier and exercised more, my mind became calmer and clearer. The sun tanned my skin and the fresh air revitalised me. I was sleeping better, and I was enjoying living on my own, in a basic bungalow overlooking the great stretch of Haad Yao Beach, on the west coast of the island. So with the power of Mother Nature, the island eradicated all the stresses I had accumulated from living in a big city. I rediscovered inspiration for my life in Thailand.

I went to yoga three times a week, overlooking the jungle and all its different shades of green. The yoga was wonderful. It relaxed my over-active mind and toned my, then, under-active body after sitting at my laptop for too many hours a day. I also became friends with the crazy Koh Phangan yoga crew who were an open-minded, interesting crowd that provided lots of entertainment during my time on the island. Hanging out with them was never boring, and I always rode back to my bungalow through the night air on my motorbike, hair blowing in the wind, smiling and amused at the events of the evening. *I've got to write a book about all this one day,* I always thought.

One night, I was invited to 'Jet's Party' in the jungle. Jet was a Scottish expat who lived in a tree house in the middle of the jungle, up a very undulating dirt track. He would invite couchsurfers to come and stay with him in exchange for helping him to build his tree house village and to help with his permaculture farm. I rode on my motorbike up the dirt path to his party with a friend I'd met on the island. Lip-glossed and short skirt on, I was expecting the kind of party I was used to in Bangkok.

When I arrived, it was clear that I looked totally out of place, although nobody made me feel it. They were all too busy doing their own thing. The party was full of die-hard hippies wearing nothing but fisherman pants and dancing as if spirits had possessed their bodies (spirits of the ethereal kind rather than vodka and gin). There were dreadlocks and bare chests everywhere. People were banging on bongo drums whilst rave music played loud into the night air, and coloured images were being projected into the dark, leafy jungle.

There was no alcohol to buy at the party, only chai tea that some of the yoga girls were selling. One of the guys passed round a hip flask that contained 'oolong', a love potion he'd been concocting on his stove all day, made from a mixture of Thai herbs and various other ingredients. He told me that it was a strong aphrodisiac. After just splitting up with Jake a few weeks earlier, I decided that I didn't need to be falling into the arms of a random guy after taking a sip of the potent oolong. I stayed clear.

My yoga teacher Trent, his wife Eleanour and three-year old daughter, Mist, who was being home-schooled, were all at the party. Trent was a very unique character who originally came from California, and his confidence intimidated me at first. He had long red hair and I never once saw him wearing shoes, or any kind of shirt for that matter. He floated around the island in an orange cape that seemed to extend from his fisherman pants. Eleanour, his wife, was pretty and gentle. I really enjoyed her yoga classes. I wondered what kind of relationship they had and how they had ended up here? One morning while I was working on my laptop on the balcony, Trent called me out of the blue and asked if I wanted to go for breakfast. Why not? Over banana smoothies in the Island Café in Chaloklum he told me his fascinating life story.

Trent had been brought up in one of those hippie communes in California in the sixties. His upbringing had been unconventional to say the least. He told me that, as a youngster, he lived amongst lots of families and had many 'Mother figures' who took care of him. When he was aged 15, he went off to the streets of New York to experience being homeless 'just to see what it was like'. Living off packaged ready meals or any other food that was out of date and had been thrown in the dumpsters round the back of supermarkets, he told me that he never went hungry.

By several twists of fate, Trent spent various stages of his unorthodox life being an artist, a chef and a DJ in Mexico. He had met Eleanour, in a nightclub in Rio de Janeiro, and they had moved to Thailand together to start a yoga school. Yoga, he said, was always drawing him in, and it was only a matter of time, before he gave into it and became what he was always meant to be. Trent's story, over breakfast (it didn't matter how much of it was fabrication), once again made me smile at how there are so many different ways to live your life.

Another memorable character that I hung around with in Koh Phangan was an Australian guy, about 40-years old, called Devon. Devon was completely off the wall, in every sense of the word, and had a massive tattoo of a mermaid right across his chest. The mermaid, he told me, was a friend of his that he had met one night when he was sat on the rocks looking out to sea - tripping on acid of course. I liked him a lot.

So the story goes, although Devon never told me this himself, he had been a drug dealer in a former life (it seemed that every expat in Thailand had a secret past), and he had an unending stash of cash that was supporting his life in Koh Phangan. He was also trying to sell his love potion 'oolong' to yoga and holistic centres. You'd see him out and about on his motorbike around the island, carrying bottles of the stuff in his backpack and selling it to various centres.

Devon was a close friend with a punky girl from California, Lyric, who had bright purple hair, piercings, tattoos up each arm and enormous boobs. People whispered that she had been a porn star back in the USA. I'd also heard rumours that she had been involved in a hit and run accident, which meant that she was now literally 'on the run' in Thailand and could never go back home as she would be arrested. I could think of worse places to hide out than Koh Phangan. Like I said, everyone had a story and you just didn't know which ones were true. Identity as an expat in Southeast Asia is a fluid thing, and with no one able to call you up on your past, you could pretty much reinvent who you were and create a new history for yourself if you wanted to.

A typical conversation between Devon and I over dinner would be:

Devon: "What did you do last night?"

Me: "Oh, I went to the night market, got some food, went to Chok Dee Bar for a drink and caught up with friends. Then I did some work. Nothing special really, what about you?"

Devon: "I had a real good long chat with Mother Nature."

Me: "Oh yeah? How is she?"

Devon: "Amazing man. I went back to The Source."

While my logical side was giggling inside at what my evening dinner conversation had become, I asked questions like "Really, how is the old gal?", "What was she wearing?", "Tell her hi from me!" Who on earth had I become?

Devon strongly believed in the power of manifestation. For those of you not familiar with this, it is the power of thought to influence the Universe, as explained in the best selling book, *The Secret.* The philosophy tells us that the Universe is abundant and you can have anything that you want, as long as you believe that you can have it. The idea is to picture yourself already possessing the thing that you want, so that you can encourage the Universe to bring it to you. If you want money, imagine you are already rich. Want a partner? Imagine them already lying next to you in bed and leave them space in the wardrobe. Money, fame, a dream house, the perfect relationship, you could have anything you wanted as long as you truly, *and I mean truly,* believed you could. Apparently famous people throughout history, the big names like Einstein and Jesus, were in on *The Secret* and used the magnetic laws of the Universe to change the world. Devon had recently used the power of *The Secret* to manifest himself a pole dancing, 'angel healing' girlfriend (very appropriate). Maybe I should give this manifestation thing a go.

I had always been rather open-minded and intrigued to explore alternative viewpoints that veered from the norm. I always enjoyed a lengthy, in-depth discussion about the meaning of life, and I am fascinated by ideas that question reality and the way that we see things. Reading about quantum physics, religion, space, time and spirituality blew my mind, and made me feel like there was so much that we didn't understand about our incredible existence on this planet. Why not have a guess at the meaning of life with some crazy theory or other?

I have always thought that there could be more to this world than we realise, and that maybe, one day I would discover it. Perhaps I would find a time tunnel or just spot something a bit out of the ordinary that would finally convince me that the world is an illusion, although a very convincing one (Einstein said that). I plan to be a hippie granny and take hallucinogenic drugs with tribes in Peru when I am in my 80s, so I'll let you know what it's all about then. Keep an eye out for the book.

One night Devon read my 'Angel Cards.' The Angel Cards were a pack of cards with different characters on them that were supposed to tell your fortune when you turned them over. I had never had much time for this kind of thing but I humoured him, and I must admit that part of me was intrigued. Devon had recently become obsessed with the cards, and was now using them to ask things like, "What type of burger should I order?" and "Should I go to the Half Moon Party tonight?"

It was a Sunday night, after the weekly Thai buffet, movie and discussion night at the yoga centre, and we were watching a film under the stars that was being projected onto the white wall of the yoga centre. On a hot night, palm trees blowing in the wind against a dark outline of mountains against the clear black sky, it was the best cinema I had ever been to. Devon took me to one side and told me to pick three cards.

One card represented my recent past, one my present and one my near future. The cards I picked were Peace, Blessings and Freedom. Peace represented my past which was upside down, signifying that my recent past had been full of conflict (could this signify the Red Shirt conflict in Bangkok and my arguments with Jake?). My 'present' card was Blessings, also upside down, which meant that I had blessings all around me, but I was shutting them off. My final card was Freedom, which meant that I could have everything that I wanted if I could just let myself be free. It sounded pretty good, but I didn't really believe in all that. Or did I?

The wacky friends I made in Koh Phangan made sure that I never felt lonely. I even developed a kind of routine to my days here, which always helps to give meaning to life I think. I was still enjoying my daily yoga, riding past elephants in the morning on my way to class. I would 'salute the sun' facing the beautiful beach and swaying palm trees that surrounded the yoga studio, buy tropical fruit from the local market to eat with my muesli and start work on my balcony overlooking the sea in the late morning. I would head to the beach in the afternoon and swim in the sea or sunbathe on the sand. I made friends with the local guys at the chilled-out beach bars and two lovely Canadian girls, Jessica and Sarah, who had opened a cool gourmet burger bar in Haad Yao. Life was easy and fun, and I was enjoying working on developing the magazine – with lots of new inspiration and stories!

One inspirational work spot was the serene Art Café in Sri Thanu, with a folk-indie music play-list and the best 'muesli, fruit, yoghurt' on the island. One morning, I got up early and headed to my bohemian 'office' on my rented scooter. As I manoeuvred around the palm-tree-fringed road overlooking the beautiful shallow waters of Haad Chaopao, a very tall guy in very tight Speedos and nothing else, came running out, in a panic, in front of my bike.

It turned out that he was Italian, couldn't speak a word of English and was very sunburnt and dishevelled. I reckoned that he had gotten completely lost after being out partying all night at one of the 'moon parties' on the other side of the island. He had certainly walked a long way from Haad Rin and was now desperate for a lift home. I sped off down the lane with the gangly 'Speedoed' wonder on the back of my scooter. He was holding onto me so tightly that I wondered if he had ever been on a moped before. I made it back for my breakfast at the Art Café and smiled. My trips to work were certainly different to driving up the M62 motorway to Manchester.

I also took regular trips to the nearby backpacker diving hub, Koh Tao, which was a great place to find advertisers for the magazine, and a great place to hang out with the fun island diving crew for a few days. One week, Pearl, Monica and one of Pearl's friends from home came to visit, and we spent a week at a dive school in Koh Tao gaining our PADI Open Water Diver certificates. I had been nervous that I would panic underwater, but the watery world had a strange way of making me feel calm, and I fully enjoyed the experience. Southeast Asia was full of incredible diving opportunities, and I was excited that I now had a licence to explore a whole new world.

There were other goings-on in Koh Phangan that I didn't take part in, but nevertheless intrigued me. If you haven't guessed it already, Koh Phangan was a hub for the 'healing arts'. Reiki, didgeridoo sound healing, chakra realignment therapy, tantric workshops, shamanic healing, aura cleansing, neuro-linguistic programming, re-birthing and other new age events took place at any time of year on the island. If you looked for it here, you could find it. Trent commented that the hard-core party scene of the east coast on the island contrasted nicely with the harmonic 'healing' crowd of the west coast. You could detox, retox and detox many times over. One of the stranger events that took place at one of the yoga centres under the cover of darkness, and certainly not advertised in their leaflets, were the DMT evenings. Devon had experienced them loads of times and he invited me along to see what it was all about.

Apparently, DMT is a chemical that is released in your body when you sleep which prevents you from moving around. It is said that humans naturally release copious amounts of the chemical when we die. Taking the drug when you are alive, therefore, is believed to recreate a near-death experience. Recently, backpackers have been flocking to Peru and Brazil to have Ayahuasca experiences, a potent plant root which contains the chemical DMT.

Having been terrified of death my whole life (as a child I used to wake up crying about the fact that one day I would die), this sounded like a hellish experience to me. Trent agreed. He said that he had taken DMT once and had gone through a traumatic experience, where he totally felt like he was about to die. It offered no enlightenment he said, just terrified him about the onset of death all the more. This was not something I wanted to explore.

Devon, on the other hand, had 'died' many times, and he did it in the middle of a circle at the yoga centre. He told me that every time the experience was the same. Angels dressed in white would come for his body and gently lift him up, taking him down a long black tunnel, back to 'The Source'. He told me that he always smiled when he was 'dying', an experience which would take a few hours, and he came out of it feeling refreshed and reborn.

Perhaps the drug recreated a sense of what you thought would happen when you died? If you were comfortable with the thought of dying then perhaps you had a lovely experience. I, on the other hand, would have no doubt gone through a tormented nightmare. I certainly didn't risk it.

After the DMT evening, we all went out for a pizza at an authentic Italian restaurant in Chaloklum. Sat in plastic chairs overlooking the pier, it was a magical spot. Before we began eating, all of the yoga crew put their hands on the middle of the table and started to perform a strange 'transferring of energy' ritual. One by one, they put their hands on top of each other, slowly drawing out the bottom hand and putting it on top. They were silent whilst performing the ritual, very serious and stared into each other's eyes the whole time.

This whole hippie thing was getting a bit much for me. I was still feeling a bit freaked out by the DMT 'dying' show. I just wanted my pizza and to taste something that I knew was real – like cheese.

"What the hell is all that about?" I asked Trent.

"Oh, it's just that your hand goes dead and it feels tingly and nice. We do it cos we think it turns the girls on." He gave me a cheeky smile and a wink. I burst out laughing, and wondered how much of this he really believed in and how much he was playing the part of hippie yoga teacher in Thailand. He threw his orange cape over his shoulder as the sea breeze began to blow.

18

A Stranger in My Homeland

After living in Koh Phangan for six happy months, I took a trip back to England for some grounding, and to catch up with friends and family I hadn't seen for over two and a half years. Returning to England for a three-week 'holiday' from my new life in Thailand was a complete and utter shock to the system. Reverse culture shock hit me hard, and I had forgotten so much about life in England that I felt like an alien in my birth country. I hadn't considered two and a half years to be that long, yet when I arrived it felt like I'd been away for ten years - or more. It wasn't that things had drastically changed. More the opposite, they hadn't changed much at all. It was me who had changed without even realising.

"But Nikki, this is the next step! You have to consider the future." That was my old school friend, Emily, across the table at the weekly quiz at our local pub in Manchester. To my amazement, the 'next step' she was talking about, was having children. With an engagement ring on her finger, a brand new Mini Cooper sat in the car park outside the pub and a four-bedroom detached house in suburban northern England, I suppose for Emily, it was the next step. For me, on the other hand, the next step was quite different. I wasn't even on the same footpath.

Whilst Emily was planning a family, I was planning which country I would live in next. After deciding I wanted a change from laid-back beach life in Koh Phangan, I was considering going to live in Malaysia, Vietnam, or the Philippines perhaps. All the belongings I had were on my back, and I felt free to wander wherever I pleased. However, when I told friends in England that I hadn't decided which country I would live in when I returned to Southeast Asia, they would all respond with the same incredulous amusement. They would laugh, roll their eyes with a look of 'rather you than me' and say, "Oh Nikki, what are you like?"

What was I like? I started to worry. To begin with, during my trip back home, I didn't have any shoes or adequate clothing for one of the coldest winters England had experienced in 100 years (trust me to pick it), so I'd been borrowing sweaters from friends and old-fashioned coats and boots from my mum, (sorry Mum). On a night-out, I was outraged by the ridiculous, latest fashions and the fact that everyone seemed to be wearing shoulder pads and platform shoes (the 80s were back - did I miss something?).

I had absolutely no interest in following fashion in Thailand, and arriving in England after living on a tropical island for the past six months, I had one pair of pink flip-flops to my name. For a few weeks in Koh Phangan I didn't wear any shoes at all, after losing them at a local beach party. This was much to the delight of Trent, my yoga teacher, who had said that wearing no shoes would make me more grounded. This has yet to be confirmed.

Whilst getting dressed to go out to a trendy Manchester night club on New Years Eve, I asked my friend, "Jeans and a nice top will do, right?" She was looking at my outfit with a disapproving sideways glance. "Wear this," she responded and flung a twinkly dress at me. Unlike Southeast Asia, there are certain dress codes to adhere to when going on a night out in England. Everyone here smelt nice, they had clean hair, perfectly shaven legs, plucked eyebrows and no three-week old dirt underneath their fingernails. I was getting the hint that I needed to brush up a bit.

Furthermore, when socialising with people back home, I felt oddly inappropriate. I had stories to tell about my travels and the quirks of running a business in Thailand, but they were stories that my friends back home couldn't really relate to. Friendly, yet vacant smiles looked back at me as I tried to tell my tales. I didn't want to be the one going on about my life in Asia and boring people with, "Do you know how much this meal would cost in Laos?" even though I couldn't help thinking it. On the other hand, I certainly couldn't keep up with conversations about careers, new cars and gadgets, dating, TV, films and the latest music and festivals. In a way that I had never imagined, I felt out of touch with modern society and decidedly uncool.

There were other cultural nuances and social etiquettes that I'd completely forgotten. Putting your napkin on your knee, queuing for toilets and lifts, giving people just a little more personal space, crossing the road at designated pedestrian crossings. At people's houses, I found myself looking for the bin at the side of the toilet to discard my toilet paper, as I was so used to not being allowed to flush 'solids' in Southeast Asia. And how could you clean up properly without a 'bum gun'? I hadn't realised that Southeast Asia had gotten under my skin so much and had begun to change my habits and personality.

Going out to restaurants, I'd have to stop myself from tucking into my meal as soon as it was laid down in front of me. If you waited for everyone else to get their meal before you started to eat in Asia you'd be starving! Many times in Thailand, I would be at the 'ordering a dessert' stage, whilst other people at the table hadn't even been served their main meal. And, when I left restaurants in England and said my thank-you's and goodbyes, more than once I started to bow at people in a Thai style 'wai' - a gesture of gratitude I had become so used to.

I also developed a form of Tourette syndrome when buying train tickets and snacks, *"F*** OFF, HOW MUCH? I could buy a plane ticket for that!"* No matter how much I tried to brace myself, I couldn't help but be shocked at the cost of day-to-day things in England. So used to haggling for goods in Southeast Asia, I had to hold back on asking shopkeepers if they could do me a 'special price'. Here in England, there were no cheeky deals to make and no tuk tuk men pestering to take you to your destination for 'cheap cheap my friend'. It all felt rather serious and lonely, without the constant street life and hassle from vendors.

Perhaps the most unusual thing I realised is that you can't just talk to people in England. They will think you are weird. In Thailand, it is completely acceptable to see another farang on the bus, strike up a conversation with them, ask them where they are heading for the evening and see if you can join them. When I first arrived home, I made small talk with everyone, everywhere. On the train, in a café, walking down the street. So how long have you been in this city? Where are you from? Where are you going? I soon learned that asking someone where they are going in England is considered stalker behaviour and likely to get you into trouble. "She's been away for a while," my friends would apologise on my behalf. 'Away' began to sound like a euphemism for a mental institution.

In a bid to catch up with as many friends as possible, I rushed from house to house, friend to friend, going out in different cities across the UK, and getting a glimpse for a day or two into my friends' lives. I met new fiancés, boyfriends and pets, set foot in new first homes, heard about new babies on the horizon and caught up on all the gossip I had missed over the past two and a half years. I laughed about old jokes, reminisced about school and university days and cried with joy to see everyone. Yet, despite wonderful welcomes and hugs from friends who would always be friends no matter where I am in the world, I somehow felt disconnected, like I didn't belong to the general order of society in England anymore. It stemmed from not having what many would call a 'normal job'.

Aside from the day-to-day experiences, what shocked me the most about coming back home was the clear order of everything. Emily had hit the nail on the head with her 'next step' comment. When you are living it day-to-day you don't ever step back to realise it. Yet now, as an outsider in my own country, I saw a clear pattern at work and a set way that things were organised in England which was very different to my unconventional life in Southeast Asia.

First of all, I never knew what day of the week it was in Thailand. Working for myself, I didn't have to clock into the office at a set time anymore (I was never very good at this when was living in England anyway). I had no daily structure and didn't follow the 'five-days on, weekends off' rule that many people's lives in the world are determined by. Time was an entirely different concept in Thailand and, to be honest, a lack of routine had been one of the things that I'd been finding most difficult to cope with. At times, I craved some kind of structure and routine to my day. Without team support and office banter, I felt a constant challenge in self-motivation. However, I knew deep down that I would struggle to fit in with such a regimented system again.

Then, there was the pattern that extended to the journey of your whole life. I'm talking about going to school, passing your driving test, going to university, getting a job, buying a car, getting engaged, getting married, getting a mortgage, buying a house, having kids, and then supporting the kids through all of the above until your retirement.

At 26, my group of school friends were mostly starting to reach the engagement stage. Before coming back home, I had wondered if I would be envious of this. Being well and truly single in Southeast Asia, there had certainly been times when I'd felt lonely and romanticised the safety and comfort of home life, meeting someone and settling down happily ever after. Meeting someone was definitely something that I still wanted, and I guess you never know when you will find someone special. I certainly didn't want to force 'the next step' if it just wasn't right for me. I was truly happy for all of my friends who had found a life partner, and promised I'd come back for all of the weddings. When and where they would get an invite to mine, I had no idea.

One Monday morning during my trip back to England, I woke up on a friend's sofa (generally my sleeping arrangement for the three weeks whilst I was back). Waking up at 7am, when it was still dark in England and freezing cold, I had a flashback of getting up for work in the advertising agency in Manchester where I had been an Account Executive for two years. I had memories of hearing the heating click on, which meant I had fifteen minutes left in bed, desperately not wanting to get up and feeling immediately stressed about the mountain of work I had to get through that day. In the winter, I would scrape ice off my car and drive an hour to work on a traffic-clogged, grey and dark motorway. That life just wasn't for me and at the time, it had made me stressed and miserable.

Almost to myself I uttered quietly, "I'm glad I don't do this anymore," just as my friend walked in ready for work.

"Oi!" she exclaimed, "I have to do this for the rest of my life!"

At 7am, it was too early to get into the fact that she didn't. She had options outside of the structure that her own society had created for her. And, if she dared to step away from that norm, she would realise that far from being limited, there are so many different life paths she could take. As scary as it may seem to try something different and forge a life overseas, it is possible, perhaps even easier, to flourish in a different set of circumstances. If it's not working for you personally, you do not have to follow the accepted and respected pattern set by society, schools, the media or your parents. We had a cup of tea and my friend went to work.

19

Malaysia and Singapore

After my eye-opening trip to England, I returned to Southeast Asia and wondered where I would go next? I felt like I needed a change from island life in Koh Phangan, but I didn't fancy returning to the hectic city life of Bangkok. Plus, all of the friends that I had made in Bangkok just eight months earlier, had now left the city. I didn't know one person who was still living there - an example of the transient nature of life in Thailand. Yes, it was time to start afresh. But where would I go?

I spontaneously booked an AirAsia flight to Kuala Lumpur. I had been thinking for a while of expanding the distribution of the magazine and trying to secure advertisers in Malaysia and Indonesia. It seemed like now was a good time to do this. These days, I was making a decent wage from the magazine (30,000 Thai baht or the equivalent of 600 British pounds each month), which went a long way living in Thailand. I was also making a little extra money from the occasional

TEFL course we sold through the website and our affiliate agreement with the TEFL school down in Phuket. But how far would this money go in another, more expensive, country? Travelling around and going out for dinner and drinks every night in pricey England had left me with absolutely no savings when I had returned to Southeast Asia.

Seeing friends back home on the career ladder, putting down deposits on houses and getting mortgages, had left me with slight concern that I wasn't thinking seriously enough about the future from a financial perspective. It had given me a kick up the bum (more of a sick, panicky feeling in my stomach actually) to make a plan to achieve bigger things with the magazine. I wanted to maintain an unconventional lifestyle, but I didn't want to be impoverished doing so. In a kind of competitive hankering, I wanted to be on the same financial level as my friends, even though I was doing things in a completely different way. Was this possible? I pondered life choices on the AirAsia flight to Kuala Lumpur, over an expensive tuna wrap. And, not for the first time (you'll notice this recurring theme), I wondered if I should pack it all in and go back home to 'settle down'.

When I found myself in KL amidst a choice of highly-priced backpacker hostels, I thought I'd try to do what is known as 'barter' in Southeast Asia. I would ask the guesthouse if I could stay with them for free, in exchange for advertising in the magazine. I was just around the corner from Jalan Changkat, Bukit Bintang, which is a popular nightlife spot in KL. One guesthouse seemed very interested in what I was offering.

"We will design you a quarter page advert for free and put you in the next issue of the magazine. I just need to stay here one week while I go around to see other businesses in KL," I said. "We print copies of the magazine all over Southeast Asia, so people will notice your hostel and book online before they arrive here. It's a great opportunity and you won't pay a thing!"

The middle-aged, Bangladeshi owner of the guesthouse smiled and said, "Okay, it's a deal!" I was pleased that I would save some money, and hopefully make a solid business connection here for the future.

"Unless…", he continued, before I could close my folder and pick up the sample magazines to leave, "…there is another deal that we can make?" I looked at him, puzzled. He was a large man with a receding hairline and piercing eyes, and he continued to peer at me intensely above his little reading glasses.

"Well, we can also give you a link on the website…" I began to explain.

But before I could finish my sentence, he rubbed his hand along my thigh and said, "No, I mean, is there another deal that we can make?" I jumped up and quickly removed his grubby hand from my leg, horrified at his suggestion. "A negotiation of services?" he continued.

I couldn't believe that the hostel owner had tried to make a move on me, in this unprofessional and highly disrespectful way. I also couldn't believe that he was actually surprised when I turned him down! Did he really think that I would sleep with him in exchange for a room? I left the hostel immediately and decided to pay for things the normal way at the next hostel.

I did experience quite a lot of sexism during my time in Malaysia, which I had never really experienced in the same way in Thailand. Unfortunately, many of the Malaysian men that I tried to work with didn't seem to have much respect for a young, white girl trying to run a magazine in a male-dominated Asian business world. I found it tough to be taken seriously.

To get out of having to stay in a noisy backpacker hostel whilst I worked on the magazine, I decided I would try to find an apartment on a short-term basis in KL. I was also trying to go out and make friends on the 'Wednesday Ladies Nights' along Changkat Bintang, in the hope that I might find a potential housemate. After much determination, with little reward, nothing seemed to be working out the way I hoped. The prices of apartments were three times more expensive than I was paying in Bangkok. Plus, many landlords wanted a one-year contract, which I felt that I couldn't commit to.

I was getting desperate to start some kind of life here in KL. I needed to get back into a routine again so that I could get down to work. Staying in dorm rooms and working in a backpacker hostel during the day wasn't an ideal living / working situation. Plus, living on a tight budget in expensive KL, my hostel, one of the cheaper ones, although friendly, was rather dirty and had recently been affected by bed bugs! In truth, like most girls at age 26, I wanted a steady group of friends, clean nice clothes and also, I'll admit it - a boyfriend. I really wasn't sure that the life I was leading at that time was a sure fire way to get me those things.

If I'm being honest, one of the reasons that I'd wanted to leave Thailand and start a new life in Malaysia, was partly due to a strange concept that we called 'White Woman Syndrome', (WWS). When I first moved to Bangkok, I had noticed it when I was out in bars and nightclubs. One night, I had begun chatting to a group of guys on the dance floor at the end of the night, as I realised that they were from Manchester. I was smiling, dancing and flirting with them, like any normal single girl might do. An American girl came up behind me, fiercely tapped me on the shoulder and growled, "Scouring for men at the end of the night are we?"

It wasn't just this incident that made me realise the competitive nature of securing a decent expat man in Bangkok. If you tried to talk to a guy in a bar, it wasn't uncommon to be approached by a group of girls who would come out of the shadows to protect their 'male', like a goose protecting their goslings. With most Western men snapped up by Thai women, and Western women seemingly uninterested in dating Thai men, there just weren't enough Western men to go round!

So, when confident, independent women moved to Bangkok and became expats, something strange began to happen to their psychological state. They wore the perfume that is well known to repel men of all nationalities, 'L'eau de Desperation'. This stemmed from a phenomenon that I have already touched on. Overall, Western men come to Thailand to look for young Thai women, who, speaking in very general terms, behave submissively towards their Western men. A strong, opinionated Western woman was just not what these guys were looking for. This situation left a lot of sexually frustrated, confused, angry and bitchy white girls out there!

On the whole, my friends and I had laughed and joked about the dreaded WWS. Yet deep down, we all thought, that when the time came to find a boyfriend, Bangkok was certainly not the place to be. Part of my decision to move to Malaysia was that I could perhaps live a more settled life and find a steady boyfriend at some point in the not so distant future.

Back in KL, I was sat over a teh tarik (a delicious hot Malaysian sweet tea) in Aji Café, on the outskirts of the hectic China Town. I noticed another European girl sat alone on a table, and I went over to talk to her. Her name was Sofia and she was a supply teacher back in Switzerland. Her life pattern at that time was that she would work hard for six months in Switzerland (hating every minute of her job), and then go out to Malaysia for the next six months to 'recharge her batteries' as she called it. She was blonde, attractive and gently spoken. We discussed life, relationships and dreams over many teh tariks in Aji Café (as a Hindu restaurant, they didn't serve alcohol and this was probably a good thing for us!). Together, we nearly, maybe, sussed it all out.

Sofia at 40 years old, and me at 26 years old, were both in a similar position. We wanted something different out of life and didn't want to follow the conventional path, yet we still wanted to fulfil the tradition of finding a life partner and having children one day. As the Pussycat Dolls sung: "I don't need a man to make me happy!", but is this really true for many women if they admit it to themselves?

At 40, Sofia was obviously leaving it a bit late to have a family, the ol' biological clock ticking and all - and apparently her mum kept reminding her. I think women have this sense of time running out perhaps more than men do, due to this fact of life. I suspect that this makes women innately more impatient (well that's my excuse anyhow). I have always been aware of my female friends trying to organise things, set up homes and move relationships onto the next stage. This seems to be a trend amongst women, much more than men, because I think men feel that they generally have more time than women do. Or perhaps, they don't even think about it at all!

Like many girls, I nurtured the dream that I would find 'the one' at exactly the right time in my life. On holiday in Spain when I was younger, I'd heard the phrase 'media naranja' which literally means 'half orange' - your perfect match or soul mate. I wanted to believe that my media naranja was out there now, living his life, struggling, achieving, thinking, working and dreaming and one day our paths would collide. Did I believe in fate? Did I believe that things happened for a reason?

I was only 26 at the time, so I reckoned that I didn't need to worry just yet (I am 29 at the time of writing this, and still no closer to finding 'the one' – which collision course is he on? *Hurry up!*). Deep down, I was conscious that I didn't want to spend my entire life getting into ridiculous situations and writing stories for people to laugh at, only to find myself left on the shelf at the end of it all – the scruffy backpacker shelf.

Sofia and I discussed all of this and more. We talked about past relationships and ones that were in the pipeline (this was a shorter conversation). It was exactly what we both needed at the time – a good girly chat! One night we went to a popular backpacker and expat bar that was owned by the Indian millionaire playboy, David Devar, who I'd met with earlier that week to discuss advertising his huge empire in the magazine. More than once during the meeting, he had put a hand to my face and shushed me in a further display of sexism that I experienced here in Malaysia.

I got chatting to an older guy in his 50s, who had been living on some remote Indonesian islands and had just flown back to KL to renew his visa. He was friendly and his stories were very interesting. He told me amazing tales about living with indigenous tribes in the jungles of Kalimantan, crazy tales of black magic and strange occurrences. Tanned, wrinkled skin, dog-eared cowboy hat and well-worn trekking shoes, he was every bit the old explorer. He had obviously shunned the life of 2.4 kids, wife and grandkids for a life of adventure. But was he happy? He had stories to tell and I found him to be more intriguing than most middle-aged guys that I had met back home in England, but he had not a penny to his name (nor cared by the looks of it).

I remember talking to my brilliant friend, Annabelle (who later became Deputy Editor of the magazine), about this encounter and many others like it in Southeast Asia. You meet many unconventional characters in Asia; people who don't really fit into general society back home and are drifting with seemingly no focus or plan. Was life just about experiences and nothing else? Or was there more to it? What were we all doing here in Southeast Asia *exploring?* Should we just go home and *get a job?*

"It's just another story to tell the grandkids!" Annabelle had said.

"Yeah," I replied, "but at this rate they'll be somebody else's grandkids!" We both laughed nervously.

Sofia left KL and travelled back to Switzerland for her six-month work stint. Having a terrible phobia of flying, Sofia travelled the lengthy journey from Malaysia to Europe and back again, by cargo boat - which cost around US$2,500 and took around six weeks! It was an adventure in itself, she told me.

So, here I was, back on my own again. I felt the inevitable twinge of sadness as I said goodbye to someone that I had become so close to in a short amount of time. The transience and constant breaking away was something I still dreaded. I decided to get out of the city for a while. I needed to get away from the pressure of trying to find a housemate and an apartment. I had been in KL now for around two months, and I was still trying to make some kind of permanent base here.

I caught a bus to the Cameron Highlands, a high-altitude hill station, that had been used as an escape from the city by the English colonials back in the 1930s. The area was named after British surveyor, Sir William Cameron. Complete with a golf course, black and white thatched cottages, tea plantations and strawberry farms, it was said to replicate a 'Little England' amidst the tropics. I could just imagine the old, eccentric, British expats indulging in afternoon tea as they sat by a roaring fire, trying to cure their homesickness in Malaysia. Due to the altitude, the temperatures in the highlands were remarkably cooler than the city (I bought socks for the first time in months!), and I felt ready for a mini adventure. Would the Cameron Highlands be the escape that this British expat needed to cure her own unsettled feelings?

I arrived in the small settlement of Tanah Rata where shops advertised tea and scones next to roti canai (Malaysian flat bread), and I booked into a small hostel that seemed cheap and cheerful. Looking at all of the touristy jeep tours and bus tours available, I decided to shun them all, get up early in the morning and explore the area by myself. At 9am, I picked up an A4, one-sheet, paper map from the hostel that had black lines for the trekking routes in the mountains, and set off for the highest peak, Gunung Brinchang. Whether I was following the map correctly or not, I spent most of the journey following the road looking like a hitchhiker in need of a ride.

The region was beautiful: undulating lush and leafy landscapes, rolling mist swaying over the hills and occasional glimpses of bright green velvet swathes of tea plantations. Workers in the tea fields waved to me and looked puzzled at a young Western girl out here trekking alone. If only Sofia were here to share the scenery with.

The Cameron Highlands is famous for the 1977 disappearance of the American Thai-silk magnate, Jim Thompson, who had been trekking in the area. His body has never been found, and it is still a great, unsolved mystery today as to what became of the millionaire entrepreneur. Some people say that he was assassinated for his involvement in spying activities, others say that he was eaten by a wild animal, or fell into an animal trap that had been built by aboriginal hunters. I hoped the predators, whoever they were, weren't around today.

I trekked on alone, and managed to get off the road onto a narrow forest path that was covered in thick undergrowth with vines hanging down from above. It began to pour down and the muddy track became complete slush in a matter of minutes. I had been trying to make it to the viewpoint, Gunung Brinchang, which was a recommended point to admire the scenery of the area. I crawled under bushes and over broken trees, fell over in the mud, scratched my legs and got bitten by bugs. I walked over precarious canopy bridges, found the track and lost the track again and again. I wondered why I hadn't seen another person along this 'popular' route. After what seemed like hours and hours, the canopy started to thin. It was beginning to get dark, and I was exhausted after having trekked all day. I was beginning to worry that I was getting very, very lost.

With every bit of strength left in my arms, I hauled myself up over a muddy hill on my hands and knees to see what was over the top. My head popped over a ledge to come face-to-face with about eight coaches and a large crowd of Chinese tourists pointing cameras in my face. No, I was not the long-lost wild animal that murdered Mr. Jim Thompson. I was just a stupid English backpacker who was lost, and now completely covered head to foot in black mud! I must have looked ridiculous. I trudged on by, as the Chinese tourists giggled and clicked their cameras at me, getting back to the hostel late that evening.

That night at the hostel, I took a hot shower and decided on an early night after a hard day's trekking. It was proving impossible to sleep however, due to a very active rat that was scuttling above me in the floorboards, back and forth all night. My body was aching from the walk and I was in need of a good night's sleep.

The next day, after only a few hour's sleep, I hired a motorbike on a whim and visited a strawberry farm and a tea plantation. Sitting overlooking the hills writing postcards to my mum and grandma back home, the loneliness (brought on by my tiredness) started to creep in. That night, I tried to sleep, but the rat was at it again, this time relay racing back and forth with its mate and giggling (or so I imagined).

Loneliness. It washes over you like a big wave. I don't think I had ever really felt it like this before. I don't think I had ever truly given into it and admitted how I felt. For a solo traveller, it is definitely something that you have to learn to deal with, but something that people rarely like to talk about. I think that the fear is, once you admit to it, it's like you are letting it sneak in and torture you even more. So, you just push it away and try to ignore it. You can feel just as lonely in a crowded city as you can in a solitary beach hut. It is a state of mind. And my least favourite state of mind.

'You'll meet loads of people when you are travelling!' were the words that I'd heard before I came backpacking. They were the same words that I'd also repeated to people to encourage them to leave. And it was completely true. However, after a while, you just want someone who knows you, someone you don't have to go through the small talk with. Someone to share every significant and insignificant moment with. You become tired of making connections with people, only to say goodbye to them three days later. Friend after friend had become an email address and a Facebook picture. Now that this was no longer just a backpacking trip for me, but a lifestyle choice, I began to really worry. Would I be able to hack such a transient lifestyle in the long-term?

In Asia, where everybody is so outspoken, what makes it worse as a solo female traveller is that taxi drivers, travel agents, bus drivers, waiters ask you constantly: "You alone?", "Just one person?", "Table for one?", "Room for one?", "Single?", "No boyfriend?", "No husband?" *Yes, just one. Completely, absolutely, totally alone. Single, yes. Just one, yes you have it right. Try not to burst into tears.*

You look around at other people who are having an amazing time on a once-in-a-lifetime backpacking adventure. "Wow, you have the dream job!", "I wish I could do what you do!", they say. You start to feel guilty for harbouring lonely feelings when you should be having fun. You push them aside. *What is the matter with me? I should be grateful for what I have. I should be on a permanent high 24/7, because after all, aren't I living the dream? Isn't this what I always wanted?* Wherever you are in the world, life will have its ups and downs. It took me a while to realise that what makes the ups and down worthwhile is sharing it all with good friends. I was fed up of being on my own. Something had to be done!

I got out of my bed (the rat smiled), started to browse the Internet and pondered my options from here. Did I want to make a base in KL at all? Should I go back to England and try to run the magazine from there? Should I go back to Thailand? I spotted something on Facebook and started to read an interesting travel blog by a fellow blogger that I had come across in circles online, Johnny Ward. His words concerned me. Was I ever going to be a normal person again? Had I been ruined by travel?

"I think it's fair to say that the general consensus is that travel is good for you. It enlightens us, broadens our minds, helps us take a more holistic view of our lives and the relative ease in which we grew up. I am a huge advocate of travel and believe all of that without doubt. However, very few people discuss the potential damage that travelling could cause. What if this lifestyle of ultimate freedom, where a day without a cool new experience is seen as a 'boring' day (forgetting the fact that in the 'real world' people do the same thing, day in – day out, for decades), causes us to shirk commitment?

Living on the road, travelling so much, constantly meeting new and interesting people from all walks of life, our senses are constantly stimulated. New brief relationships burn brightly for a few days but are extinguished before they have a chance to flourish due to the weekly sleeper train leaving Kathmandu tomorrow morning - and you have to be on it!

Then when you do re-settle, is something always going to be missing? Can you face a stable (stagnant?) social group and the same job for the next two, three, ten years? Can you meet that one girl/guy and know that they are enough, that they will supply you with the same excitement that you had on the road? If you can, that's great but if you can't - what then? My question is this – has travel caused that, or was that in your personality long before you booked your ticket?"

(Johnny Ward, www.onestep4ward.com)

I called my dad. I needed him to add a bit of logic to the situation. "Never make decisions when you are emotional," he had always said. I broke down to him on the phone. "If it was easy, everyone would be doing it Nikki," he said again.

He encouraged me to come back for a few days to Pattaya and talk things over. After dinner and sharing a bottle of wine with my dad, the world had always seemed a better, more exciting, interesting place. Always telling me the truth, constantly encouraging, but not mollycoddling, my dad was always in the background egging me on and giving me the best advice he could. The truth is, most of what I did was to make him proud of me, so that I could share all of my experiences with him.

"Go back to KL, then go to Singapore as you planned. Finish the job that you started, getting advertising for the magazine and sorting out distribution, then come back to Thailand. We'll figure everything out and make a plan about where you are going to live." It seemed so simple, and so I did all of that and headed back on the AirAsia flight to Thailand.

After a few days in Pattaya, I headed north to Chiang Mai where my old housemate Monica was now living. She'd been raving about how cheap it was and what a fun place it was to live. She seemed to already have a ready-made group of friends that would welcome a wandering expat. Would I find my home here?

20

Songkran in Chiang Mai

With a super-soaker strapped to my back, I ran through the sweltering heat of the city, which had become a war zone in a matter of hours. Thankfully, the most lethal weapon out there that day was a toilet bucket filled with ice-cold water. It was Songkran Festival in Chiang Mai and time for the Thai people to celebrate the Buddhist New Year.

Spiritually, like in many cultures, New Year means new beginnings, washing off the previous year and starting afresh. The watery madness that exists today evolved from a Buddhist tradition dating back thousands of years. In the old days, people used to pay respect and wish each other good luck by sprinkling blessed water on each other's shoulders and washing Buddha statues to symbolise purification. Today, however, no man, woman or child across the land remains dry for three days of complete mayhem in the world's biggest water fight. Garden hoses, water pistols and buckets filled with water are chucked at innocent passers-by. In Chiang Mai, the dirty water of the city moat is used as readily available ammunition for cheeky kids. Cheesy Thai pop music blasts from bars, people dress in the traditional brightly coloured, flowery Songkran shirts and the Old City becomes an all-day party!

Chiang Mai was a new start for me. I had been living in the city for six weeks now, and I was enjoying every minute of it. I had taken to the streets of the Old City that day with a new group of friends I'd met who were all staying for at least – wait for it – three months or more! We'd all got over that mandatory "How long are you staying for?" question, and had decided to become great friends. As a group, we opted not to get too close to anyone who said that they would be leaving in a few days 'on the slow boat for Laos' – immediately identifying them as a backpacker. We had already experienced the transient nature of expat life in Thailand, and were all at roughly the same stage of our journey in living abroad.

Upon arriving in the city with Dad and Ying, who had decided to take an opportune marketing trip to check out the city with me, Dad and I had driven around the city on a rental scooter looking for an apartment. I had found myself a gorgeous little apartment in a very local area of the city which was costing me only 10,000 baht per month (around 200 British pounds), complete with a small gym, 24-hour food delivery and a rooftop pool! After looking at around 20 apartments, I had shortlisted it to the final two, and then finally plumped for this one after seeing a bunch of hunky Australian guys drinking wine and watching the sunset in the pool. Things seemed too good to be true (although the hunky guys did turn out to be Jehovah's Witnesses - and married ones at that!).

Despite my indifference for Chiang Mai as an adventurous backpacker, it turned out that the city was actually a fantastic place to be an expat. There were lots of WiFi cafés. that made inspirational, sociable work spots, and there were weekly events such as the Thursday Quiz at the UN Irish Pub, the Tuesday Salsa Night at Second Floor Gallery and the Wednesday night Open Mic at the North Gate Jazz Bar. Plus, there were plenty of opportunities for exciting weekend breaks in the gorgeous countryside surrounding Chiang Mai.

By chance, my good friend Pearl had also found herself in Chiang Mai at this point in time, and together we met the wacky and wonderful,

Scottish teacher, Gemma. Every weekend, we would hop on our motorbikes and head off in any direction to explore the surrounding countryside. Since my lonely days exploring by myself in Malaysia, things were certainly on the up.

Having a more stable life and work environment, things were going increasing well with the magazine, and I was even managing to save around 100 pounds per month with the cost of living being so low in Chiang Mai. We were receiving more and more submissions from writers, and gaining more advertising support. I had recently launched an online forum for backpackers to share ideas and ask questions, and had started to make videos for YouTube to share on the website. Our social networking pages were becoming more and more popular with encouraging comments daily.

With the laid-back lifestyle in Southeast Asia, it was still a challenge to get advertisers to confirm in time for print deadline, or writers to send their high resolution photos in time. "I dropped my camera off the side of a long-tail boat and lost all my pics!" and other excuses made the list. They always made me smile, and I realised how much I loved this unpredictable part of the world.

The best excuse came from a Cambodian photographer: "I'm so sorry that my photos are late. I had planned to send them to you in an Internet café as soon as I arrived in Phnom Penh. However, on the way from Siem Reap our bus accidentally hit a cow and was delayed. What took so long was that the bus driver moved all of the luggage out of the compartment under the bus and into the main cabin, to make room for the cow!"

Running a business in Asia was never normal. When his photos finally did arrive (he had snaps of a family of seven, a pig and a rooster all crammed onto one motorbike), they were certainly worth it. I was starting to think that I really did have the dream job, well, at least *my* dream job, after all.

One day, I received an email from the owner of a huge global travel magazine, asking questions about the audience I had been growing over here in Southeast Asia. Would I be interested in some kind of collaboration? I wasn't sure what he meant, but I thought I might as well set up a Skype meeting to find out more. That day, I had cycled to the city and was late getting back due to getting a flat tyre and having to push my clapped-out old bicycle home through the traffic-clogged streets. I arrived back to my flat one minute before our meeting. My hair was a mess and I had a smear of dirt across my face. I hoped he wouldn't turn his Skype video on, but he did.

The marketing director peered at me, slightly disconcerted, from the other side of the video, which may as well have been a porthole into a different world. Our lives were a stark contrast. He sat there in a smart office with his shirt collar and tie, while I sat there with my linen, hippie top, wind chime dangling in the background, onto the balcony where my tomatoes had been growing in the sun, dogs barking down the street and sun beating down making beads of perspiration appear on my forehead.

"I reckon that my company is worth between 3-5 million pounds right now. And with an Asian market who knows…" he continued. "It's all about profits. I know you've grown up a good little business over there. But just think, you could be working for us with sale targets and bonuses. We'd make you Regional Sales Director of Southeast Asia. You could make a lot of money. Our plan is to make this global and sell out to a multi-national company for big money in three to five years."

Three to five years. Three to five million pounds. Who knows what might happen in three to five years? After a lot of listening and not much talking, I said goodbye, told him I'd "be in touch" and pressed the 'End Call' button on Skype. I closed my laptop and went to pack for a weekend's adventure in the mountains.

Gemma, Pearl and I were heading off for a weekend in Chiang Dao, a paradise of jagged mountains and bird watching, just an hour north of Chiang Mai. Upon arriving in the gorgeous village rather early in the day and filling ourselves up with delicious fried rice at a street-side stall, we had decided to press on. The day was young and the weather was fantastic. The heat rippled off the road, and the countryside was breathtaking. We turned left out of Chiang Dao and set off for the middle of nowhere, passing hill tribe villages where people still wore the traditional purple and black velvet 'Hmong' clothing.

We drove through mountains, past miles and miles of mango and papaya trees and endless amazing views. As we ascended higher and higher into the mountains, the weather was becoming colder, and mist was rolling in from the horizon. We stopped to put on our jackets and discussed whether or not to continue down the road. Captivated by the scenery, we had driven much further than we had realised. Looking at the map, it actually made more sense to carry on to the backpacker hub of Pai, rather than return to Chiang Dao. We hadn't booked a guesthouse for that night, but had three solid hours left of daylight to find one.

We studied the map and there was, indeed, the dotted line of a dirt track coming up on our left that would take us right into Pai village. Pai was a haven for the traveller, and we knew that if we made it there, we would be rewarded with beers, great food and good live music for the night. 'Impassable in rainy season' the map said. Oh well, I had thought naively. *We aren't quite in the throes of rainy season yet - it is only just beginning. Surely experienced (ahem) Honda Click drivers like us will be fine!*

An hour later it was chucking it down with rain and freezing cold.

"It's too dangerous," said Gemma shouting through sheets of rain, "we can't ride in this!" We had passed through the final settlement of Wiang Haeng and turned left onto the dirt track that we reckoned led to the promised land of Pai.

"Just a bit further?" I suggested, looking sheepishly at the dirt track that was fast becoming a slippery mud chute. Pearl studied the map, with water dripping from her eyebrows.

"It's another 60 kilometres!" she screamed. After a lot of falling off, getting caked in mud, stuck in mud, skidding in mud, revving and spraying each other trying to get out of said mud, we had been forced to call it a day. We were now stranded in the middle of nowhere and it was getting dark. We left our motorbikes under a rickety shelter and trudged back to the main road, with a plan to hitchhike to a nearby village.

Like three drowned rats, we stuck out our thumbs and shivered in the hope of a lift. It wasn't long before a pick-up truck stopped and a friendly hill-tribe family beckoned us in. We were soaking wet, but the mum refused to have us sit in the back of the truck that was open to the rain. Instead she made us squash into the backseat of the truck, where we apologetically dripped on baby clothes. In broken Thai, we asked to be taken to a hotel, if there was one close by? After driving through hill-tribe villages mile after mile up here, we weren't very hopeful of a decent lodging for the night.

About fifteen minutes down the road, the dad stopped the car at what can only be described as a cowboy ranch. After some discussion and enthusiastic smiles, we were ushered in and fussed over by the staff. Walking in through saloon doors, to the sound of Johnny Cash playing on the speakers, was one of those surreal moments in Thailand where your world stands still for a moment and you have to remind yourself where you are. We spent the night drinking hot toddies, attempting small talk with some Stetson-clad locals and singing along to country music's all time hits, from Kenny to Dolly! Thailand's unpredictable nature had surprised and warmed my heart again. It was these moments of living in Southeast Asia that made everything worthwhile.

Life in Chiang Mai was good and I was happier than ever, with a nice place to live, good friends and a good work routine. And, they always say that love strikes you when you are happiest in yourself and least expecting it!

One night, Gemma and I were walking out of the late night backpacker hotspot, Zoe in Yellow, at 2am, not quite ready to give up partying, even though we had drank enough red bull vodka buckets between us to make the Full Moon Party crowd proud. The only place that was open late in the city was a dodgy nightclub, on the other side of the city, frequented by 'ladies of the night' named, appropriately, Slinky's. We wobbled onto the street, giggling and chatting and started trying to find the way to Slinky's where neither of us had ever dared go before.

"Let's ask this guy!" I pointed.

"What if he doesn't know?" Gemma hiccupped.

"Of course he knows where Slinky's is, look at his stupid hat!" I shouted, well within earshot of the Western guy in the hat getting off his motorbike across the street. He grinned at us.

"It's just up the road on the left, but I don't know why you want to go there; it's full of prostitutes."

"Sounds like our kind of place!" Gemma and I joked.

"Well, if you really want to go, it's just up the road on the left, two minutes," said the English guy, who was definitely more sober than us.

"But where?" we demanded.

"Jump on the back, I'll take you," he said.

"Great!" So Gemma and I hopped on the back of the motorbike, without helmets or a care in the world, with a complete stranger. I made sure that I was the one sitting directly behind the guy as I'd decided that I quite liked him. I smiled to Gemma as our hair blew in the wind and we waved to passers-by, "See you at Slinky's!"

When we arrived at the seedy nightclub, the handsome English stranger said, "Ok girls, have a great night!"

"What! You're not coming with us?" I slurred.

"It's not really my kind of place, girls."

We dragged him into the nightclub, and Gemma provided us all with tequila shots and a Chang Beer chaser. We were the only Western girls in the night club that was full of older men, a few Thai girls in short leather dresses dancing against poles and half-naked girls parading around the dance floor. We knocked back about five tequila shots each, and the Thai girls started to get annoyed at Gemma for trying to dance with their men. After a few hours of trying to drunkenly chat up our new friend with the worst lines ever, I wasn't in any fit position to drive my motorbike back home. As Gemma negotiated a tuk tuk, Craig (the stranger) and I sat by Chiang Mai moat and shared our first kiss.

After our initial drunken meeting on the Friday night, Craig and I met on a sober Sunday afternoon in the Old Town. The night before, Craig had given me his number, but I had obviously forgotten his name at the point of typing it in and had received a text from QUIRKY in my old Nokia brick, asking for a first date.

Craig started to tell me about his life. He was 37, quite a bit older than me, but with boyish good looks and amazing blue eyes. He was from the north of England and had been living in Chiang Mai as a teacher for five years, after leaving a stressful career as a restaurant manager in England. I liked him instantly, and from day one of our relationship we had great fun and didn't stop laughing. Craig lived in a house outside of the city, and at weekends I would lie in the hammock writing articles, while he cooked for me and we chatted for hours. We would hop on the motorbike at weekends and go for a 'pootle', as he called it, around all of the little Thai villages, stopping for a drink in a 'Mom and Pop' shop along the way.

After seeing each other for a few months, we took a trip to my beloved Koh Phangan. It felt great to be showing Craig a place that had been so special to me, and my experience here on my favourite island was very different now, with a boyfriend, than it had been alone. We watched the sunset every night with cocktails, ate at all of the amazing restaurants on the island and swam in the clear blue sea in the day.

One night we had been drinking and chatting in a beach bar, and

Craig was telling me more about his childhood and his family. We were sharing secrets and really getting to know each other. Craig was talking about his Uncle Bobby – a guy that he had admired and loved growing up, and who had sadly passed away a couple of years earlier. He took out his wallet and pulled out the only photograph that he had of his uncle - a small black and white passport photo and handed it to me.

"I don't usually share this with people," he said. At that moment, a gust of wind blew the photo right out of my hand and down the beach. I gasped and ran after it in the dark, crawling around on my hands and knees in the sand, searching for the photo that I knew could never be replaced. It was hopeless.

I trudged back to the bar, tears in my eyes, feeling dreadful for losing something that was so important to Craig. "I'm so sorry," I said.

"Sit down," he told me. He held my hands and looked me in the eyes. "If Uncle Bobby could see me sitting here, with the girl of my dreams, happier than I have ever been in my life, he would laugh out loud and smile at what just happened."

Life was amazing, and I was falling in love in a place where I had never thought it possible.

21

Internal Affairs

Catherine Dickson had emailed me to ask if there were any opportunities available for an internship at *Southeast Asia Backpacker Magazine*. 'What timing!' I typed in my email back to her. 'We're actually just opening up an internship program at the moment.' Of course, I hadn't even thought about the possibility of hiring an intern, and was both flattered and excited that this bright, young girl considered *SEA Backpacker Magazine* a valued company with which to spend the second year of her university summer.

Over the two years that I had been running the magazine, we'd had a few requests for 'work experience'. However, with my haphazard lifestyle, lack of office, not to mention my penchant for a good lie-in, I just didn't think that I would be able to organise a structured enough setting for a young protégé to learn anything. Cathy, however, was different.

Six months earlier, I had met Cathy, via Skype, from a WiFi café in a shopping mall in Kuala Lumpur, and I had decided instantly that she would be a great sidekick, sorry, intern. Cathy was studying Geography at the University of Sheffield and had straight A's in A-Levels. She had been travelling throughout Thailand, Laos and Vietnam, which is where she had picked up the magazine, and had already shown initiative in getting in touch with me about an internship when there wasn't even one advertised!

Over Skype, I'd been trying to sound as professional as possible, but I think she sussed out my unconventional ways right away. We clicked immediately and Cathy decided to come to Chiang Mai for three months from July to September. I sent her an email explaining the situation:

About the company:
We are a small publishing company currently based in Thailand, but the nature of the work means that travel is an integral part of the job. The work is unconventional – meaning it is by no means a nine-to-five. Every day is different. We have a permanent graphic designer and web designer based in Thailand, and the writers and contributors are travellers all over Southeast Asia who submit stories to the magazine. Breaking into new territories and literally doing things that have never been done before in Southeast Asia is an exciting adventure. It is a constant learning curve and one that requires an attitude of 'anything is possible' and in this wonderful part of the world – it really is!

What are we looking for?
SEA Backpacker Magazine is at a rapid growth stage and we are looking for an enthusiastic individual who can help us grow and at the same time gain incredible, unique work experience in a fascinating industry, in a booming part of the world. We are looking to take on an intern from 1 July – 30 September who will be based with us in Southeast Asia for three months. The intern will essentially be 'executive shadowing' the Director of the company, Nikki, gaining one-on-one tuition in all aspects of the publishing industry and working on exciting projects. Travel within Southeast Asia will be a fundamental part of the role and from day one you will be working as part of the team rather than as an observer. There may be some preparation required during the month of June and if the internship proves successful in the eyes of both S.E.A Backpacker Co.,Ltd and the chosen intern – there may be opportunity for future employment.

"When shall I book my flight?" Cathy typed back.

I decided against picking Cathy up from the airport on 'The Joker' (which was the name of my rather temperamental motorbike at the time), and instead picked her up in a songthaew (shared taxi) with a driver. I'd already rented her a room on trendy Nimmanhaemin Road in the most upmarket area of the city. Popular with students and expats, the road was lined with cafés, restaurants, massage parlours and boutique shops. The road was to become our office for the next few months as we built the magazine over many an iced latte.

Cathy jumped into work with the magazine right away, and, at first, I was shocked at how quickly she picked things up. She would complete the tasks that I had given her in a matter of minutes and I was in a bit of a panic thinking of new things to keep her busy! Over three months, Cathy helped me to build the website, adding articles and videos, and helped with social networking. She introduced me to things online that I had never even heard about!

I taught her how to use the program InDesign so that she could help to design adverts, and, eventually, the magazine. By day, we would work in cafés on our laptops or visit potential customers in the city to try to get advertising contracts. By night, we were out socialising and making contacts in many of the busy bars around the city. We

166

were working hard and playing hard, and the whole internship idea was turning out to be a great success!

After one month in Chiang Mai, we decided to travel to Cambodia so that I could show Cathy the ins and outs of a sales trip and see how many new customers we could get for our next issue. We caught the overnight bus from Chiang Mai, stopping a night at my dad's house in Pattaya so that the two of them could meet. I'd been telling my dad so much about my intern-wonder, and likewise, I'd been telling Cathy about my dad, who had been a huge inspiration for me to start the magazine in the first place.

Dad, Ying, Cathy and I had all gone out for a beautiful seafood meal overlooking the beach and had a great night. The next morning, we caught the bus across the border and headed to Siem Reap, the starting point of our sales trip. Over the next week, we would travel to Phnom Penh, Sihanoukville, Kep and Kampot - destinations in Cambodia with burgeoning backpacker scenes. We booked into the lovely Rosy Guesthouse in Siem Reap, which we had managed to stay in for free, in exchange for an advertising package with the magazine.

The next day, we set off around the town, going in and out of cafés, restaurants and adventure companies introducing the magazine. Ying and I had been here just two years earlier doing the rounds, but of course, as is the nature in Southeast Asia, everything had changed! On the first day, we managed to get three sign-ups for advertising (one of which Cathy had sealed the deal all by herself!), and things were going very well.

The following day, Cathy had a day off to explore the legendary Angkor Wat Temples. She had decided to get up at 5am in time to see the sunrise over one of the most famous landmarks in all of Southeast Asia. That night, after dinner, Cathy went to bed early to make sure she was ready for her excursion the next day.

After Cathy had gone to bed, I stood on the balcony of Rosy Guesthouse amidst scented orchids, a gentle breeze blowing in the hot, humid air and people walking along the riverside below. I reflected on the last few months and smiled. I had found happiness in Chiang Mai. Business was going great, I was developing a great rapport with my new intern Cathy, who seemed as passionate about the magazine as I was, and what's more I had made a good friend. I was also in the beginnings of an exciting new relationship with Craig. I was enjoying having a guy who cared about me, to relate all of my adventures to when I returned 'home'. A child cycled by the river below and two monks went by on an old rickshaw. It was a beautiful, still evening in Cambodia. I was proud of myself, feeling lucky and blessed, and wanted to revel in the moment. *Things just can't get any better,* I thought. I looked at my phone. It was too late to text Dad, who I usually liked to tell when life was great. I'd ring him tomorrow.

22

The Day Everything Changed

The next morning Ying called me on my mobile, which surprised me, as we had only been gone a day or two. "Why don't you come back and do the magazine here, Nikki?" she asked.

"What are you talking about Ying? You know we've booked our flights back from Phnom Penh to Chiang Mai next week. We've got meetings lined up here and things are going great. We're not ready to come back yet. What's the matter?"

I couldn't make out what she was getting at, and I reckoned it was one of those 'lost in translation' Thai-English things. She spoke so fast and I was only half listening as I was packing our day bags, eager to get started with our day of marketing. There had been a few hilarious language cock-ups between us in the past, my favourite being when Ying had asked me to help her friend with his business cards. His company was involved in the fumigation of expat houses in Thailand's insect-plenty climate, and Ying had asked me to check his business

169

card before printing:

> 'WE WILL KILL ALL OF YOUR INSECTS,
> COCKROACHES AND PETS.'

Explaining to Ying how very different the missing 's' made the meaning in the word 'pests' - I couldn't stop laughing.

This time, Ying was acting strange. What could be the matter? After a lot of trying to fabricate some kind of story as to why I should come home, Ying finally told me the truth in clear English: "It's your dad. We have been to hospital and they have found a brain tumour. You need to come home now."

After that phone call, life was never the same again. I immediately packed up all of my things into my backpack and checked out of the hotel. Cathy had just arrived back from her Angkor Wat sunrise tour, and, in a panic, I told her I was checking out and that she would have to continue the sales trip alone.

"You don't know the details yet," she had said. "Try to stay calm, I will look after everything here. Don't worry!"

I decided against taking the slower tourist bus and instead hopped in a banged-up old taxi. It took me three hours, at break-neck speeds along dusty roads, all the way to the Thai-Cambodia border of Poipet and Aranya-Prathet. From there, I took another three-hour taxi ride straight from the border to my dad's house in Pattaya. "Drive fast!" I screamed.

Along the way, I was trying to stay calm as Cathy had suggested, but, of course, my mind was working overdrive. This was my dad who I loved more than anything else in the world. My dad. A brain tumour? I thought that I would wake up any minute from this ridiculous nightmare. This wasn't happening. Was it real? Had Ying got it all wrong? If she *were* telling me the truth, would there be an operation? Would my dad be okay? I tried not to let panic set in and worry about the worst-case scenario. That was just not possible. This was *my dad*.

In the taxi on the way, I desperately tried to ring my mum who was back in England, but my phone was out of credit. She finally called me and I queried, desperately not wanting it to be true. "It can't be serious?" I had been wondering why Dad hadn't called me himself. Was he unable to get to the phone? Was he at the hospital? Was he in pain now?

Drive faster, taxi! Mum had said that she had received a text at 4am from my dad that had caused her to leap out of bed and call me. It read: 'I am very sick. I have brain tumour. Nikki needs you now.' We both sobbed on the phone, but we tried to think positive, until we heard further news. I promised my mum that I would call her as soon as I got back to my dad's house and found out more about the situation. *Drive faster!* Forget any 27-hour bus journey, this three-hour taxi ride was the longest journey of my life.

I got back to the house and Dad was upstairs in bed, in serious pain. He was frowning and screwing up his face in anguish, and he held me and cried when he saw that I had arrived.

"It will all be okay," I reassured him. "It won't be anything serious. It definitely won't be cancer. They will just take it out and you will be fine."

Holding my hand tightly, my dad whispered, "I'm not sure this time, Nikki. I can't tell you if it will be okay." I think, at any age, one of the hardest things that a parent can admit to a child is that they just don't know if things will be okay. I had to be strong.

The Day Everything Changed

The next day, my mum arrived all the way from England. Since receiving the text message, she had booked the first flight out and had taken a taxi from Bangkok Airport to Pattaya. We all drove to the hospital together with my dad in the car, who was now silent and hardly able to walk due the excruciating pain he was experiencing in his head.

While my dad was given morphine and had finally drifted asleep, free, for now, from the terrible pain, the doctor told us the facts. From the X-ray, they had found a grade four glioblastoma tumour on the right hand side of my dad's brain, which was, indeed, cancer. It was operable, but ultimately incurable, as the tumour was known to be particularly aggressive and would just keep growing back no matter what treatment they tried. I looked at the doctor in amazement.

"Even if we operate..." the doctor said, "and that is your choice, your dad has around a year to live."

I ran outside screaming and crying. I could not believe this was happening to me – to my dad. He was only 57. He was fit and healthy, and had never smoked or taken drugs in his life. He drank moderately, had always played sport and looked after his body, and he now played golf three times a week. What's more, he absolutely *loved* life. He already made the most out of every day and lived life to the full – he didn't need a wake up call. He didn't need his life to be cut short like this. It just wasn't right. This could not be happening to him – it was just not fair. Cancer is never fair.

Everything had happened so quickly leading up to his diagnosis. Ying explained that the night before, Dad had been out playing snooker with one of his friends. The snooker cue kept slipping off his left hand as he was trying to steady it to hit the ball. He kept shaking his hand, thinking that it was a little bit of cramp, and thought nothing of it. That night, when he walked to the car after the game, he had dropped all of the snooker balls onto the floor. Trying to pick them up, he had been unable to make the grabbing shape with his left hand. Now he was really starting to panic, thinking that he was having a stroke perhaps

His friend had driven him home and Dad had ran in the bedroom where Ying was sleeping. Ying said, that by this time, my dad's left lip had started to twitch and she knew something was wrong. Ying drove my dad to the hospital immediately and the doctor took an X-ray of his head. Doctor Pichai, who was to become an incredible support to us all in the months that followed, had told my dad the harsh truth that very first night.

In the days that followed, we had to make a quick decision about whether my dad was going to have an operation. If they didn't operate, he could be dead within weeks. Of course we wanted to go ahead. My mum and I drove up and down the motorway from Pattaya to Bangkok getting second opinions with brain surgeons. Every time, we hoped that when we showed them the scans that they would say, "No, no that's not a tumour – they have got it all wrong. Your dad will be fine!" I felt a duty to my dad to be thorough in my research, and to find the best surgeon in the whole of Thailand to conduct the operation. It was the only time in my life when my dad couldn't take control of the situation, and I had to be strong for him.

Doctor Pichai performed the operation in Bangkok-Pattaya Hospital on 7th August, removing 60% of the brain tumour. He had explained that his goal for the operation was to remove as much as possible, allowing for the longest time and greatest quality of life for my dad. A tumour on the right hand side of my dad's brain meant that it was his movement on the left hand side of his body that was affected. If it had been in another area of his brain there might have been personality changes or inability to speak.

Still in denial, we were hoping that once the majority of the tumour was removed, Dad's life could go back to normal, and somehow we would find a way of making sure that the tumour would never grow back. Despite the doctor's words that this type of cancer - also known as the 'Kennedy tumour', after President Kennedy's brother who died of the disease - always recurred, we still had hope.

After the operation, Dad recovered his movement marvellously. Within a few days he was walking around the hospital, and was sporting a trendy hat over his newly shaved head. Doctor Pichai was pleased with how my dad's body had responded after the operation. I felt that I could see in his eyes, even though he had probably seen this scenario a hundred times before, that he too believed that it was unfair for such a disease to strike a healthy, strong and happy man.

It was the first time that the two of them got chance to really discuss what was happening. Never one to 'beat around the bush', my dad appreciated Doctor Pichai's straight-talking bedside manner. I think the two of them had a great respect for each other, from the very beginning until the very end. Ying reckoned that the two of them had been brothers in a past life.

We were all still in shock and finding it hard to comprehend what was happening. Doctor Pichai told us that we should begin to think about what treatment course we wanted to pursue. The treatment that was described was always focused on 'buying more time' rather than 'finding a cure'. As far as the doctors were concerned, there was no-one on earth who had ever survived this disease and it was important to face facts.

The pathologist recommended a dual treatment of powerful chemotherapy and radiotherapy that would cost US$60,000 and had no real guarantees of prolonging my dad's life. It certainly had no guarantee of prolonging my dad's *quality* of life. He would have to come into the hospital every day to receive radiotherapy, and would be given tablets of chemotherapy, which had strong side effects. On the positive side, people have been known to live up to three years with this treatment. I looked at my dad and I knew what he was thinking.

"If I am going to die, I am going to die in the state that I am in. I don't want to suffer chemotherapy that will make me sick and make what time I do have left miserable. As I have lived my life up until now, I want to be able to live each day to the full. Even if treatment will prolong time, what is the point of that if I am not happy and able to do the things I love with the people I love? I don't want my family to suffer with me through that over an extended amount of time. I have never believed in expensive cancer treatment anyhow, and I don't want to throw money at something now, in desperation, that we already know will not work. I have always been a believer in nature, so that is what we'll look at now. In the land of herbs and ancient medicinal plants – I'd rather look at alternative forms of treatment. Let Mother Nature do what she wants with me."

The ever-inspirational, awe-inspiring man that I was so proud to call my dad. Even now, lying in a hospital bed in a weakened state, after having been given the worst news that anyone could ever imagine, he was surprising me and inspiring me to lead a better life. My eyes welled up with tears (as they are doing right now again writing this).

"You are just amazing, Dad," I had said, and meant it with every single cell in my body.

Dad was discharged from the hospital after about a week. My mum, and Cathy, who had now arrived back in Thailand from her travels in Cambodia, flew to Chiang Mai to stay in my apartment, while I went to stay at my dad's house. I had already begun to look at alternative forms of cancer treatment, and read into everything I could about glioblastoma brain tumours on the Internet. It seemed that the doctors were right. Apart from a few miracle cases that had dubious facts surrounding them, rarely anyone survived this particular type of cancer. I watched documentary videos about conspiracy theories behind cancer treatments and pharmaceutical companies. I read about homeopathic and natural remedies, and scoured anything online that I could find that would offer some hope.

While Ying looked after my dad physically, cooking healthy meals and caring for him, my research into alternative treatments was all that I could do to keep my dad's spirits up and keep us all going. I threw myself into it like a school project.

The Gerson Therapy was fascinating. It had been developed by a German-born American physician called Max Gerson, who discovered that something as simple as an alternative diet could cure chronic diseases such as tuberculosis and even cancer. After suffering from migraines since being young, Gerson had experimented with different diets in order to rid himself of the pain. He discovered that eating a plant-based diet of organic fruit and vegetables, no meat or animal product, teamed with raw juices, coffee enemas and natural supplements miraculously cured him of his malady. Gerson began to prescribe the diet to patients with chronic degenerative diseases, with astounding results. He claimed that 446 out of 450 patients of skin tuberculosis who had been sent home by the hospital to die were cured by the diet therapy. Apparently, Gerson had treated and cured hundreds of patients of whom conventional treatment had failed to cure.

"Let food be thy medicine and medicine be thy food," the great Greek physician Hippocrates quoted more than 2,000 years ago. It seemed so simple. Could it be that we had forgotten the healing powers of nature in lieu of mass production and huge profit-making pharmaceutical companies? I began to research further, watching documentaries about food production, learning about the pesticides and hormones that were being sprayed and pumped onto our food today. The things that I saw shocked and concerned me, and made me wonder if mass food production was causing cancer in the first place?

I found other therapies that extolled the forgotten benefits of the healing power of nature. Each natural remedy condemned expensive chemotherapy treatments as frightening consequences of a profit-driven capitalist society. The Joanna Budwig diet, which consisted of organic cottage cheese mixed with organic flaxseed oil, was said to have cured thousands of cases of cancer. There was the controversial Burzynski Clinic in Texas, which used antineoplaston therapy to supposedly cure cancer patients. I also found incredible claims of the power of thought and meditation in healing cancer. An American biologist named Bruce Lipton was, supposedly, bridging the gap between science and spirituality, claiming that genes and DNA could be altered by a person's beliefs. If this were true, and this was all future science that was yet to be taken seriously, then patients would be able to literally 'think' their way to recovery.

But could these alternative therapies be taken seriously? Were they simply money-making fads that played to desperate people when they were at their most vulnerable, so-called 'Quack Treatments'? Or, as the conspiracy theories suggested, were they valid treatments that had been suppressed by large pharmaceutical companies in order to sustain the monopoly on cancer treatment. You can't patent an organic apple. And after all, cancer was a hugely profitable, multi-million-dollar industry.

Question things. That is what my dad had always taught me. Do not believe everything that you read in the newspapers or see on TV. That is exactly what I was trying to do now – in order to save the man that I loved most in the world. I wanted to believe in all of the conspiracy theories, if it meant that there would be a cure for my dad's illness. I had always tried to look at things differently and consider alternative ways of seeing the world. And, I had often thought that there was a lot wrong with mass-produced food and our unhealthy modern lifestyles. So was there a cure out there? Or was I wasting my time looking for a grain of hope where there was none? I refused to feel completely helpless and be passive in my dad's progressive illness. I wanted to remain in control, and research helped me to believe that I was.

Ying had also been doing some research. Rather than Internet research, the Thai way was to discuss everything with friends, family, the shop-keeper, the woman at the market, the delivery guy and the post office staff. Usually, someone's brother's auntie or uncle knew a friend of a friend who had been in exactly your situation and could offer help. In this way, Ying discovered renowned Doctor Sommai Thongprasert, a 91-year old Thai oncology doctor turned herbal cancer specialist. He had apparently been curing terminally ill cancer patients from his clinic in Singhburi, eastern Thailand, with a mixture of five specific Thai herbs.

Throughout this whole period of 'research' my dad was intrigued and enthusiastic. He was constantly amazing me with his positive attitude, and he was even talking about writing a world-shattering book. The book would be about how he had been cured by a natural herbal treatment in Thailand, and it would shed doubt on expensive conventional medicine. During those days, we rarely cried or dwelled in misery, and the three of us stuck together with our mission to find a cure.

We had decided to visit the famous Doctor Sommai, which was a five-hour drive from Pattaya, and we packed the car to stay the night in Singhburi. Apparently, people from all over the country drove to visit the doctor every day. By 8am every morning, he would have a queue of hundreds of people out the door of his tiny wooden clinic.

We set off in the car and, after not long, were forced to take a diversion, making our journey an overall nine hours, rather than the five hours we predicted. The diversion was due to dangerous flooding in Thailand at that time and a lot of the roads had been blocked off. Even on the main highway, we passed houses at the side of the road that were a third covered in water. There were motorbikes tied up with ropes in the trees to prevent them from getting waterlogged. This strange, ever-adapting, resourceful country never failed to surprise me. Perhaps it could surprise me now with a miracle cure for my dad?

We rose at 6am in the morning, and Ying had already paid one of the guys from the hotel to go and stand in the queue for us at the doctor's surgery.

"Mai pen rai," she had said. "I will make sure that we are seen by Khun Mor." (Khun Mor meant Doctor in Thai).

We arrived at the surgery and managed to see Doctor Sommai after waiting only about an hour. After everything that I had read about the man on the Internet, I was eager to look closely at the 91-year old 'magic doctor'.

Doctor Sommai was a man of few words. He asked my dad to explain his problem as he looked over the X-rays carefully. He touched my dad's head, which now had very short black-grey hair spiking out, looked into his eyes and prescribed him six-weeks of herbal tea, five times a day. He recommended against chemotherapy, told him to eat a vegetarian, even a vegan diet if possible, no alcohol, sugar or fat and keep exercising.

We drove back to Pattaya, and Dad began his alternative tea treatment right away. After drinking a full cup of the foul-smelling, thick liquid mud that Ying had been boiling on the stove all the day - that had made the house smell like a forest – I think he started to realise that this treatment may not be 'the cup of tea' he had first thought.

Over the next few months, Ying made delicious vegetarian meals, doing everything with a mushroom that she possibly could. Coconut curries, mushroom stir-fries, delicious pineapple-rice dishes – the Thai cuisine certainly suited the vegetarian option very well.

Out of support, Ying and I also became vegan. I gave up chocolate (one of my loves!), and I even stayed off the wine for around three months. One night, when Ying was away at her mum's house in Isaan, Dad came to talk to me while I was sat in the garden. He had a cheeky look on his face. "I feel like steak, chips and red wine," he said and smiled.

A little indulgence was what we both desperately needed. We got dressed up and got in the car to go to one of my dad's favourite restaurants in Pattaya, where we enjoyed an amazing steak with blue cheese sauce, over a bottle of red wine, just like the old days. My dad whispered to the waitress to keep the evening a secret from Ying, and we had great conversation, almost, but not quite, forgetting the small problem that my dad had a brain tumour.

Most of the time, we felt like the brain tumour was almost a silly inconvenience. My dad should be playing golf, enjoying the sunshine and being happy, while I should be building the magazine. This ridiculous, stupid thing that was happening was just unnecessary and no one really had time for it. But it was happening, and we couldn't stop it. No matter how hard we tried to forget it didn't exist, research the hell out of it and find out every bit of knowledge there was to know about it, we couldn't make it disappear. This was a problem that none of us knew how to solve.

At this point, I didn't know what I believed in anymore. I didn't know if Doctor Sommai's herbal treatment would work, if we had been right to give into 'a little of what you fancy does you good' with the steak and wine, or if indeed, the vegan diet was doing any good anyway. After all of the shock, heartbreak, pain, hope, and confusion over the last month, I flew to meet Craig on my favourite island of Koh Phangan, for some much-needed healing for myself.

He greeted me with open arms and I wondered what on earth I would have done without him. We had only been dating a few months, and this bombshell was enough to make any new boyfriend run a mile. He didn't have to be by my side through the biggest challenge in my life thus far, but he had no intention of letting me go through this alone. He promised me that he loved me and would cope with all of my ups and downs through this life-shattering time. We watched sunsets, and I felt safe in his arms in my Koh Phangan. *Can't time just stop now like this? Forever like this?* I prayed.

One morning, I went to a yoga class at a nearby school on the beach in Sri Thanu. I was interviewing one of the yoga founders for the magazine and I ended up telling him about my dad. It was always the thing foremost on my mind.

He told me that, by chance, there was a young couple currently staying at the centre who had recently been all over Thailand researching alternative therapy for illnesses and cancer. I should definitely speak to them. They were sat on another table and I immediately poured my heart out to the lovely couple. They told me a story about a friend of theirs back home who had been the inspiration for their trip. He had been diagnosed with a terminal brain tumour when he was 21 years old. How devastating! He had been operated on, but the doctors had told him, as they had said to my dad, that the tumour would grow back and that he didn't have long to live. "No way," he had said. "I am only 21 years old and your twenties are the best time of your life. This is not happening to me!"

With diet and daily meditation, apparently, he had managed to prevent the tumour from growing back throughout the whole of his twenties. Then, at aged 29, just weeks before his 30th birthday, the tumour struck again. Was it the fact that he had focused so strongly on staying alive in his *twenties* that had made the tumour go into remission for so long? Was this *The Secret* at work or was it just coincidence? At 29, however, his life was a different story. He had met the love of his life and was engaged to be married. He also had a child, a son, on the way. "No," he had said, "I must see my son grow up!" Apparently, the guy continued his powerful thought exercises and diet, and is still alive today with his son now at school.

Could this hopeful and miraculous tale be true? Why would this young couple lie about this story to me? And if so, could my dad heal himself?

Did I believe in miracles? I looked out at the pink, red, yellow, blue and green sunset setting over the Gulf of Thailand, palm trees swaying in the breeze and the sea sparkling. Yes, I did believe in miracles. Yes, I did.

23

The S.E.A Backpacker Office

With my dad carrying on with his alternative treatment and diet at home, I went back to Chiang Mai to try to carry on with my life as best I could. In the meantime, Cathy, my intern-extraordinaire, had basically taught herself how to use InDesign and had been busy getting the next magazine together. I was shocked (and thrilled) that the magazine had been progressing so well without me, and was so grateful that she had been able to step in and help with tricky things while I was out of action. She had even found a few more customers in Cambodia and they needed invoicing. It was business as usual. Both of us managed to laugh at the fact that her internship was certainly turning out very differently than we had both thought! Cathy's devoted efforts kind of kicked me back into gear as I realised that life and business must go on – no matter what.

"You're going to need this magazine if anything happens to me, Nikki. You will need a focus. So don't let it slip, don't give it up. Keep calm and carry on." My dad's wise words, which I knew were true.

So I didn't. Let it slip that is. I threw everything I had into growing the flourishing business that I had built thus far. The hard work distracted me, and nights sat up late on my laptop answering emails took my mind off everything else that was happening. Ideas of how to expand the business were jotted down in lists, spray diagrams and on Post It notes. It was like going back to the beginning – I ran everything by my dad, almost in a panic - thinking that one day soon I may not be able to do so.

When I was in Koh Phangan with Craig, I had met someone that was to become a big part of my life and business for the next few years. Her name was Annabelle, and she was the owner of a funky, burlesque night-club back in London, that was now running without her and enabling her to travel. She was charismatic, full of life and inspirational. We clicked immediately. After Annabelle's initial email asking if she could contribute articles to the magazine, we had both discovered that we were in Koh Phangan at the same time and had decided to meet. 'I can't do tomorrow I'm afraid,' Annabelle had written over email, 'I'm currently tangled up in a love triangle with a Swiss guy and his Thai girlfriend, called John. Yes I said John!' I knew I was going to like her.

One afternoon, sitting in a beautiful infinity pool that overlooked Ang Thong Marine Park on the west coast of Koh Phangan, I revealed everything about the business to Annabelle after only knowing her a few days. I felt like I could trust her immediately, and I didn't mind sharing money and business problems with her, things that I normally wouldn't have shared with others. After all, she had experience herself with running a successful business back in the UK. In turn, Annabelle told me about her ambitions and her desire to write. We formed a friendship, and decided that we could help each other in very different ways. A week later, Annabelle became Deputy Editor of *Southeast Asia Backpacker Magazine* and helped enormously with the next stage of the ride.

Together, we found someone to help with sales (always the most crucial and most difficult part of running the business), who was to become our Sales Director; and we picked a candidate for an Online Manager who was to help with social networking and the blogging side of things. Ying, who was now unable to commit time to the magazine as she was looking after my dad full time, told me that her sister, Suchada, was in-between work and could we use an accountant? I was beginning to build a team. And now, our small team needed an office.

One day, whilst wandering through the Old City of Chiang Mai, I came across a small room for rent at 8,000 Thai baht/month. It was in a busy area of the city with backpacker hostels all around. I would get a lot of footfall from backpackers here. Wasting no time, the next day I laid down the deposit. I have often found that sometimes when you want something to happen so badly, it kind of falls into place, and this is what was happening now, at rapid speed! Craig, and a friend of his from work, spent the weekend painting the disgusting red office walls a much more pleasing white, and I printed a huge SEA Backpacker logo out to stick on the back wall. My mum, who was still in Chiang Mai at this point, helped me to kit out the office with furniture from a nearby store, and we were ready to open within weeks of renting.

The doors to the SEA Backpacker Office opened, and thus began a new stage in my life and the life of the magazine.

In the first week of opening, I bought an old scrapbook from the market and turned it into a 'visitors book' for people to write a message in when they dropped by the office. I bought three pin-boards to put up on the wall: one for events in Southeast Asia, one for insider tips to Chiang Mai and finally one for traveller messages. I started the board with a fake one to get people going... *'DAVE, We've got on the slow boat. We still have your passport!'*

I made cardboard signs that read; *'Fruit shake break – Back in 10 min'* and *'Massage time – Back in one hour'*. I hoped that people would catch on to the personality of what this very different 'office' was all about. It wasn't an office, it was a 'hub,' a creative space for travel and dreaming. I wanted the office to be an embodiment of what the magazine stood for - 'a travel diary for everyone.' I wanted people to pop in, ask for travel advice, and write anecdotes and tips in the visitors book. They could look at the huge map on the wall and browse through back copies of the magazine, which were all laid out in date order on the shelves. It was a place to get inspiration for your backpacking trip, and there were beanbags and a comfy leather couch where people could relax and chat.

After a few months of being open, people started to notice the little unusual office. Craig had been in a bar down town and had rung me to say that he had just heard two backpackers talking. One had said to the other: "Hey, do you know where the SEA Backpacker office is? I came here to Chiang Mai just to check it out!" Despite everything else that was going on in my life at the time, I watched the sign being erected above the door to the office, looked up from across the street and felt proud for everything that I had achieved. And the visitors started to flood in.

At the beginning, it was difficult to get any work done with people entering through the doors and asking a myriad of questions (some rather ridiculous), at any hour of the day. With other members of the team out on the open road researching articles or taking sales trips, most of the time it was just Suchada and I in the office. With Suchada's limited English (and non-existent backpacking experience), it was me that was left to answer the majority of the travellers' questions.

"What's the quickest way to get to Laos?", "When is the next Full Moon Party?", "What else is there to do in Chiang Mai apart from trekking and going to see a Muay Thai show?", "Are the buses in Vietnam okay?", "Where shall I go next?", "Where can I find pickled onions in Chiang Mai?", "Should I get a tattoo?", "Do I have Dengue Fever?" *Go to a Doctor!* Sometimes, I wondered how people managed to make it out of their own front door and onto the aeroplane in the first place.

Some travellers had trouble figuring out exactly what the purpose of the office was. One backpacker walked in and placed his smelly laundry on my desk while I sat at my laptop and said, "Can you get it done by Tuesday?" We were not a laundry. We were not a hostel. We were not a travel agency. We were not a bar. One rather attractive traveller walked in and asked, "Can you tell me the way to your house?" I blushed and started to giggle before I realised that 'Your House' was in fact, the name of a hostel up the road.

Prize for the weirdest visitor went to a strange gentleman who handed me a business card saying that he was an 'Alchemist of Spirits'. He walked into the office wearing white trousers and a purple waistcoat over a bare chest, holding a huge knobbly stick (supposedly his staff), and proceeded to smell every object in the room before finding his way to my desk. Thankfully, he didn't smell me.

"I can turn your hate into love and your love into hate," he asserted.

"Hi...", I said, unsure of what to make of this bizarre character.

How on earth was I going to get rid of this weirdo so that I could get my 95 emails answered? "Erm… would you like to see our media pack to see if you'd like to advertise your alchemy services to backpackers?" I suggested.

At that point, an American woman walked into the office to tell me that she had found a copy of the magazine in her library back home in San Francisco and that every issue was being collected there. "Wow! Amazing," I replied in astonishment wondering how on earth the magazines were finding their way to San Francisco. Somebody must have been subscribing through our new online system!

As I sat in my office chair smiling with bewilderment, the Alchemist began a debate with the American woman about her 'negative aura' that went on for quite some time. I looked up at the two of them from my desk, one sat on a bean bag, one propped up against the wall on his 'magic shaft'. They were debating furiously and I reckoned this could go on for some time. I rolled my eyes at Suchada and she smiled at me. If only she could imagine this scenario taking place in a day-to-day 'office' situation back in England. It was a different world. I laughed to myself and nipped out to get a fruit shake for 20 baht up the road.

On days when I really had to get important work done and deadlines ticked off, I decided to put up a cardboard sign that read: *'Magazine work in progress – DO NOT ENTER!'* It was shamefully ignored as people continued to peer through the blinds and ask me questions at my desk.

One afternoon, a hostel owner from up the road brought in a bottle of SangSom whiskey at 2pm in the afternoon and declared a 'welcome to the neighbourhood' party. I tried to decline, but it was no use. It seemed that an end to my workday had come early and there was nothing I could do about it. When I hung up my *'Yoga Time'* sign on the door two hours later ready for my evening class, I wasn't sure that I was in a fit state to be doing downward dogs!

My days at the office were mostly happy times. Santose, the friendly tailor next door on the left hand side, would pop in to ask questions about English words from his dictionary or would sit on the step outside playing his guitar. He was working for a group of tailors in Chiang Mai and most of the staff were actually Burmese or Nepalese. They were always extremely friendly and helpful towards me. On the right hand side, there was a Thai travel agent called Pep. When I first opened the office, Pep was very curious as to the nature of my business in case it could have been competition for his travel company. Indeed, I think everyone was intrigued by, but never indifferent towards, the new white girl doing business in town.

"What are you actually selling?" Pep had asked. "Are you selling tours – same me? You are just giving free advice – but why?" As backpacker after backpacker poured into the office to chat to me, I had started to wonder that myself! Crazy farangs.

Every day, I would buy a delicious lunch from one of the street-side cafés in the area: fresh organic produce, stir-fries, curries, the famous local Chiang Mai dish, khao soi (chicken curry soup); and of course, Western food whenever I wanted it. I would order my breakfast from the little café opposite: muesli, fruit yoghurt or mixed omelette on toast, and often the waitresses would bring it right over to my desk. It felt nice to have my 'regular order' and to be recognised in the area with smiles and waves everywhere I went. I felt like I was becoming part of the community.

In one issue of the magazine, we had written a 'Local Portrait' article about a lady called 'Tip'. Tip was the much-loved, locally famous, fruit shake lady in Somphet Market, just two minutes around the corner from the office. We had a full colour photograph of Tip covering a page in the magazine, and had printed a poem that a couple of travellers had written about her and her admirable work ethic as a single mum with her own business. The poem was called *The Fruit Dance*. Tip had received so much extra custom from the article that she came into the office to thank me personally. She bought an SEA Backpacker T-shirt for 300 baht and brought me a gift of a glorious mango and strawberry fruit shake!

Moments like this made everything worthwhile. I stopped by her stall the next day and saw that she had laminated the article and put it up on the wall behind her fruit shake stand. She beamed at me and told me to visit for free fruit shakes any time. I made sure I always paid.

Although during low season it could get a bit quiet, there was always a lot to do in the SEA Backpacker office, and the visitor book was being filled rather nicely. I had found a good base and felt settled for anything that was to come.

S.E.A Backpacker visitor book, October 5, 2012:

'Thanks for being an inspiration and for reminding people to follow their hearts, sometimes this is the most challenging thing to do. What we find when we travel is more valuable than what we look for. Keep up the good work!'
(Sonia - San Fransisco - Barcelona)

24

Welcome to the Philippines

I had met Anna, like many other work contacts that later became friends, when she emailed me asking if she could help out with the magazine. She had sent the email from the island of Bohol in the Philippines, to ask if she could help to build the Philippines destination section of our website. Anna was born in New Zealand, and had moved to the Philippines with her engineering company when they had begun a project in the troublesome province of Mindanao. She had since fallen in love with the 7,107 islands (visiting as many as she possibly could!), and had started an NGO and a travel company called Flip Flop Tours.

The company arranged for backpackers to visit remote islands and have an authentic Filipino experience at various local home-stays. The money that backpackers paid for accommodation went back into providing the local village with electricity, a reliable water supply and other amenities that are so taken for granted in the Western world.

Anna was also involved in various micro-finance projects in the Visayan Islands, of which Bohol is a part.

Anna had invited me along on the very first 'Flip Flop Tour' to discover more about the company, and to experience the archipelago for myself. The Philippines is famous for its amazing white sandy beaches, wreck diving, lively festivals and Spanish colonial heritage. Being a Catholic country, I was about to experience a very different culture from the Southeast Asia that I was used to. It was a great opportunity to showcase the country in the magazine, and to show that we were forging new ground and reaching new backpacker destinations. I'd also managed to wangle a meeting with the Philippines Tourism Department who had just launched their 'It's More Fun in The Philippines!' marketing campaign. I was eager to talk to them about partnering with the magazine in order to get more backpackers to visit their under-celebrated shores.

The timing was right, but I was in two minds about whether to go. My dad had recently had a scan which had shown that despite his herbal treatment, the tumour was continuing to grow, albeit at a much slower rate than it had been. I went down to meet Dad and Ying at Bangkok-Pattaya Hospital, where Doctor Pichai was strongly recommending radiotherapy to prolong my dad's life. I could see that my dad didn't really want to go through with the treatment as he didn't have any faith that it would have much effect. On the other hand, he didn't want to go against the advice of the professionals, especially Doctor Pichai, who he had trusted from the beginning.

In the end, my dad decided to start a six-week course of five-days on, two-days off, radiotherapy treatment at Bangkok Hospital. So that they didn't have to drive up and down the motorway every day from Pattaya to Bangkok (two hours), they had decided to rent a small apartment in Bangkok for six weeks and I went to stay with them there for a few days. My dad was to begin the second week of treatment just as I was about to fly off to the Philippines.

I told my dad about the opportunity and he strongly persuaded me to go.

"What are you going to do? Sit here and watch me? No, get on the plane, Nikki. You'll be back in two weeks!" This was much easier said than done. As well as worrying immensely about my dad and his treatment, not to mention wanting to spend as much time with him as possible, I had developed a rather ridiculous fear of flying that seemed to come out of nowhere. The owner of a travel magazine with a phobia of flying – just great! I had never really 'enjoyed' flying, and much preferred to be on solid ground, but up until this point, it was never a real problem for me. I would get the jitters before taking off, and then I would be fine. Since my dad's illness, however, this slight nervousness had developed into a fully-grown phobia - palms sweating, almost crying at take-off, heart-banging fear.

The only explanation I can offer as to the cause of this new panic is that my dad's diagnosis had led me to believe that anything could happen. Day by day, we get through our lives with a notion of 'it'll never happen to me' (and most of the time it doesn't), but now, with the inconceivable happening right before my very eyes, I was starting to question the probability of the unimaginable. If my dad had less than a 1% chance of getting a brain tumour (1 in 140 people), then could a plane fall out of the sky? The odds of dying on a plane are actually more like 1 in 11 million, so I believe!

"What do you expect with everything that you are going through, Nikki?" my mum said. On the outside I was trying to be calm, hold a business together and continue with my travels and life as normal. However, on the inside, strange things were taking place in my body and to my personality that were sure signals of what I was experiencing. Later, I realised that my fear of flying was caused by the fact that I was deferring my fear. Instead of facing up to my real fear - that my dad was going to die - I had created something entirely new to worry about. It meant that I could be strong in the face of awful circumstances on the one hand, but then fall apart at something seemingly so small.

I arrived in the Philippines and Anna's boyfriend met me off the ferry from Cebu Island to Bohol. It was pouring down with rain and the sea was very choppy on the boat over to Bohol. I had been crying non-stop all of the way since leaving Bangkok Airport. I just felt so far away from my dad. I reckoned that I would get off the boat, say hi to Anna and then turn around and go right back. Yet upon arrival, I chatted with Anna, her boyfriend and their lovely friends from New Zealand and I decided to give it one day. If my dad was taking things day by day, then I decided that I would too. If I still felt the same tomorrow, I could easily get a return ferry to Cebu and leave on the first flight back to Thailand.

Anna and Co. didn't waste any time getting me into the swing of things and ready to experience authentic village life on the small island of Bohol. What a unique welcome I received! In true Filipino style, we were greeted into the tiny village of Balilihan, in the northern jungles of Bohol (where we would have our home-stay), by a unique song that had been composed especially for our arrival. An extremely cheerful Filipino guy wearing a brightly coloured shirt, who went by the name of 'Goody', led the serenade as he strummed a high-pitched ukulele: "Welcome to Bohol, we are the land of the noble man." At the same time, the local women of the village adorned us with handmade bamboo garlands around our necks. The scene felt more Hawaiian than Southeast Asian, and it was a wonderful introduction to the fabulous hospitality that the country is famous for.

In the Philippines, small communities known as barangays are led by a barangay captain who is aided by a council. It is a system that is unique to the Philippines, and from an outsider's point of view really seems to promote harmony and togetherness. Events take place at the local barangay hall, and teenage hipster boys mingle with exuberant toddlers and well respected grandparents. It's funny, I just couldn't imagine the juvenile 'hoodies' hanging out with grannies back home on the streets of Manchester.

Wafts of exotic scents began to drift from the town hall where the women of the barangay were preparing a Filipino feast for us. Eager as I was to try my first traditional Filipino home-cooked meal, it wasn't dinner time yet. To build up our appetites, a group of cheeky local kids had challenged us to a game of basketball and were now waiting for us on the court outside the barangay hall. In the Philippines, basketball is the most popular sport, dating back to the early 1900s when the Americans introduced the game and built courts in many communities. The Filipinos have embraced the game with a passion and as we found out, are incredibly good at it! We suffered an embarrassing defeat; six twenty-something girls beaten by five eleven year-old boys half our height.

Then it was time to eat. A feast of chicken adobo, jack-fruit stew, sticky rice and other delicacies were served on a traditional bamboo plate with coconut leaves, all washed down with a glass of very sickly coconut wine – mixed with chocolate powder and raw egg. Saraap! (Delicious!) Before eating, we gathered around to pray to God for the food we had been given. It was a strange contrast, coming from mostly Buddhist Southeast Asian countries, to witness such a devout belief in Catholicism here. I could see, at once, that the religion was a very important part of people's everyday lives.

The Philippines is one of only two predominantly catholic countries in Asia, the other being East Timor. The influence dates back to the arrival of Ferdinand Magellan and the Spanish colonials in 1521. During their 333-year occupation, the Spanish managed to build a church in almost every city and town, and the growth of Catholicism has since spread rapidly throughout the country, with Filipinos vehemently upholding the faith. That night, on my first night in the Philippines, arms raised high in the air dancing and singing hymns on the basketball court, I praised the Lord 'Halleluiah' more times than I had done in my entire life.

A local band had been invited from a neighbouring barangay, and you could definitely detect the Spanish influence in the music as acoustic twangs drifted into the night air. I drank more coconut wine and chatted with two very intelligent sixteen-year-old local girls who were looking for good husbands. Their requirements being: "Stable job, reliable, religious, not smoke, not drink, be enjoyable and good to look at." *Good luck girls!*

Although other barangays in the area had experienced visits from foreigners before, Balilihan Barangay would be the first to actually have guests stay overnight, and they were extremely excited to be our hosts. As the remainder of the 'El Niño' (monsoon rain) pummelled down on the wrought-iron roof of the barangay hall, we slept like babies on thin mattresses on the floor. It had been just the day I needed, full of family, friends and love. Even though I wasn't part of this community, the Filipino people had certainly made me feel like I was. And, even though I hadn't told anyone about the trauma I was experiencing 'back home' in Thailand, I felt like I was understood. I enjoyed the warmth and life of these people around me. I decided I would give it one more day. One more day.

Waking to the sound of roosters is an experience that is common everywhere in Southeast Asia, and shortly after the crowing stopped, a few of the nosier kids came running and giggling into the hall to invite us to breakfast. In a similar fashion to the previous evening, we had to earn our food first, with a trek up the small mountain behind the village where breakfast was to be served. A table laid out with fresh mangoes, eggplant omelette and fried fish was set up next to a giant concrete crucifix overlooking a view of undulating green hills and jungle. The Philippines was a green and luscious land and, in these parts, very under-developed.

After breakfast, some of the locals offered to take us to the nearby waterfall so that we could shower. With no running water in the village, the options were either the ever-torturous cold bucket shower or the more natural approach… we chose the latter. After a half-hour motorbike journey up dirt tracks, through lush rice terraces, tropical jungle and by wooden huts, we arrived at the waterfall. I was expecting a stream and a trickle of water where we could splash our faces – not Niagara Falls! The waterfall was very high, several-tiered and a truly spectacular sight. Standing under the powerful force of the falls with tons of water gushing down upon our heads was an exhilarating feeling. There was no other tourist around. A site like this would have been swarming with tourists and signposted to death in other parts of Southeast Asia.

That morning, we left the home-stay village and went back to Anna's house, where I was able to get phone signal and call my dad to make sure everything was okay. He sounded positive on the phone and the treatment was going okay. I told him all about the home-stay, and he was intrigued to see my photos when I got back, saying that he would love to visit the island one day. His words spurred me on to continue my adventure so that I could excite him with possible future adventures of his own when I got back to Bangkok.

"Are you sure that you don't need me to come back?" I asked. The answer was of course no, and my dad encouraged me, as always, to explore, dream, discover.

Anna's house was very interesting, located in a tiny village clinging to the edge of the ocean, with a deserted, windswept beach as her backyard. Her house had no running water, and there wasn't a mirror (not even a hand held one) in the entire three rooms that consisted of their living room, bedroom and kitchen. I imagined how many girls at home (including me) in image-obsessed England would cope without a mirror in their house!

Anna and her boyfriend were the salt of the earth, and it was no wonder that the local Filipino people had welcomed them into their village as if they were born there. Next door's children, roosters and chickens wandered into the house on a whim, and would stay and watch you as you ate your cereal or brushed your teeth. There was always a friendly guy in a neighbouring house who would help with a dodgy motorbike engine or deliver some fresh water to your back door. It certainly was the simple life. I reckoned that not many people back home could adapt easily to this lifestyle.

The next day, we set out on a three-day banca adventure. The banca boats, with far reaching wooden balances on either side, are unique to the Philippines. Everybody says that you haven't been to the country if you haven't set sail on a swashbuckling voyage in one of these shaky vessels. The three days sailing turned out to be an unbelievable adventure as we anchored the boat at various remote paradise islands.

Some of the islands could be walked across in an hour, some islands had just one palm tree growing on them; on some of the other islands, locals glared at us due to the lack of foreigners that visited the area. Pulling onto the shore, through bright turquoise waters, and creating the only footsteps on the sand on the most exquisite beach you've ever seen in your life was an amazing experience.

We stopped for a night at the beautiful and mystical island of Siquijor, infamous for witchcraft and shamanism all over the Philippines. Apparently, people would travel far and wide to this island for miracle black magic cures, or even to put curses on people who had wronged them. Spending the night in a colourful, bohemian beach house on the northern coast of Siquijor, treating ourselves to an amazing fresh seafood barbecue, we managed to avoid the witches that night.

On the way back to Anna's island, we encountered a storm in our tiny banca. Everyone knew that the Philippines was desperately prone to some of the worst weather in the world, and I was constantly reading reports about typhoons, tsunamis and storms that proved fatal to the local inhabitants. The boat was rocking like mad as the captain tried to steer, nonchalantly, through the sheeting rain. There were eight passengers on board, and we wrapped a plastic sheet around our bodies in a futile attempt to stay dry as the waves lapped over the sides of the boat. The captain had discarded his broken compass over the side of the boat (I had watched him in disbelief as he had thrown it), and you couldn't see even a metre ahead of you in the thick mist and rain. I had no idea how the captain knew which way to go – and there was no land in sight. Anna and the others, who were very used to sailing, having been brought up in sea-faring New Zealand, seemed unconcerned. My eyes scanned the horizon as I desperately tried to spot land.

Just as quickly as the storm had arrived, the rain stopped, the sun came out and turned the area, once again, into a tranquil paradise.

"Look, dolphins!" our captain shouted. Sure enough, swimming right next to our boat, was a school of dolphins that had seemingly risen out of the stormy waters to enjoy the return of the sunny weather. With tears in my eyes, I wondered about life and all its beauty, and all its horror. Maybe the fact that it was so fragile, so doomed to end, made it all the more beautiful.

25

Witch Doctors & Herbal Remedies

I arrived back in Bangkok after completing the originally planned two weeks in the Philippines. I had been fighting worry the whole time I had been away, and I was now nervous to see how my dad looked. Had his condition or appearance changed at all in this short amount of time? Dad and Ying picked me up from the airport in the car, and we were to go straight to the hospital for the results of my dad's latest scan. Dad had put on a lot of weight from the steroids he was taking alongside the radiotherapy treatment. As a keen footballer, tennis player, golfer, walker, runner and active sportsman all his life, I had never seen my dad with what now looked like a 'beer belly'. He told me how much he hated his appearance. We laughed it off, but I could see that he was annoyed and felt helpless about his body changing, regardless of anything he could do. Back in his house a few months ago, I'd seen him exercising and doing weights every morning for at least two hours. His determination and fight was remarkable.

At Bangkok Hospital, we were once again told the news that my dad was going to die. With each new appointment, you hope the news will change, but it never does. The radiotherapy, herbal treatment from Doctor Sommai and a healthy diet were not working to prevent the growth of the tumour. Straight from Bangkok, we drove to see Doctor Sommai in Singhburi, to get his advice and ask him if there was anything else we could do at this late stage. After waiting a few hours to see him that day, the magic doctor concluded that there was nothing that anyone could do. Along the journey thus far, hope had been spurring us on. There had been a tiny chance that something that my dad was doing might just cure him. Now we were faced with the inevitable reality, that from day one, I think my dad accepted before any of us.

Just after his diagnosis, while we were all still in shock, my dad had called me and said, "Nikki, I've worked it all out. I died in a car accident that night."

"What are you talking about?" I asked, as a shiver went up my spine.

"I wasn't sick up until that point. I had been enjoying my life. I died in a car accident that night on my way back from snooker, and the time I have now is a bonus," Dad said decidedly.

At the time I couldn't work out if Dad was being spiritual, if he had gone crazy and actually thought this to be the truth, or this was a metaphor for how he wanted to look at things. When I realised what he was trying to say a few moments later, I was overcome with emotion. I was taken aback with admiration for his incredible logic and positive attitude to life. If he was already dead, then the rest of his life was a bonus, which he should appreciate every moment of. Thinking in this way turned the scenario from a negative into a positive one. It meant that he had extra time, rather than dwindling time. He had been given something, rather than something having been taken away. It was an amazing way to deal with things, a very Buddhist approach – perhaps the way we should look at life all of the time anyhow? All of our life is a bonus already. From that point on, my dad accepted his death, and, although at times he was annoyed and frustrated at what was happening to him, he was not afraid or in denial of death. I can only hope that when my time comes I deal with it like he did.

While my dad accepted his fate, Ying on the other hand, was not accepting it in the slightest. She desperately looked for anything and everything that offered hope of a cure for Dad's terminal illness. In Thai culture, as I had already discovered, nothing was black and white. There was always an alternative way of doing things. I hadn't realised that the 'black magic' side of things and belief in animism was so strong, despite an apparent devotion to Buddhism; but I was about to find out. Even though I had already been living in Thailand for four years at that point, there was still so much that I didn't know, so much that I would never have discovered if my dad had not been ill. The country never ceased to surprise me.

First of all, Ying invited her own dad to come and stay at the house with us. I'd met Ying's father a few years ago, back in her home village in Isaan, and I was aware that he was a highly spiritual man who meditated every day, and was something of a religious guru in the local village. Together, Ying and her dad visited the temple and came back with medicine from the local monks that looked like a bunch of black twigs. She gave my dad brown, smelly, boiled drinks and sprinkled strange leaves and soil into his porridge. She soaked flannels in herbal muddy liquid and placed them on his forehead as he was doing the sudoku in the newspaper. She rubbed the area around his tumour every night with tiger balm, until my dad fell asleep. I was so glad that my dad had someone to love and care for him in this intimate way, during that time.

Every day at 8am and 6pm ritually, Ying's dad would perform his magic on my dad. He would sit over my dad on the sofa and chant verses in Sanskrit language. He would, then, hold my dad's head and gently blow onto the area where the tumour was growing. Dad said he always felt a sense of calm during the 'magic' hour, and I think he was willing to give anything a try, also for Ying's sake, who was buoyed up by the belief that the magic could be working.

Next came the smoking. You would think that for someone with cancer, the last thing that you would recommend for them to do would be to smoke, but this was a different kind. Ying had discovered (from a friend of an auntie's brother's cousin) that Thai people with cancer had been visiting a family far out in the countryside east of Pattaya. They were administering 'smoking therapy' for patients in a terminal stage of the disease. According to Ying, they had cured a woman with stomach cancer and a family member with breast cancer. "Why they not cure brain tumour?" Ying asked.

Willing to give anything a go, we drove out two hours to the middle of nowhere to visit the Thai family that were administering the bizarre treatment. It was a Thursday, and Ying had specifically chosen this day as auspicious. Thursday is a day when Thai people start something significant or new, like get a hair cut for example. Ying was filled with hope already about the potential success of the treatment.

We arrived at the house amidst palm trees, mango trees and high grasses, and sat on the balcony in the tropical heat while Dang, the man of the house, prepared the mixture. I was a little dubious. Ying had already agreed that we would come to his house for the next three weeks on Tuesdays and Thursdays, and we were paying 5,000 baht (US$150) for each session. We hadn't seen the smoking apparatus yet and we had no idea of the ingredients in the mixture that my dad was going to smoke. Ying and Dang chatted at a hundred miles an hour in Thai and I was getting a bit frustrated. I kept interrupting and trying to ask, what I thought, were sensible, serious questions about the smoking treatment and my dad's health.

"Farang no believe in anything!" Dang said.

It upset me that I had been easily dismissed as a foreigner who did not understand Thai culture. All along the way, I had been trying so hard to understand. I learnt by asking questions, and I felt helpless that I had no control over anything anymore. Reason and analysis was out of the window in favour of anything that offered a glimmer of hope, even if it seemingly defied logic. Dad seemed to go along with anything in an effort to please Ying - and what could he do anyway? It would become really difficult for me to support something that in one way, I knew was offering my dad hope, yet in another way, I didn't really believe in.

The smoking apparatus consisted of a ceramic pot with coals in, and something that looked like pink salt (the medicine) sprinkled over it. The coal was then covered with a kind of toilet plunger with a hollow bamboo handle, and then wrapped around with a wet cloth so that none of the smoke would filter out into the air, but all pass up through the stick. Once the pot was set alight at the bottom, Dad would then stand over the bamboo stick and, with a short plastic straw, inhale the mixture as much as he could. He had to breathe in a certain number of breaths (according to superstition), and then rest for so many minutes.

The whole thing gave off a very potent smell, and I had to step away from the balcony as the smoke was aggravating my asthma. What was I allowing my dad to do? Yet what could I do when my dad saw hope in the therapy and Ying was determined that we were going ahead? Ying was using the best of her Thai local knowledge and doing what she truly believed was helping, but, at this point, she was unable to see anything from my point of view. When we knew that there was no conventional treatment that could cure Dad anyhow, was I wrong to quash hope in Ying's outlandish ideas? We carried on.

A few weeks later, after Dad had been rushed into the hospital after a particularly horrendous headache, Doctor Pichai told us that it could be weeks that my dad had left to live. In the hospital bed, my dad was high as a kite on morphine and suggesting that we all go out for an Italian meal. He was talking so fast and getting really annoyed with us for making him stay in the hospital when he wanted to go out eating, drinking and dancing! His childish protests were quite hilarious, and I couldn't believe that we were all finding a reason to laugh amidst the tragic circumstances. My dad called his own mum, my grandma, who, in her eighties, was sobbing on the phone so far away from her son.

"Don't worry, Mum!" Dad said. "The worst that can happen is that I can die and we don't even know what that's like yet!" he laughed. From the hospital, I called my own mum and she decided to fly out to be with me for support.

Dad was discharged from hospital and we went home. My mum arrived the next day, as did Ying's sister, Suchada. Throughout this time, Suchada had been in Chiang Mai keeping up her receptionist role at the office really well, whilst I had been pre-occupied with my dad. She had been taking English lessons, and her communication level had really come on since the last time that I had seen her.

Over the next few days, we all chipped in making dinner and looking after my dad, who was now unable to walk freely around the house. It was so heartbreaking to be carrying my dad everywhere he wanted to go, and seeing his frustration at not being able to do things for himself. The tumour was growing and weakening the left side of his body to such an extent that he no longer had control over his movement. He was losing his independence and this was the worst thing that could ever have happened to him.

Ying was continuing to look for miracle cures and things were getting really desperate. She decided that we needed to up things a level, and began looking seriously into Thai black magic and local shamans who could offer hope to the hopeless. She brought home a magazine one day that had photographs of Thai amulets, tattoos and strange men dressed in leopard skin cloaks. She declared that this was our next step. I sighed.

We were to visit the 'Por-Poo'. Despite the overarching Buddhist philosophy that pervades Thai culture, those who get to know Thailand beyond the two-week holiday, will discover that the animist beliefs are still very powerful. Shamanism and black magic date back thousands of years, and Thai people (often in desperate situations) find themselves turning to local magic men (Por-Poo) in times of need. The next day we got my dad dressed and into a wheelchair, and drove to Pattaya. Parking in the car park of a Chinese restaurant, we walked over to a building that I had never noticed before. How I had missed such an elaborate, multicoloured monstrosity I shall never know!

The building was like a horrifying children's theme park. The walls were manufactured to look like a cave and the cheap plastic was painted a sickly brown. The entrance was the mouth of a tiger that you walked through to get into the building, and gaudy, brightly coloured statues of snakes, bears, ladies dancing, dragons and any other mythical creature you can imagine greeted you as you walked in. The room was packed with people, and there was a canteen and toilet facilities on one side and a cloakroom, where people had left thousands of shoes, on the other side. Out of respect, you had to take off your shoes to enter the building, as you do upon entering most Thai houses and shops.

At the far end of the room stood Por-Poo - the man that we had come to see. There was a long queue of Thai people, holding small bunches of flowers and queue numbers, that were kneeling down in front of him quietly. Ying ran off to get us a number and my mum, dad and I looked around the room in a cross between astonishment, horror and intrigue.

As my dad's case was serious, Ying had made sure that we swapped our ticket number with someone else to get further along in the queue to see the mighty Por-Poo. I couldn't believe how many people were here and were relying on the Por-Poo for some kind of divine intervention to help their life situation. While we waited, I wheeled my dad's wheelchair to the front to get closer to the action. The Por-Poo himself was an unusual character indeed. Dressed head to toe in leopard skin, with long grey curly hair down to his waist and a tiger tattoo on his back, he looked like a kind of caveman cartoon, like a baddy in a Flintstones movie.

In Thai, this character (full name Por-Poo Puttareusi Thepnorrasing) is believed to be a reincarnation of a hermit and an acquaintance of the Buddha, who went off to live in a cave and pursue shamanism. His magic is white and benevolent, and he is believed to have the powers to heal cancer, disabilities and other ailments. If you haven't got a serious ailment, it is still extremely lucky to see Por-Poo, and hundreds of Thai people all over the country visit him for a variety of different reasons. With a cheeky smile and swigging a Leo Beer in-between seeing 'patients', I wondered how serious this Por-Poo was. I very much doubted that he was the reincarnation of an ancient hermit. I also saw the huge pile of money, the 'collection' that was being carried around the room on a brass platter. Por-Poo was taking 100 baht from each person that he saw that day. I feared that this was just a huge money-making spectacle, preying on the most vulnerable.

I looked around at the Thai visitors, each one of them serious and solemn as they waited to see the magic man. One other foreigner, queuing up with his Thai wife, looked decidedly out of place and equally baffled by the whole thing. I felt so sorry for my mum who, having not witnessed anything like this before in Southeast Asia, was experiencing serious culture shock. She was trying, for my dad's sake, to remain calm and collected. After having been to the Hindu

Thaipusam Festival in Kuala Lumpur, and seen people enter trances through their faith in religion, and even insert spears into their cheeks and hooks into their backs without showing pain, I felt more equipped to deal with this than my mum. However, we were here, this time, for a very different reason than tourism and voyeurism. This was personal.

The queue was slowly going down and it was getting nearer to my dad's turn. A woman in front of us, her hands held together in a wai (Thai prayer), knelt before the shaman. He poured a liquid over her head and all over her body, washing away the evil spirits. The liquid was a concoction of water, lotus petals and chopped-up limes - a kind of spiritual 'sangria'. In one hand, he held a long metal shaft (think 'the devil's stick') and tapped her on the head quite violently as if knocking some sense in, or out, of her being. The woman began to moan uncontrollably, and then contort her body into twisted shapes in a kind of effort to release something - a trapped demon perhaps? In front of a captive audience, she knelt down on all fours and began barking loudly like a dog to the room. I sat in utter amazement, wondering if this was real, mind over matter, some kind of brainwashing or a complete performance? It was one of the strangest things I have ever seen.

"Move out of the way so the dog spirit doesn't enter you," Mum said.

We looked at each other in shock – what the hell was happening to our lives? Here was my amazing mum trying to protect me, like she always had done, in a completely bizarre environment. My wonderful dad was sat next to me, terminally ill in a wheelchair, while his Thai girlfriend was negotiating us a better position in the queue to see a strange shaman that I was sure was a big fat fake! The scene became even more surreal when one of the 'organisers' began filming the novelty foreigners on her iPad, whilst dancing to the music, and taking photos of us next to Por-Poo. One of the photos, I believe, appeared in the next issue of their marketing magazine!

When it was my dad's turn to have a bucket of water chucked over him, nothing out of the ordinary happened. No dog, cow, cat or tiger spirits exited or entered him, and he just looked cold, wet and a bit sad. *Never again* I thought as I wiped his face with a towel and helped him to change his shirt. I think I had finally reached the point where I was going to stop respecting Thai culture to the ends of the earth. From now on, I was going to put my foot down and stand up for what I believed, from my own culture, was true and respectful.

The next week, when Ying tried to take my dad for his 'follow up' treatment, I stood over my dad's bed (my dad was now speaking less and less) and said a firm NO.

"But he must go three times to get better!" she cried. Even though Ying was doing her absolute best, and her heart was in the right place to try to find a cure for my dad, I felt that she was clutching at straws. I wasn't going to see my dad soaking wet and looking uncomfortable again.

I stroked my dad's head as he lay in bed asleep; I cried silently and told him that everything was going to be okay. He woke up suddenly and whispered in my ear.

"Hey Nikki. I had a terrible dream that I had a brain tumour and I was going to die," he mumbled to me, like a child. "You know those dreams when you wake up and you are so glad it isn't true?" he said.

"Gosh, Dad," I said, "don't be silly, everything is going to be okay." I held my breath and tried not to scream.

If I wasn't going to let my dad participate in the shamanic rituals, Ying was determined to carry on with it herself. I walked down to the kitchen the next morning to find the kitchen kitted out like a shrine. Along the sideboard, there were 18 red roses, 18 pink lotus flowers, 17 fresh eggs, 17 boiled eggs, different types of red fruits in the odd numbers of 3, 5 and 9, as well as 'pha trai jee worn', a brand new set of monk's ordination robes. Ying and Suchada were going off to see 'Por-Put' or 'Yomarat' (the opposite of Por-Poo), which I decoded in Thai was the equivalent of the Devil. Ying told me that she was taking sacrifices to ask for my dad's life back from the Devil - who was the one taking it from him.

In the following weeks, Ying also built a Spirit House in the garden of the house, a bright green and gold glittery structure that covered half of the grass on the lawn.

"We should have had one before!" Ying said.

In Thailand, Spirit Houses are very popular and almost all Thai houses have one in the garden or front yard, so that spirits, which would normally haunt the house, can exist peacefully outside. If you didn't have a Spirit House, it was believed that the spirits would live inside the house with the family and cause problems. Thai people would never risk not having one. Had he been in good health, I know my dad would not have been too happy about the new construction in his manicured, landscaped garden.

A huge ceremony was held for the grand opening of the Spirit House. At 6am, all the Thai women from the neighbourhood arrived in their best clothes and bearing various Thai dishes. Por-Poo was invited as he was to perform the main ritual and blessing. There was a massive feast of every fruit and vegetable you could imagine, and a pig's head and trotters on an enormous plate – none of which the guests were allowed to eat. All of the food would be given as an offering to Por-Poo after the ceremony. *So he can scoff it down with his Leo Beer!* I thought cynically. I could not wait for the day to be over.

Por-Poo drove off in his white BMW and waved. I hoped that would be the last time we would ever see him.

26

A Thai Funeral

After the Spirit House ceremony, I had decided to travel back up to Chiang Mai for a few days as we had a pre-arranged 'Photography Expedition' taking place at the SEA Backpacker office. A year before, the talented Flash Parker had approached me with the idea of hosting a photography course in Chiang Mai, and I had offered to help with promotion and advertising through the magazine. It was an exciting idea that I wanted to be a part of, and it would be great for the brand and reputation of the business.

Again, I didn't know whether I should leave my dad at this stage. I was torturing myself about whether or not I should go. With my dad now unable to speak, it was my mum's words that encouraged me. She promised that she would stay and take care of things, and reminded me that my dad would want me to go and make the photography course a grand success! In truth, I was in desperate need of a break from the house, yet I felt dreadfully guilty at leaving, even only for a few days. I also wanted to see Craig, hug him and have him tell me that everything was going to be okay – even though it almost certainly wasn't. I decided to go and would be back on a flight within an hour should anybody need me.

Back in Chiang Mai, on the night before the photography course, I visited the office, closed the door and sat alone by lamplight. It had been more than tough keeping the magazine going through all of the trauma we were experiencing, and I had barely gotten the last issue out to the print shop at all. Did I have the energy or motivation to carry on through such hard times? I opened the SEA Backpacker visitors book, and found it filled with pages and pages of encouraging, inspiring comments. While I had been in the Philippines and at my dad's house, the lovely Suchada had been loyally keeping the office open every day. People had continued to pop by and write a little note in the book. One read:

> *'SEA Backpacker Magazine. My best travel buddy in seven months travelling through eight wonderful Southeast Asian countries. Thanks for guiding me with inspiration and recommendations. I LOVE YOUR MAGAZINE!'*
> *(Isabelle, Chiang Mai, 30/08/12)*

Another…

> *'What time is it? Now. Forever and always. Now.'*
> *(Anon 24/10/12)*

Life inspiration returned to me at a time when I most desperately needed it. If, at times, I had offered encouragement to people through the magazine, here I was, getting it back tenfold now. How could I ever give this up?

Over the next three days, the photography course was a great success and an amazing experience. Although I had spoken with Shawn (AKA Flash) over email and Facebook lots of times, I hadn't actually met him in person before, and he was everything I thought he would be - hugely passionate about photography, endless bags of energy, fun-loving and above all, a really nice guy. Our business partnership quickly developed into a friendship and we made a great team during those three days.

Dylan Goldby, from Australia, was co-presenting the workshop, and he was also a very talented photographer, a friendly guy and had a wicked sense of humour. All together, the three of us pulled off a great course. The guests, who we treated more like friends, were absolutely thrilled with what they had learnt and experienced during the tour. Whilst Shawn and Dylan led the workshops each day, I picked out the places in Chiang Mai to visit for the best photography opportunities. As it was the Loi Krathong Festival in Thailand during that time, also known as 'The Festival of Lights' (we had timed it perfectly!), it wasn't difficult at all to find the most amazing scenes that just begged to be captured on camera.

Loi Krathong Festival takes place on the night of the full moon in November, marking the end of the rainy season. Night skies all across the country become illuminated as glowing lanterns are floated into the air, and rivers and lakes glisten with candles as tiny boats are set afloat in honour of the Goddess of Water. The roots of the festival lie firmly in Buddhist origins, and the beliefs centre upon the concept of 'letting go' or 'being freed' from your troubles. As the lantern or boat is launched and drifts away, it is believed that people can be released from their 'dukkha' or suffering and make a wish for good luck in the future. The name of the festival comes from the small lotus shaped boats, which are called 'krathong', and are made of banana leaves and filled with candles, incense and other offerings. The boats can also contain locks of hair, photographs or symbolic remnants of the past. It was my favourite Thai festival, not only for the beautiful scenes, but for the sentiment behind it.

On the last night of the photography tour, I left the rest of the team and went to meet Craig so that we could share some of the festival together. I set a lantern off into the night sky as he held my hand and I let go of my own 'dukkha'. I remembered a few years ago when I had been a lone backpacker in Chiang Mai and had set off a lantern from the Rooftop Reggae Bar. My only hopes were fun, love and excitement over the coming years. I never dreamed that I would be working here four years later, setting off a lantern with a boyfriend and praying for my dad to die peacefully. It was a strange moment and one that I will never forget.

As soon as the photography course was over, I called my mum. "Come back now." She said it with an urgency in her voice that I hadn't heard before. I started to look at flights online, but everything was completely booked up with people flying back to Bangkok after the festivities in Chiang Mai. Being Thailand's 'capital of culture,' Chiang Mai was a popular place to be during festivals, and I couldn't get a train or a bus either! I finally managed to book myself onto an overnight bus that would arrive at 7am the next day into Pattaya. After a sleepless night on an uncomfortable, over air-conditioned bus, I arrived back in Pattaya and was met by mum at the bus station. I could tell already by her face what had happened.

"Your dad has died, Nikki," she said.

He had passed away just an hour before I arrived home. *Maybe he wanted it this way* I thought.

The next few days were some of the most difficult days that I have ever experienced in my life and I honestly don't know how I managed to deal with it at the time. When telling friends and family about the experience later, I felt like I should leave bits out because I didn't want to upset them too much. I could see tears forming in their eyes as they felt my pain. However, like anyone who has gone through difficult times will tell you, you find a way to cope and carry on through it, because that is the only thing that you can do. You must go on.

First of all, the way that various cultures deal with death is strikingly different. The rituals involved in post-death are meant as a comfort for the people of that culture, not to outsiders. In English culture, everything that follows death, from the funeral proceedings to the final goodbye, seem to be for the purpose of comforting close relatives, making it easier for them to deal with the passing. The Thai culture, at this unusual time, offered no help to me.

Before my dad had become really ill, he had spoken to Ying and told her that she should arrange a funeral according to Thai culture and that he didn't want anything special. As he had been living in Thailand, I think he felt that it would have been unnatural to perform an English funeral, and he wasn't religious in the slightest. However, I don't think he had much idea about what Thai funerals actually entailed. None of us did.

When my mum and I arrived back at my dad's house from the overnight bus, there was already a chaotic atmosphere in the house. Neighbours and people from the local temple were fussing around, and rushing up and down the stairs carrying various items. I had no idea what was going on or what I should do to help. I was immediately frowned upon by the neighbours for wearing an 'unlucky' pink top (I had just arrived off the bus!), and was told by Ying to shower and get ready to go the temple. In a state of shock and panic, I went along with everything that I was told to do that morning: wear this, do this, carry these belongings to the car, re-arrange these things in the house, get this food ready, and various other tasks. My dad's body lay in the bedroom upstairs where he had died just hours before. Personally, I was afraid to enter the room. I had never seen a dead body before, and I knew that my dad would not have wanted me to be left with a disturbing image of him.

Finally, my dad's body was carried downstairs in a haphazard fashion, by the security guard, the man from the temple, Ying's elder brother, her dad and some other people that we did not know, and laid into the back of a pick up truck in a blanket. I was horrified to be told that I would be the one to drive the pick-up truck, with my dad's body in the back, to the temple. I did as I was told. Along the bumpy journey, Ying's dad sat in the back of the truck, crouching over my dad with an umbrella, to stop the hot sun beating down on his body. There seemed to be very little regard to dignity and I was welling up with sadness and anger inside, yet I felt that there was little I could do to change things. This was not my country or culture.

We arrived at the temple, and my dad's body was laid out on a folding table with a white cloth placed over him. My mum and I were told that there would be a ritual taking place before putting the body in the coffin. As well as around 15 Thai people, there were five very confused farangs at the service that day, as a few of my dad's golfing friends had turned up out of respect to watch the proceedings. Nobody really explained to us foreigners what was going on, and we nervously followed everyone else, as we formed a queue near the body.

Copying carefully what the Thai lady in front of me was doing, I could see that you had to pick up a handful of rose petals from a bowl on the table, dip them in water in another bowl, and then place the petals onto my dad's hand. The only part of my dad's body that you could see was, in fact, his hand, which was protruding from under the white cloth and was now very white itself. One by one, we queued up to perform the ritual, and a monk stood at the front of the table, guiding people.

As I approached the table for my turn, I lowered my head and took a deep breath. I had told Ying and the monk that I was certain that I did not want to see my dad's face. I remembered a few months ago that my dad had been very much against the idea of me seeing his dead body. He had been adamant that I should remember him as he was, with no disturbing images haunting me for the rest of my life. I respected this, and I was glad that this was his wish. However, when I approached the bench, for some reason, the monk whisked back the white cloth and I saw my dad's white face. Perhaps if I would have been prepared for this, I could have dealt with it much better, yet, this way, with everything being such a shock, I had no chance to control my emotions. I began to cry.

I could see from the looks on some of my dad's friends' faces that they were finding this very difficult too. How different this was to the funerals of England, where everything is concealed and the cold realities of death are hidden as much as possible from family and friends. Even in open-casket funerals in England, the body is dressed up in a way to disguise death, and the deceased person is made up with powders, jewellery and make-up, to look their best. In this way, the truth of death is indeed hidden, yet the relatives are spared certain images that may torment them forever. They are, at least, comforted that their loved ones look peaceful and content in death. I questioned later - is it better to hide such natural facts of life and death or display the harsh truth?

When my dad's friends were asked to lift the body from the table into the gaudy white and gold coffin below, I could see that they were very uncomfortable. Here they were, holding the body of a friend, whom they had played golf with not so long ago. Everything about the day was poorly planned and awkward, and one of them nearly tripped up whilst placing the body in the coffin. I tried hard to separate the fact that this was my dad, with what was going on, and desperately tried to retain composure.

None of the Thai people cried or seemed to be struggling with their emotions like I was. In Thai culture, as I had discovered during other times, there exists a compartmentalising of feelings. Perhaps this was the way that Thai people had learnt to deal with potentially upsetting circumstances. They have an unusual way of expressing emotion when the time is 'right', as deemed by religion and culture, and not a moment before or after. I have never seen a Thai person lose control or break down due to their emotions, like Westerners are almost encouraged to do. "Let it all out. Don't hold your emotions in or bottle things up," parents and friends tell us.

We are taught from a young age to let our emotions out when they surface, not holding back the tears, and allowing yourself to cry or feel sad whenever you want to. According to modern Western psychology, suppressed emotions only lead to problems, psychological issues or even physical issues, in later life. I believe this to be very true, and have experienced stress and pent up feelings causing me physical distress. Some Thai people, on the other hand, believe that instead of letting emotion out, the moment you break down, you are actually letting a 'demon' in, and then you may never be able to stop crying!

A friend of mine who was teaching in Chiang Mai, had experienced the unusual way that Thai culture deals with death, when a little boy in her class died tragically, in a motorbike accident, at 13 years old. The head teacher had interrupted her during a lesson to announce the news to her and the rest of the class, and my friend had immediately started to cry.

"What's the matter, Teacher?" the children had inquired, trying to find an answer as to why she could be crying. "Did you see a ghost?"

My friend thought it so strange that they did not understand why she would be crying at this tragic accident and the loss of such a young life. The children seemed unperturbed.

On the way to the funeral the following week, the kids had laughed and joked on the bus all the way there – could it be that they did not care about their fellow student? Yet, during the ceremony, my friend could see that it was now time for them to let their emotions out. She saw the children and teachers cry their hearts out - perhaps at the time when it was allowed, seen as appropriate. I am not sure if this is a true explanation – or an attempted explanation by an outsider trying to make sense of a part of Thai culture that I found rather cold and disturbing. I do not profess that I know the real answer. It seemed at this point that the more I learnt, the less I knew, about anything.

Thai funerals last for three days. The major ceremony, when the body is cremated and the spirit is laid to rest, takes place on the third and final day. The body is meant to remain in the temple for three days, whilst family members and friends visit to pay their respects, and bring flowers and other gifts. In the centre of the temple, there was an enormous photograph of my dad in a gold frame with twinkling fairy lights wrapped around it. The frame sat above the coffin, surrounded by hundreds of tropical flowers and large clocks of different shapes and sizes. For some reason, clocks seemed to be the most popular gift offered to the temple during the funeral. Was it something to do with the passage of time? Again, as I questioned the presence of the clocks, trying to give some meaning to the act, I found no answers.

Every day during the next three days, we had to visit the temple to take my dad breakfast, lunch and dinner, and place it right next to the coffin. I am not sure if this was to appease his spirit as it lay in a sort of purgatory state before heading to the afterlife. Or, did they think that my dad was potentially still alive until his body was sent off to the spirits during cremation? Either way, I resented this act and thought it was pointless and ridiculous, nevertheless abiding by it quietly. It was hard enough to make our own dinner and force food down to carry on through the unpredictable days. Taking food to place at my dad's coffin, which we knew would not be eaten, only to take it away again when the next meal was ready, was unnecessarily upsetting, especially because we knew he would have loved what we were cooking had he been alive!

One day, I took 'scouse', a northern English dish of meat and potato stew, to the coffin. It had been one of my dad's favourite meals, and it had upset me to cook it the first time without him here. The monk at the temple saw the small bowl I had dished out and told me off for not giving my dad enough to eat. It seemed that every effort I was making to respect Thai culture was not working. I kept getting everything wrong, and every little mistake I made added to my distress at the time.

While Mum and I tried to do everything that was expected of us, just to get through each day quietly, it became apparent that something was wrong. In all of the panic getting my dad's body to the temple, we discovered that he had not been registered as deceased and therefore we did not have the necessary death certificate. By law, you were not allowed to cremate a body without this extremely important document. The document was all the more important because my dad was a British citizen in Thailand. The certificate was proof of what had happened to the body overseas.

A Thai Funeral

As we had failed to get the body registered, we now had to arrange for someone from the hospital to come out to the temple to perform the necessary medical necessities. It seemed to take forever to organise and would delay the funeral for another few days. Once the visit was finally over, Ying and I followed the ambulance in our car to get the certificate that we needed. It took hours of waiting in a very busy and basic local hospital whilst Ying and I sat nervously in a morbid room that was full of coffins waiting to be filled. After this upsetting experience, Mum and I had to then drive to Bangkok to visit the British Embassy to give us a final certificate of 'release'. It was an unbelievably stressful and anxious few days. Would the ordeal ever be over?

When we finally arrived back with the certificate, thankfully, people were now preparing for the final day. My mum and I were exhausted from all of the activities, after driving up and down the motorway to the British Embassy in Bangkok. We both just wanted the whole ceremony to be over, so that we could actually start to come to terms with my dad's death in our own, personal way.

On the final day of the funeral, we awoke early, dressed in black and took a deep breath, hoping that the day would pass as peacefully and uneventfully as possible. At 9am, my dad's friends and Ying's family and friends gathered at the temple. Five monks took to the stage with microphones and sat cross-legged in a line. I sat on the front row, which was reserved for family members and close friends, and I had to take a garland of flowers to the head monk for the proceedings to begin. The five monks unravelled a white piece of string between them and started to chant in Sanskrit.

A few of the Thai girls in the audience played on their phones during the ceremony, and one even wandered off to make a phone call in the middle of the proceedings. I imagined the social inappropriateness of someone answering his or her phone during a funeral in England. But this was not England – as we were reminded again and again – we were very far away from anything that we were used to!

Thankfully, the final ceremony was calm, symbolic and actually rather touching. After a final prayer, the coffin was placed in a kind of tower where it was to be burnt, and the head monk started the fire with a single piece of lint. All of the members of the congregation walked up to the coffin and lit a piece of paper with a candle. One by one, we placed our small flames onto the coffin, which was now burning fiercely with smoke rising from the chimney at the top of the tower. As you walked up to the tower with your piece of paper, you were given a chance to say your own personal goodbye. It was the only moment during the whole ceremony when I felt some kind of relief.

Once the ceremony was over, Ying, Suchada and I had to drive back to the house in silence, carrying the gold picture frame of my dad. Again, I had no idea as to the meaning of this activity. I drove, Ying held the photo in the back of the car, and Suchada held an incense stick, which was not allowed to burn out fully until we reached the house. I had to drive fast. The only time anyone spoke was when we went over a bridge and Ying said, "Don't worry darling, we're going over a bridge now – just follow us."

The photo was then taken up the stairs into the room where my dad had died, and the incense stick was left to burn out in the house. Once the incense stick had burned out, we were allowed to talk. I guessed that this symbolised that my dad's spirit had now left us and left the house. Suchada told me that the house was now 'ghost free'. After this ritual, people started to arrive at the house for what was deemed as 'the wake', and I decided that this was where I could show people a side of my dad that was familiar to me. I put on an Amy Macdonald CD, a Scottish folk singer that my dad loved, and it blasted out of the speakers as people arrived.

"So goodbye. You were my world and my life. I just want you to know, that I left that body long ago. So long ago." Amy's words, to a song that my dad had repeatedly played over and over again during the last few weeks of his life, were bizarrely appropriate.

27

A Backpacker in Hong Kong

After my dad's death, I moved back up to Chiang Mai to spend time with Craig and to try to get on with business for the next six months. I threw myself into work passionately, in order to take my mind off recent events. My deputy editor, Annabelle, was still working for the magazine, helping out immensely in terms of creativity and support. She joined me in Chiang Mai to talk about future plans and how we were going to take the magazine to the next level.

A lot of the problems that I had been facing recently with the business were partially down to the fact that the company was based in Thailand. First of all, it was very difficult to employ another foreigner legally, due to the difficult process of work permits. Being an English-language magazine, this made it very difficult to employ Thai people with a level of English that was good enough to write and proofread, for example. Plus, Thai people, in general, were not as interested in backpacking in Southeast Asia as a foreigner would be. Add to this difficulties with banking, delays with international transfers, tricky licences that you needed to do various things, as well as high legal fees to run the business in the first place. The whole thing restricted growth in a big way.

I had ideas about creating a backpacker trip booking system on the website, possibly expanding to include other regions of the world such as South America or Europe, or even writing a series of travel guide books. However, I didn't feel that Thailand was a good enough base from which to grow the company. Politically, the climate of the country was turbulent, with regular coups that ousted the government every few years. Although civil war never actually broke out across the country, it wasn't exactly a risk that I wanted to take with the future of my business and livelihood. The political demonstrations not only affected the delivery of magazines, but they affected tourism, deterring people from visiting the country, plus the entire morale of the Thai backpacking scene. As businesses lost custom, advertising was the first thing to go. It made sense all round to try and grow the magazine so that it didn't solely rely on the Thai market. I needed to create a solid base from which to expand our reach throughout the Southeast Asian region and potentially the world.

Another thing that had been troubling me recently, was the office. Since the opening, it had provided me with a stable place to work, had served as a drop-in information centre for backpackers, and had done wonders for our reputation in demonstrating that we were serious in doing business in Southeast Asia. However, with my more international ambitions, I wondered if Chiang Mai was the right place for an office – or if indeed we needed an office at all? After all, I was a digital nomad and only needed WiFi in order to do my work. What was the point paying out for office rent every month? If the magazine grew, it would mean that I would need to travel more, not less, and there was little point of an office if I was never there.

My lifestyle was also changing. Whilst my dad had been ill, I had desperately needed a base, some stability and a place that I could go every day to have structure in my life. Yet now, circumstances had changed. I was growing restless of Chiang Mai and I felt restricted by an office office that I felt compelled to go to every day. It seemed that my backpacker itch was alive and well.

I had already begun to look into alternative hubs for the business that offered more stability than Thailand and would allow for global growth. I was looking into places where you could have a 'remote office', an address that was just a lawyer's office, while staff worked from anywhere in the world. From my research, I discovered that the thriving Asian hubs of Hong Kong and Singapore were regarded as the best, most stable bases for doing business in Asia. Initially, I had thought that these two places would be way out of my league financially. However, when I looked further, I found that Hong Kong, as well as being one of the easiest places in the world to set up a business, was also one of the cheapest!

Hong Kong also beat Singapore on a few other attributes. In Hong Kong, unlike Singapore, a foreigner could own a business 100% and did not need to have a local, native business partner. The fact that I didn't actually fully own my business in Thailand had been troubling me. With my dad no longer here, Ying wanted to go her own way in terms of work and she didn't really want to help out with the magazine anymore. This was of course totally fine, as we had very different ideas about doing business anyhow, but long-term, I didn't feel that she wanted the responsibility of being a silent business partner. Even if she didn't directly work for the magazine anymore, as 51% share-holder, she could still be liable if something went wrong. And, from my point of view, if I wanted to grow the business dramatically over the next few years, I felt that I needed 100% ownership and control.

Annabelle and I took a trip to Hong Kong in March. "Pack your heels!" I told her. "We're going to Hong Kong!"

As well as a 'recce' to investigate business opportunities, we were also planning on having a jolly good time. A 'blow-out' was much needed after everything that I had been through, and Annabelle was a fantastic ally to have along for the ride. It was a new year, and I was feeling hopeful about business and the future for the first time in ages. Restaurants, nightlife, shopping and exploring – we were ready to treat ourselves to a visit to the New York of Asia!

Before flying to Hong Kong, I had been to visit Max, the owner of Vietnam Backpackers' Hostels, who had now become a good friend and somewhat of a sounding-board for my business ideas. Max had spent a few years working in Hong Kong, and he put me in touch with a lawyer there, who immediately arranged a meeting for the day after I arrived in Hong Kong. Everything seemed very efficient and smooth, and there were no language difficulties or cultural confusion. It was a breath of fresh air after struggling for years doing business in Thailand. I knew I was going to like Hong Kong already! 'Fong bin' was a Cantonese phrase that I had started to use in Hong Kong, which meant 'convenient' or 'easy' in local language. It was exactly the opposite of the Thai 'mai pen rai', and I was ready for a big dollop of it!

Arriving in Hong Kong, the pace and the vibrancy of the city was amazing. Skyscrapers towered over us, the sea glittered across the impressive harbour, and trendy bars and restaurants served expensive food and drink to rich, young professionals. Compared to Chiang Mai, the chic bars, posh shops and sophisticated business people made me feel out of place and a bit intimidated with my flip-flops and backpack. Who did I really think I was, believing that I could set up a business in a place like this? However, my research was not wrong. Despite the glitz and glamour, it was very cheap to set up a business in Hong Kong, and, although I felt it, I was in no way out of my league here. I was excited and nervous at the same time.

Unbeknownst to Annabelle and I, we had arrived during the hugely popular rugby event, 'The Hong Kong Sevens'. It was proving absolutely impossible to find a place to stay, due to the hoards of tourists that had packed into the city to watch the biggest sporting competition of the year. After snorting at the ridiculously high prices we were being quoted for the tiniest rooms on the planet, we made our way, pitifully, to the notorious backpacker ghetto of Chungking Mansions. This 17-story tenement block in the heart of Hong Kong, is the only affordable way for travellers on a budget to experience this incredible city.

Packed with more characters than a soap opera, with currency exchanges, cheap trainers, laundry, mobile phone shops, food stalls and visa services, the building harbours a mish-mash of Hong Kong's recently arrived immigrants, international traders and budget-conscious backpackers. "Watches, watches…", "Copy handbag…", "Tailored suit madam?" As you cram into the tiny lift and ascend up the floors to your guesthouse, backpack squashed against the door, and body pressed against the face of a small Indian lady, the claustrophobia starts to creep under your skin. You feel like you want to run outside into the street, scream and take a long deep breath.

A Backpacker in Hong Kong

'Ghetto at the Center of the World', as described in the title of Gordon Mathews' book, Chungking has gained iconic status since Kar Wai Wong's 1994 movie *Chungking Express* (a favourite film of Quentin Tarantino, apparently). A transit point for goods sold all over the world, Mathews estimates in his book that up to 20% of mobile phones used in sub-Saharan Africa pass through the building at some point. We checked into a room the size of a shoebox, with no windows (forget about a fire exit) and a bathroom that you couldn't quite stand up straight in. Yet we were paying 300 HKD (around US$40) in one of the most expensive cities in the world, so what did we expect?

The next day, I got dressed in the cramped bathroom, put on my heels and best dress, and caught the underground to the central business district of Hong Kong for my meeting with the lawyer.

"Where are you staying?" the sophisticated female lawyer had asked in polite conversation before our meeting.

"Oh, just a hotel in Tsim Tsa Tsui." I had said. I imagined that she would be mortified if she really knew where this entrepreneur-backpacker was staying!

I had a list of questions for the lawyer and I went through them one by one during the meeting. I'm sure that some of them made me sound like I was totally out of my depth, but if I didn't ask then how was I ever going to know? The lawyer was calm and considerate, and she answered my queries thoroughly. After the meeting, I had made up my mind that Hong Kong made total sense for my growing brand. The new business was to be called 'Backpacker International Limited' - allowing for world domination plans! Annabelle and I thought that it sounded pretty high-end and professional. We celebrated over a Greek meal and a glass of wine in the trendy Soho district.

It takes all of three days in Hong Kong to set up a company. The efficiency of the country is incredible. Things happen so fast that you hardly realise what you have done. Business - opened. Bank account - opened. Credit card - why not? After my meeting with the lawyer, I was sent to open my business bank account in the biggest bank that I have ever been in my life, the HSBC Headquarters in Hong Kong.

I arrived at the enormous glass building late for my meeting, sweaty and out of breath. Getting off at the correct tube station, I had walked in the opposite direction in my six-inch heels to the bank. (The heels were meant to impose an air of sophistication and power.) Along the way, the heel had broken on my shoe and I was forced to purchase some horrendous purple wedged flip-flops in the street outside the bank. Flustered and slightly embarrassed by my attire, I went to the wrong floor in the lift several times, before finding the 'new business accounts' department. I approached a very smart, suited receptionist, who told me to take a seat in a large waiting room that

was filled with immaculately dressed Chinese businessmen. I grinned at everyone in the hope that I could deflect attention away from my inappropriate shoes.

"Backpacker International Limited, two o'clock," the bank manager called out to the sea of expensive suited-and-booted male entrepreneurs. I raised my hand at the front of the room and smiled. She glanced down at my purple shoes, exposed toes with chipped nail varnish on show. Backpacker International - of course it was me! I hobbled after her thinking that I should have called the business something less obvious, like BIL. Then she would not have seen so easily through my disguise of backpacker dressed as businesswoman!

The bank account was set up in a flash, and I walked out of the intimidating building, threw away my stupid shoes, bought some flat pumps and felt a pang of excitement. It was a sunny, fresh day, and I walked along the harbour feeling excited and exhilarated about the future and where the magazine and this new business move could take me. I now owned a business in Hong Kong! *Did you hear that, Dad?*

28

South American Dreams

I flew back to Chiang Mai and spent the next few months winding the Thai company down. One day, while I was working at the office, a young American girl called Grace came in asking if we had any work experience opportunities? She was teaching English in Chiang Mai and had Tuesday and Thursday afternoons free, so was wondering if she could come by the office? She wanted to help out and learn about what was involved in running a travel magazine. Grace was enthusiastic, full of energy and inspired me all over again about what I was trying to do with the magazine. I said yes immediately and this became the start of a great working partnership and friendship.

With Grace helping out with the website and Annabelle continuing to write and edit articles for the bi-monthly magazine, I had time on my hands to look into other projects that would grow the business and expand the reach of the magazine. With more and more people interested in doing internships or work experience, I decided to create the 'SEA Backpacker Ambassador Program'. It became a way for backpackers to get involved with the magazine as they travelled in Southeast Asia. The program would be mutually beneficial to both the magazine and backpackers themselves. The way it would work is that backpackers would write articles and keep us up to date with news and events across Southeast Asia, and, in return, we would reward them with free dive trips, VIP passes to festivals or free nights' accommodation at the various hostels we worked with. The program was to become a great success in the coming years, as it meant that we were able to bring more talented people on board. With a network of backpackers on the trail in Southeast Asia, we had our eyes and ears to the ground across the entire region.

Our first ambassadors were Chase and Charla, an adventurous couple who had driven a car from London, through Turkmenistan and Uzbekistan, to Mongolia in the wacky cross-country race, 'The Mongol Rally'. They were now living and working in Bangkok as English teachers, and they wrote articles for the magazine about news updates in the city, festivals, yoga, Thai football, craft beer and more! Then there was Ben, who made up one half of *The Hungry Backpackers*. He was into off-the-beaten-track foodie experiences and wrote articles about must-try local delicacies and street food. There was also Samantha, the flashpacking pole dancer, and Melanie, our spiritual ambassador, who wrote advice columns for soul-seeking backpackers who had come to Asia to 'find themselves'. We also took on Amy Lou, an expat teacher living in Chiang Mai, who celebrated everything about the city from its tea shops to its markets and, finally, Will, A.K.A. *The Broke Backpacker,* who prided himself on travelling on a shoestring. With a good mix of people, the diversity of the articles on the website and in the magazine grew.

Later, we'd bring on board several formidable 'couples' ambassadors, twosomes who were exploring the world and earning money together with their joint travel blogs. In becoming ambassadors for *Southeast Asia Backpacker Magazine,* the ambassadors were able to increase popularity and expand the reach of their own blog. They could share their own articles on our website and through our social networking channels, as well as use the well-established brand name to make connections with backpacker-related businesses across the region.

South American Dreams

We hired Jazza and Alesha from *NOMADasaurus*, who were travelling overland from Thailand to South Africa, Kach and Jon from *Two Monkeys Travel* who had recently been motorbiking through Vietnam, Nick and Dariece from *Goats on the Road*, off the beaten path specialists and house-sitters, and Tom and Anna from the travel blog, *Adventure in You*, a British-Filipino couple who were reviewing adventures around the world. Although I rarely came face-to-face with the ambassadors as we communicated via Skype, Facebook and email, we became a kind of backpacker family. We understood each other's goals perfectly, and I knew that if we happened to meet up on some shore, someplace, somewhere, we'd share drinks and laughs like we'd known each other forever.

With the ambassadors helping out with the creative and marketing side of the magazine, I was able to get started on some significant projects that had been brewing in my head for a while. The biggest of these projects, which actually came to fruition in January 2013, was 'Backpacker Bookings' - an exciting new online trip-booking portal. The website enabled our readers to actually book the trips and adventures that they had read about in the magazine. Over the years, we had experienced many of the legendary backpacker trips, such as the Halong Bay Castaways Island Trip or the PADI Open Water Diver course - it seemed only logical that we would offer backpackers the opportunity to book these through our website. Plus, we had excellent connections across the region with companies that we could trust. Although it was initially expensive to set up and complicated to work out the booking processes, Backpacker Bookings would become a much needed revenue source for the magazine in future years, as we earned a commission on each trip booked through the website.

The next step in expanding the magazine and propelling our brand into the future, was to create a digital version of the bi-monthly publication that people could download 'all over the world' onto their iPads or Kindles. This would expand our global audience and, in this day and age, was essential if you wanted to be taken seriously as a modern publication. I loved the tangible printed version of the magazine that lingered around in hostels for years and years. I also adored the fact that people would keep the magazine as a souvenir of their travels, or cut out articles for their scrap book. However, I knew, that one day, in our technology driven world, it would make sense, financially, to make the magazine an entirely digital publication.

One day, Grace and I met for breakfast at a cute little WiFi cafe in the Old City and Grace said that she had something to tell me. Despite the fact that she loved working with the magazine, she wasn't feeling challenged enough with her teaching job. She had decided to leave Chiang Mai at the end of the year, head back to the US for Christmas, then, in January 2014, she would travel to South America.

"South America?" I laughed at this serendipitous little twist. I showed her the beginnings of the website that I had been building which would one day become *South America Backpacker Magazine* and her eyes lit up. She had no idea that I was planning to reach out to a new continent and expand the magazine globally.

South America had been a dream of mine since I started travelling at the age of 23. Initially, I had thought of backpacking in South America right after my first Southeast Asian trip. I had planned to go to Australia, earn some money and then fly over to the Latin continent for a new adventure. However, as you now know, starting the magazine took my life in a completely different direction. However, I had not lost the desire to travel there. I had always been interested in learning Spanish, and I felt that, culturally and environmentally, South America was a land that would inspire and revitalise me: its music, landscapes and colours. The high Andean peaks, salsa clubs and lush Amazon rainforest beckoned…

A soon as it was imagined that I might travel to South America with Grace, and that I might use this as an opportunity to launch the second branch of Backpacker International Limited, I couldn't sleep. I grew restless of Chiang Mai. Things annoyed me about the city more than ever before. I grew annoyed at the hordes of tourists at the Sunday Night Market, and I became frustrated at the increasingly gridlocked traffic in the city and the suffocating pollution. The pollution reached horrendous levels in the city during the months of March and April that year due to the extremely damaging environmental issue, 'slash-and-burn' farming. The land is cleared ready for the next crop, but the air is left almost unbreathable. The city was enveloped in an unhealthy cloud for weeks on end, and I wanted to get out.

Also at this time, the last few members of my original group of friends in Chiang Mai were about to leave. I was, once again, confronted with the ever-transient nature of the Southeast Asian expat scene. Most of all, I was bored with the fact that life in Chiang Mai had become too easy and too comfortable. No matter how hard I tried, I couldn't suppress these feelings of restlessness.

One sunny afternoon over at Craig's house, while he sat in the garden, pottering around, making bread, watering the plants, watching films and drinking beer, relaxed and content as ever, I paced around anxiously. It was time for a change and I knew it. Over the past five years, Thailand had become my comfort zone, to the point where I felt more out of place back in England than in this exotic land. I wasn't satisfied that I had found, in Thailand, a place that I wanted to settle forever, and I couldn't help wondering what was around the next corner. Are the beaches whiter in the next bay? Is the food tastier in the next city? Are the wild and remote areas even more wild and remote in the next country? Who will I meet and what will I discover about the world and about myself? I had the travel itch for somewhere new, exciting — unknown. The addictive impulse of travel and adventure washed over me, and I knew I had to obey.

With the recent events of my dad's death, I had also come face-to-face with my own mortality. I had witnessed the reality that life is short and that you need to make the most out of every second, while you are fit and healthy to do so. Anything can happen, at *any* time. Dad had told me before he died that he had absolutely no regrets in his life. How many people can lie on their deathbed and say that? Would I?

A travel buddy and I used to have a saying that we'd use every now and again to encourage each other to make a big decision that was scary or daunting. "What would be best for the book?" The idea was that one day, when we were old and grey, we would write a biographical tale about all of our adventures. We must make sure that the content was as exciting as possible! Could epic adventure novels have been written if the author had just stayed at home in his pyjamas in front of the TV?

It's easy to stay in one place. It's easy to stick with the familiar and comfortable. It's even easier to stay in and live vicariously through friends on Facebook every night. But what if, deep down, you fancy a change? What if you harbour ambitious thoughts of travel, adventure and a life of spontaneity? And what if the move that you are contemplating means leaving behind something that is pretty good - a relationship, a job, a house? Why change something that isn't broken? Why shake things up if it isn't that bad? As Steve Jobs said: "Remembering you are going to die is the best way to avoid the trap of thinking that you have something to lose. You are already naked. There is no reason not to follow your heart."

Within a few weeks, I shut down the SEA Backpacker Office, and peeled the sign off the wall, breaking every single one of my finger nails. I shed more than a few tears as I kissed Craig an emotional goodbye at Chiang Mai International Airport. We both promised that we would rekindle our relationship in another place and another time, further down the road, but we both knew that we probably wouldn't. The paths of our lives were bound to change and we'd meet new people - and become different people ourselves. With no doubt in my mind that I was doing the right thing, I jumped on a flight back home to England to touch base with the Motherland before setting off on a new adventure.

As always, it was a culture shock returning home to find most of my friends married, pregnant or expecting. I greeted brand new babies and heard about the wonders of ovulation sticks and breast-feeding suction cups. I felt out of place and like a wild gypsy all over again, as I explained to people what I was doing with my life and why I had chosen to go against the grain. Time and time again, I was asked that question – *"Would I ever settle down?"*

One day, I went to my local bank to try to open a savings account before I set off to South America. Sat in the bank manager's dim office, looking at the photograph he had of the Cayman Islands on his wall - a tropical scene of a white beach and palm trees, I thought it ironic how many people idealise images of travel, forever believing them to be unreachable.

The bank manager almost hit the panic alarm when I had told him that I ran a business in Hong Kong, had been living in Thailand for five years and would be heading to Colombia next. Instead of Hong Kong, Thailand, Colombia, I think he heard 'money-laundering', 'prostitution' and 'drugs'. My nomadic, untethered lifestyle did not conform to bank regulations, and he was neither very encouraging about my trip, nor would he allow me to open a bank account.

"I have lived in the same house on the same street for twenty years," he continued, "...and I am happy!" *Why was he telling me this?* "Frankly, the prospect of your life fills me with dread," he concluded.

I giggled and looked at my mum who was laughing out loud and said, "Vice versa!"

A few days later, I was asked the question by one of my mum's friends, "Why do you want to travel to South America?"

I found it to be an unusual question to be asked, to which I responded, "Why not?"

There is no particular beach I want to lay eyes on in South America, no particular monument I want to see, or particular food I want to try, there is no *one* reason. Why on earth would I *not* want to travel there? Because it is there.

Is there a reason why any of us travel? Do we travel to get something out of our system before 'settling down' into the real world? Do we travel to educate ourselves? Or is it travel for the sake of travel - because such experiences bring pure joy and enrich our lives for the better?

A few hundred years ago, it was impossible for the average person to jump on a plane and explore new lands. World travel was left to the swashbuckling explorers of old, who braved malaria-infested jungles and high seas, in the spirit of adventure and, possibly, human advancement. So is it up to us, today, to take advantage of such incredible opportunities that lay before us? To explore as much as possible and learn from it as much as we can? The answer lies within each individual backpacker. It is about being true to yourself. If you believe deep down in a life of adventure, don't sell yourself short. Don't conform to other people's expectations of you.

Backpacking is not only an activity, it is a spirit, a way that you choose to live your life. You don't actually have to be sitting in an exotic location, nor wearing a backpack or flip-flops to embrace the backpacker spirit. A backpacker is someone who says yes to life and yes to adventure. A backpacker is someone who cannot, ever again, be satisfied once the exciting flutters of a new destination appears as an inkling in their head. A backpacker is someone who can take a walk down a street that they have walked down a million times before and notice something different. A backpacker is someone who is open to new opportunities and is thirsty to learn more every day about this amazing big beautiful planet we have.

Why do I want to go to South America? The same reason why I want to go around the next corner. The same reason why I want to get up in the morning. The same reason why I want to fall in love again. The same reason why I want to experience life to the full, with all of the opportunities that are presented to me, being lucky enough to be born in a country where I have the choice.

Never stop backpacking, even after you put the rucksack down.

Printed in Great Britain
by Amazon